opposing viewpoints®

chemical dependency

1990 annual

David L. Bender, *Publisher*
Bruno Leone, *Executive Editor*
Bonnie Szumski, *Senior Editor*
Janelle Rohr, *Senior Editor*
William Dudley, *Editor*
Robert Anderson, *Editor*
Karin Swisher, *Editor*
Lisa Orr, *Editor*
Tara P. Deal, *Editor*
Carol Wekesser, *Assistant Editor*

greenhaven press, inc.

PO Box 289009
San Diego, CA 92128-9009

© 1990 by Greenhaven Press, Inc.

ISBN 0-89908-555-5

ISSN 1042-315X

contents

"Codependents, as a result of living in close proximity with an alcoholic . . . develop serious psychological problems."

Codependency Is a Serious Problem

Arthur Wassmer

If you love a drinking alcoholic or a using addict, you are sick, too. I don't mean that you are sick to love that person, or that you started out sick and therefore chose an alcoholic or addict to love (though for some people that may be the case). I mean that, like any person who has lived for any period of time in a distorted, topsy-turvy, chaotic, and punishing environment, your entire system of perceptions of the world around you and your reactions to it have become distorted and inappropriate. You have gotten used to and live with conditions that are neither normal nor healthy, and your body, mind, and spirit show it.

New developments in the field of addiction treatment during the 1980s have led to the recognition of codependency as a clinical syndrome of its own, requiring appropriate diagnosis and treatment. Indeed, we have seen over and over again that unless the spouse receives some form of treatment for codependency, the alcoholic's or addict's recovery will be significantly impeded or fail entirely. . . .

A Syndrome

Addiction is a disease, so we are able to predict its course, often with amazing accuracy. Codependency isn't exactly a disease in the strictest sense, because there are no physical causative factors that we know of, but it's close enough to one to be often called a disease by workers in the field. Codependency is actually a *syndrome*, that is, a collection of psychological, physical, and behavioral symptoms that present themselves in an equally predictable order in certain kinds of persons under certain kinds of circumstances. . . .

It often comes as a shock for codependents to think that they may have problems of their own; most codependents labor under the delusion that if their alcoholic would only stop drinking, or if their addict would only stop using drugs, everything would be all right. So little do codependents typically focus on themselves and their own problems that while they are in the very midst of profound psychological, physical, and behavioral problems of their own, the idea that there may be something wrong with them usually strikes them as a very foreign idea. It is almost amazing to watch how difficult it is for them to understand that they, and not just their addicts, have a serious problem. Later, we'll see how the course of codependency directly parallels the course of addiction, but for now it's useful to note that the codependent's failure to recognize his or her own problems is the exact counterpart of *denial* in the alcoholic or addict. Just as the addict denies that he or she has a problem, and stoutly maintains that the problem has to do with the nagging wife, the demanding boss, or the impossible world, so also the codependent denies that he or she has any problem. The codependent is so convinced that his or her alcoholic is the problem that he will go on for hours describing the bad behavior and ugly situations of the alcoholic without ever referring to his or her own misery. . . .

The definition of codependence that seems most useful for our purposes follows.

> Codependency is a collection of psychological symptoms including depression, anxiety, decreased self-esteem, phobia, and obsessiveness, guilt and shame, physical symptoms such as gastric disorders, skin disorders, cardiovascular disorders, back problems, and behavioral symptoms such as "people pleasing," controlling, isolation, hyper-responsibility, work dysfunction, and compulsiveness. These symptoms present themselves in predictable order in persons who are prone to love, care for, and take responsibility for others under circumstances of chronic dysfunction in the other due to alcoholism, addiction, mental illness, personality disorder, or chronic medical illness.

Codependence almost always occurs in a

relationship in which one party has become impaired in his or her ability to function. Some of the common causes of this dysfunction are long-term physical illness, mental illness, personality disorder (a kind of psychological problem in which the individual is not mentally ill but nevertheless consistently behaves in ways that are not normal and cause problems), and, of course, alcohol or other drug addiction. Other compulsive disorders, such as gambling, eating disorders, or sexual addiction also usually foster codependency in the other partner in the relationship.

"Enabling is the behavioral symptom of some underlying ideas that, to put it bluntly, are wrong."

The codependent is usually a pretty responsible, competent person who feels a powerful inner imperative to see that things are right, that obligations are met, that appearances are maintained. As the impaired partner loses the ability to function, or at least the ability to function reliably, the codependent partner gradually begins to take up the slack, assuming more and more responsibility for the effective functioning of the relationship, and in doing so, assuming more and more responsibility for the life of the dependent. He may pay off her gambling debts, extracting meaningless promises from her that it will never happen again. He may call in sick for her at work while she sleeps off a hangover.

The more the codependent takes over the personal responsibilities of the dependent and the joint responsibilities of the relationship, the more the dependent is able to practice his or her addiction, compulsion, or other disorder in relative freedom from suffering the consequences of his failure to meet his responsibilities. If she pays the gambling debts, he will only feel freer to lose large amounts of money without worrying about how to pay the losses. He has her to worry about that.

Enabling

This pattern of assuming responsibilities that are not one's own was one of the first characteristics of codependents that was noted by the addiction treatment field, and was called *enabling,* because it enabled the alcoholic, addict, or otherwise disordered individual to continue his or her disordered behavior without experiencing its negative consequences. The idea of enabling was a hard one for codependents to take, because the implication was that the codependent somehow had an unconscious motive to preserve the status quo by helping the addicted partner stay addicted. . . .

Enabling is the behavioral symptom of some underlying ideas that, to put it bluntly, are wrong. When we enable our addict, we think (in the moment)

that we are helping. We think that if we can only intervene to avert this crisis, if we can just cover this embarrassment, if we can just prevent him or her from doing something stupid, things will get better. We believe that if we can only give our addict a break, that he will get his feet under him and shape up. We feel that it would be terrible to just stand by and let the consequences of her behavior hurt or even destroy her. Enabling is like standing in front of a dam, sticking our fingers into the little holes until we have no more fingers and toes left, as if we thought that if we could only hold on long enough, the dam would repair itself. And still the dam continues to spring leaks. We forget, deny, or don't understand the fact that addiction is progressive, that it gets worse, not better. As a general rule, the longer we can keep our alcoholic or addict from crashing, the worse the crash will be.

The more enabling that takes place, the more out of control and the less responsible the addict becomes. Gradually, the codependent takes on more and more of the job of controlling the addict's behavior—or tries to. The fact is, of course, that the responsibility for controlling one's own behavior is the proper job and responsibility of each individual human being, and except in the case of very young children, no one can do it for us. But somehow, in the heat of the day-to-day crises that mark the lives in a chemically dependent family, that fundamental fact of life gets ignored or forgotten.

Some codependents who were the children of addicted parents never learned that each person is responsible for himself, because their parents, who literally held their lives in their hands, were made so fundamentally irresponsible by their addiction or dysfunction. For them, the hopeless situation of having to control the behavior of an out-of-control alcoholic is well-known territory, and they settle into it with a kind of comfortable despair. Codependents who grew up in homes where there was severe psychological disorder or mental illness behave in similar ways.

Codependents who grew up in homes where there was chronic and severe illness learned an overly responsible and caretaking style of behavior. The family's response to the sick member was to assume a greater proportion of that member's normal family responsibilities, to pitch in and care for that member, and to accept a loved one's inability to function as a fact of everyday life. They fit right in with a relationship partner who has been rendered dysfunctional by the disease of addiction.

Other codependents seem not to have had childhood or other experience with alcoholism. Probably there is such a thing as adult-onset codependency. The most likely scenario for its development would be in a relationship with an addict or alcoholic who showed no symptoms of the disease when the relationship was forming, where the codependent partner adapted so slowly to the emerging and progressive symptoms that the changes in his or her attitudes and behavior were hardly noticeable. These folks may respond in a codependent manner to the growing dysfunction out of a framework of salt-of-the-earth beliefs. Typically they came from families in which propriety, religious beliefs, and philosophical values were placed above emotional realities. This type of codependent says things like "We don't air our dirty laundry in public," and "People like us work hard, pay our bills on time, and don't embarrass ourselves." As often as not these codependents married or became involved with their addict long before there were any obvious signs that addiction would later become a problem. They seem to have regarded each new step in the progression of their partner's addiction as a temporary aberration that would correct itself in time if only they would hold the fort while their partner was on a vacation from personal responsibility. Of course, addiction being progressive, things don't get better; they get worse and worse until finally the codependent is forced by some crisis to abandon the front of propriety and cry out for help.

Attempts to Control

Either way, the codependent partner's attempts to control the addicted partner's behavior become more intense as that behavior goes more out of control. Gentle suggestions about watching how much he drinks turn to angry harangues after each embarrassing drunk. What may have been once an equal financial partnership now sees the codependent partner playing the role of Chancellor of the Exchequer, paying all the bills and doling out small-enough advances of cash to try to prevent the addict from buying more cocaine. The codependent becomes a detective, checking the whereabouts of the addict, trying to be sure she is where she's supposed to be at all times.

When the addict can't or won't cooperate by shaping up, the codependent starts to get angry. Not that the anger is very obvious or direct, of course. Oh, no, we're much too involved in being nice, loving people. We express our anger only very indirectly toward our addicts, with sarcastically negative comments, sighs and rolls of the eyes, by sexual and interpersonal withdrawal. Or we turn our anger inward upon ourselves, becoming depressed martyrs, anxious phobics, stressed-out nags, or frantic and oppressive restorers of order. Or we get sick. Or we vent our anger inappropriately, kicking the dog, abusing our children, or screaming at other drivers on the freeway.

The more wild and out of control things become, the more energetic and manipulative we become in our efforts to get things under control. We monitor the amount of our addict's drinking or using. We locate all the hiding places and pour the booze down the drain or flush the drugs down the toilet. We develop a song-and-dance act to delay the taking of the first drink. The greater our efforts to control our addict's use, the wilier he becomes at outwitting us, and the harsher and more violent the arguments become when we win.

Psychological Problems of Codependents

You really can't blame the codependent for trying. A chemically dependent relationship is a pretty unsafe place to live. One never knows when one will be embarrassed in front of family and friends. Every phone call when our addict isn't home could be a death knell. Every drinking bout could be the end of our marriage, or result in our being physically hurt. All people, whether codependent or not, when faced with a threatening or unsafe situation, will try to do what they can to remove or reduce the threat. Attempting to control the situation is a natural, but unfortunately unhelpful, response. The only result it produces in this situation is frustration, more anger, and, ultimately, severe depression.

Research has established that when subject animals are trapped in an unpleasant, punishing, or threatening situation, their first response is to try to do something about it (the main difference between rats and codependents being that rats, apparently the smarter of the two groups, focus their efforts on escaping). Once a rat finds a way to escape his unpleasant situation, he quickly becomes quite good at it. However, if the rat is prevented from escaping, and is therefore rendered helpless, sooner or later he just gives up. He curls up into a little ball and suffers silently in a pit of rat depression, refusing food or water. If it goes on long enough, he just dies. Researchers have termed this form of giving up "learned helplessness," because the rat, having learned that he cannot escape, lapses into a profound, helpless depression.

"The codependent partner's attempts to control the addicted partner's behavior become more intense as that behavior goes more out of control."

Phyllis described the helpless depression of the codependent: "After ten years of watching him get worse and worse no matter what I did, one day I just gave up. It seemed as if I stopped feeling, stopped thinking, and stopped doing anything in my life except what was absolutely necessary to get from today to tomorrow. I don't know why. I knew tomorrow would always be just the same as today. One more fight, maybe, one more unpaid bill. Who cared anymore?

"And the scary thing was that it felt good, for a

change, not to care about anything. At least it didn't hurt. I stopped going out. I'd send the kids to the store. Then I stopped getting dressed. Who was there to care what I looked like?

"I finally knew I had to get help the morning I just stepped over his body, passed out on the kitchen floor, as if he wasn't there, and served the kids breakfast with him just lying there."

Why didn't Phyllis leave? Why did she behave like the rat who can't escape, when for ten years the front door was right there? Why did she behave as if she were totally helpless, when she could have just "left the bum," as many of her harder-headed and more pragmatic friends had advised? In Phyllis's case, the answer was that she had learned a long time ago that it was hopeless to try to escape. The eldest daughter of an alcoholic mother, she first watched her poor father practice his tolerant, long-suffering codependency for years, and more and more assumed the burden as she grew up. Children know they can't escape from their parents, because when they're little, they literally couldn't survive without them. By the time they would be able to survive without their parents, the role of codependent, depressed caretaker has become so "normal" to them that the thought of leaving their situation never occurs to them as a realistic option. Phyllis's apparent helplessness was learned, and she will have to unlearn it before she can recover from her depression and her codependency. . . .

Health Problems

Codependents, as a result of living in close proximity with an alcoholic or chemically dependent parent or spouse, develop serious psychological problems. Whether the codependency syndrome began in childhood by living as the child of an alcoholic or addicted parent or whether the problem emerged in adulthood, developing in rhythm with the spouse's emerging alcoholism, the psychological symptoms are similar. All codependents suffer from chronic anxiety, which is the result of living on "red alert." All codependents seem controlling and manipulative as they try so desperately to create a zone of safety for themselves and their families. All codependents suffer from chronic depression, the inevitable emotional reaction to the fact that no matter how hard they try, they cannot control or overcome their partner's drinking. All codependents experience serious erosion of self-esteem, except possibly those who had little to begin with, as their lives become progressively unmanageable; they experience shame and guilt over the financial difficulties, family discord, and social embarrassments caused by the family addiction. Many codependents become symptomatic with disorders of impulse control. Eating disorders, phobias, and compulsive neuroses are common by-products of the ongoing anxiety built into the codependent relationship.

In addition to these complex and very serious psychological symptoms, codependents often suffer from a variety of physical illnesses, just like their chemically dependent partners. While liver damage is seldom observed in nonalcoholic codependents, and the source of the physical problems is stress and depression rather than abuse of alcohol, the physical health consequences of codependence are scarcely less serious. Chronic back problems due to muscular tensions, low-grade infections due to psychological stress on the immune system, migraines, treatment-resistant hypertension, and gastrointestinal problems, such as ulcers, diarrhea, and colitis, are commonly seen among codependents. Cardiovascular difficulties, such as angina and stroke, may be aggravated by the stress of codependency. Alcoholism or drug dependencies, which might have lain indefinitely as latent tendencies in the codependent, are often triggered into active process by drinking or by using drugs with the addicted partner, or by drinking or using drugs for relief. Suicide is by no means unknown among codependents as the ultimate way out.

Medical problems are often complicated and allowed to become more serious because of the reluctance of the codependent to discuss with his or her doctor the real truth about how awful things are at home. The tendency to cover up, to deny, to protect the addicted spouse is like a reflex in the codependent, and as much as he or she would like to reach out for help and support, the inner imperative to keep the family secrets is often stronger still. In recent years, many more physicians have become sensitive to the possibility that alcoholism or drug abuse may underlie many of the chronic complaints of frequently seen patients, but few have yet learned to search out codependency as a chronic, underlying source of stress upon the patient.

"All codependents suffer from chronic anxiety, which is the result of living on 'red alert.'"

With all due respect to the seriousness of the psychological and medical problems associated with codependency, it is the behavioral style of the codependent that creates the most devastating and life-quashing effects. The life-style that evolves from fighting the hopeless battle to control or overcome your partner's addiction is a joyless, unspontaneous, rigid, and depressing one that precludes pleasure, negates accomplishment, and denies any possibility of establishing spiritual meaning or personal growth. Codependency is boring.

Codependents are, first and foremost, caretakers. We seem to derive our sense of self-esteem from meeting, or trying to meet, the needs of others. We create relationships with other people based on their needs and not our own. We behave as if we believe that if we make ourselves valuable to other people by meeting their needs, they will love us. Many codependents become professional caretakers, entering fields such as nursing, medicine, psychology, counseling, and social work. Usually, we are very, very good at it. No wonder! . . .

Marcia

Marcia's case fits a stereotypical picture of the female codependent. Marcia was thirty-four years old and had been married for ten years to her husband, Bill. The couple had two children, ages four and seven. Marcia is employed as an administrative assistant to the head of a large local corporation. Marcia came to treatment because she was concerned and wanted information about what appeared to be a drinking problem that Bill was developing.

Although Marcia clearly wished to keep our discussions centered on Bill and his problems, she herself appeared quite depressed to me. Generally she showed little emotion and spoke in a quiet voice. Often, however, she appeared on the verge of tears, even when the subject did not seem particularly sad. A physical history revealed that she had gained thirty-eight pounds over the past three years, was having some trouble sleeping, and was developing psoriasis. When I suggested she might be suffering from depression, however, she denied it, saying it was "only a bit of stress, probably no more than normal for a busy person." I asked Marcia to keep a log of her daily activities. She resisted this task for several sessions, stating with some irritation that she didn't see how this was going to help Bill's problem. When she finally completed her weekly log, it showed that she rose at 4:30 A.M. (she explained that her boss arrived at work at 7:00, and that he expected coffee ready when he arrived). She described her job as "meeting My Lord and Master's every need, complete from answering his correspondence and picking up his clean shirts to booking international travel arrangements and even writing a speech or two." She observed that her boss did not make her job any easier, because although he had often put in a full day's work before noon, he had an annoying habit of disappearing in the afternoon, particularly if there was drinking at lunch. She observed that covering for him was becoming a job in itself.

Marcia left work at 5:30 and normally drove straight to the day-care center to pick up Danny, age seven, and Kim, age four. She confessed that it had been a source of ongoing irritation for her that Bill, who was an outside salesperson with a schedule almost entirely under his control, almost never picked up the children. Her irritation, she was quick to state, was not because this made her day harder but because she felt guilty about the children spending as

much time as they did in day care. She would have preferred to take a job with shorter hours, she said, but the family needed to rely on her fairly substantial income since Bill's could go up and down so dramatically.

Marcia spent from 6:15 until 8:30 preparing dinner for the family and spending "quality time" with the children. Her concern about Bill's drinking had to do with the fact that he was now not home for dinner on two or three nights during the week, usually phoning from one cocktail lounge or another to explain that he was "doing business." Bill's contention was that, at thirty-eight, this was the make-or-break point in his career, and that she was just going to have to deal with the fact that for the next several years he was going to be married to his job. Marcia was careful to explain that it was not that Bill was not home to help her with the children that bothered her so much as that she was concerned about his drinking (his speech often seemed to be slurred when he called to say he'd be late) and about his driving home after drinking.

As soon as the children were in bed, Marcia's habit was to call her mother, who lived alone since her father's death (of liver disease). Marcia called every night because "Mom lives alone and just needs someone to chat with, and because I feel better knowing she's okay." By the time the phone call was complete and the dinner things cleaned up, it was normally 10:00. "By that time, I really need to get to bed," Marcia sighed, "but if Bill's not home, I can't get to sleep for worrying about him, and lately, if he is home by that time, we seem to get into stupid arguments that last sometimes for hours. I've learned *never* to comment about his drinking. That's sure to start an argument.". . .

"Codependents are, first and foremost, caretakers."

Marcia was consuming herself and her life in her compulsive need to meet the needs of others. Every waking moment was devoted to the needs of her husband, her boss, her children, her church. There was no time to take a walk, read a book, enroll in a class, watch television, or to do anything else that was solely and exclusively *for herself*. So powerful was her inner demand that she attend to the needs of others that she could not even tolerate the idea that counseling might be for her, and not to solve her husband's problem.

Marcia is typical of tens of thousands of codependent women who live with and love alcoholic or otherwise chemically dependent men. To the world around them they are saints and heroines who bear up mightily under the demands of life with a worthless drunk of a husband. To their husbands they are either uncomplaining fixtures to be both ignored and depended upon, or irritating martyrs whose silent or not-so-silent suffering fills them with rage. To the chemical-dependency counselor they are codependents in deep and powerful denial. To themselves they are no one, counting for nothing except to the degree that they fulfill their obligations and meet the needs of those around them.

Codependents are blamers. Paradoxically, they seem at one moment to blame themselves for everything that is wrong in their world and at the next moment to be blaming everyone *but* themselves. Because codependents typically have very low levels of self-esteem, they tend to be very hard on themselves, believing that if only they were smarter, or nicer, or more Christian (or Jewish or whatever), or stronger, or had a better faith, they would find the solutions to all of the problems that the people in their lives are suffering. On the other hand, because they are so little focused on themselves and their own experience, and because their own denial is so strong, they obsess self-righteously on the idea that if only the others in their lives would "straighten up and fly right," the problems over which the codependent labors day and night would not exist.

"Codependents fail to see the distinctions, or boundaries, between themselves and the people they are close to."

Codependents are compulsive people pleasers. Because they tend to believe that they are not worthy of love or happiness or getting what they want and need, their consistent tendency is to attempt to get love by meeting the needs of others, to gain happiness in the happiness of others, and get what they need and want by creating obligation in others. One bit of Al-Anon (the organization for spouses and partners of alcoholics) wit says that "Codependents don't make friends—they take hostages!"

Codependents are notoriously poor communicators. It's not that they're not verbal—most are. It's that directly communicating wants, needs, and feelings is experienced by the codependent as a terribly dangerous thing to do. Many codependents who were raised in alcoholic families learned that they could not directly acknowledge a situation for what it was. "Daddy's not drunk, honey, he's sick." Many believe that if they don't give the people in their lives what they want that they will be deserted, either emotionally or physically, so they fear expressing contrary wishes or opinions. . . .

Codependents, like their alcoholic and addicted loved ones, are deniers. Sometimes they learned to deny as children, to protect themselves from the knowledge of the awful realities around them. Often they learned from their codependent parent that reality is what you say it is ("Daddy is taking his medicine, honey, because it helps him calm down from working too hard"), so they feel that if they say things are just fine, it will make it true that things are just fine. Often codependents use denial to protect themselves from feeling a deep sense of shame about themselves and everything connected to them. (If I admit my wife's a drunk, what does that prove about me?)

Codependents fail to see the distinctions, or boundaries, between themselves and the people they are close to. They dream of a love relationship in which two become one, and there is a complete fusion of identities. They think that love means that they will be perfectly understood, perfectly accepted, and cared for. They think that in that perfect world, everything will be perfect, including themselves and their partners. They believe that all they need to do is work hard enough to shape themselves and their partners into that model of perfection, and in the end, all will be wonderful. They become confused and frustrated when others do not share their notions about what is good and right, and believe that it must be because they have failed to make themselves properly understood. Usually, they believe they know better than others do about what is good for them. They help when their help is not asked for, they advise when their advice is not appreciated, and when others fail to heed their advice or accept their help, they try to manipulate situations and people so that things come out right anyway. They can't understand when people become angry with them. They were only trying to help, right?

The Core Belief of Codependents

Codependents all seem to have a deeply held conviction, a *core belief*, that they can control themselves, the people around them, and indeed the course of history itself. Not that they would ever say so in so many words, of course. It sounds too silly, even to the codependent ear, to actually express such an idea. But the behavior of the codependent reflects the idea that if I just try hard enough, and if I work long enough at it, I can make things go the way I think they should be. . . .

Codependency, because of its intimate and reciprocal relationship with addiction, is progressive. It goes from bad to worse as the addict's disease progresses, and each new symptom of codependency is a direct response to a change in the condition of the addict. Codependents hang in there year in and year out believing that if they will only try hard enough, pray hard enough, and love hard enough, things will change.

Things will change, all right. Until you begin to work at your own recovery from codependency, things are certain to get worse.

Arthur Wassmer is clinical director of Kirkland Psychological Associates in Washington. He has specialized in treating addictive disorders since 1982.

viewpoint 2

Codependency Is a Misleading Concept

Morris Kokin and Ian Walker

Are women who develop relationships with alcoholics *different* from other women? Are they victims of circumstance, or the authors of their own destiny? Are they simply unfortunates who happen to have strayed into a web called alcoholism, or do they deliberately seek out an alcoholic mate in hope of satisfying certain deep-rooted needs within themselves? Does such a woman really want her mate to stop drinking, or does she only say so? Does she support his efforts to stop, or does she unconsciously impede his progress and undermine his attempts?

By now you might well be asking yourself, what kind of questions are these? They are surely not serious. If anything, they seem designed to give offense. Any woman who has ever been through the turmoil and terror of living with an alcoholic, whose hopes, dreams, and family life have been shattered by the bottle, could scarcely be blamed—in the face of such remarks—for feeling stunned, angry, and hopelessly misunderstood.

On the other hand, the question does exist: *Is* it just possible that such women—including those who have died at the hands of an alcoholic partner or who have chosen to take their own lives as a desperate, final solution to their anguish—deliberately committed themselves to a relationship with a man they knew to be alcoholic or susceptible to alcoholism? Is it remotely possible that these women avoid seeking help and stay in such relationships because they are disturbed people? Is it conceivable that they derive some "sick" satisfaction from such a relationship?

Let us look at some of the things that have been said in this area.

Historically, two major psychological perspectives have dominated our understanding of wives of alcoholics and influenced societal attitudes toward them. One describes these women as villains while the other sees them as victims. What is noteworthy, however, is that even when perceived as a victim, the wife continues to be blamed in one way or another for her own suffering as well as for that of her children and alcoholic mate.

In addition to the foregoing, a third perspective has also been emerging in recent years, one which tends to describe wives' behavior as symptomatic of illness. Many professionals no longer consider alcoholism to be a disease associated with just the drinker, they view it as a *family* disease—all who live with the alcoholic are said to become as sick as, or sicker than, the drinker. This so-called family disease has variously been referred to as coaddiction, coalcoholism, or codependency.

Once the disease manifests, codependents are said to behave in a manner that is not in their own best interest and that unintentionally supports and prolongs the drinking of the alcoholic. In short, this is just another way of saying that wives are somehow to blame for their own suffering as well as for the suffering of those around them.

In simplest terms, then, it does not appear to matter which psychological perspective one draws from. Whether victim, villain, or "diseased," wives of alcoholics are somehow seen as responsible, directly or indirectly, for the difficulties incurred by alcoholism. . . .

Labels That Disable

When we describe someone as coalcoholic, what exactly are we saying? To my mind the implication is that the person spoken about is somehow an accessory or accomplice to the alcoholic and all the wrongdoing that his drinking may entail. A similar case might be made for the terms "coaddict" and "codependent." Likewise, what about the word "enabler?" When applied to an unpleasant reality— such as alcoholism is—the expression takes on an equally unpleasant connotation. It is as though we were speaking about a person who "enables" a crime to take place by averting his or her gaze.

Wives of alcoholics are consistently tagged with the above labels. Not only this, they are also accused of denial, lying, covering up, protecting, excusing, and defending their mates' behavior. The fact is, the terms used to describe the behavior of these women are at best negative, at worst somewhat synonymous with the language used to describe deviant or irresponsible behavior.

The Influence of Words

The point is simple. Words influence—they can enhance or distort the way we perceive reality. When we affix negative labels to wives of alcoholics, these women start to look negative, feel negative, and suffer negative treatment at the hands of society and professionals, who should know better.

The majority of professionals who employ these labels will insist—and legitimately—that they do not blame women for causing their mates' alcoholism. Nonetheless, the words exert their own hidden effect. Living with an alcoholic is itself a very painful ordeal. What makes it even more difficult is that the alcoholic tends to deny his drinking problem and to project blame onto everyone and everything other than the bottle and himself, the most common target being, of course, the wife.

Because many people, including wives of alcoholics, are either uninformed or misinformed about alcoholism, they fail to understand the denial of the alcoholic. They thus tend to feed neatly into his itinerary of excuses and explanations. Also, since in many of his accusations there is a hint of truth, the wife is often inveigled into accepting at least some if not a great deal of the blame for his behavior. This contributes not only to feelings of guilt and shame but also to a gradual loss of self-esteem and self-confidence.

The irony of the whole situation—and it is a tragic one—is that many therapists are inclined to interpret these feelings and consequent coping styles as illness, as we have already seen. They then attach their negative labels to describe the disturbance, and inadvertently succeed in adding to the low self-esteem and low self-confidence that these women already have and that they, the therapists, initially set out to cure. In some sort of unintentional but convoluted way, they end up supporting the alcoholic's accusations that his drinking is related to his wife's disturbance or sickness.

One of the most questionable terms of all those applied to wives of alcoholics is "codependency." The expression started to become popular around the 1970s, and although its origins are somewhat obscure, the concept itself is all too familiar. It is just a new word used to dress an old idea—to camouflage and perpetuate the notion that wives of alcoholics are sick people badly in need of psychotherapy.

I will not attempt to give an exact meaning for "codependency," simply because there is no single agreed-upon psychological definition of it. In fact, to stretch a point, it might almost be said that there are about as many interpretations of the word as there are professionals using it. Some describe it as a learned behavioral problem; others say that it is a personality disorder; still others say it is something that *resembles* a personality disorder; and many others say that it is a disease.

According to some theorists, codependency is caused by living with or loving an alcoholic, who may be one's spouse, parent, grandparent, or close friend. Other theorists see the cause as involvement with anyone who is chemically dependent, and still others regard codependency as an innate part of an individual's makeup that responds to involvement with an alcoholic. To add to the potpourri, there are some specialists who claim that codependency may have nothing to do with alcohol or other chemicals but is the result of growing up in any type of disturbed family environment.

The characteristics and behavior of the individual who is supposedly afflicted with this condition are so general and all-inclusive that one wonders if there is anyone left on this planet who is *not* codependent. Codependents deny that they are involved with an alcoholic or that they have personal problems; they attempt to control others; they are confused and cannot express their real feelings; they feel depressed, angry, afraid, worried, and anxious; they have low self-esteem and low self-confidence, and they often develop stress-related medical complications.

"When we affix negative labels to wives of alcoholics, these women . . . suffer negative treatment at the hands of society."

One could go on and on describing the characteristics of codependents, but it would probably consume a good portion of this chapter—and there is really no point to it. Though there is no single definition and both the causes and characteristics vary considerably, the concept has been employed almost exclusively in connection with wives of alcoholics. Furthermore, the way these women are affected and the way they respond to or attempt to cope with a mate's excessive drinking is described as the *disease* of codependency.

There is so much wrong factually and morally with this concept that one scarcely knows where to begin to attack it. Describing women who are living with or married to an alcoholic as codependent suggests that these women are all the same—sharing the same experiences and consequences—and we know that is absolutely not true. Even when the effects are similar, wives tend to perceive and interpret the problem differently, and they also attempt to cope with the situation in a multitude of ways that can be very different from one woman to another. Perhaps this explains the numerous definitions and characteristics needed to describe codependents—so that no woman who is involved with an alcoholic will feel forgotten or left out.

A second problem with the term "codependency" is the link it establishes. Just because an alcoholic is considered to be dependent on alcohol does not make the spouse or lover *co*alcoholic, *co*addicted, *co*dependent, or *co*-anything. Why should she not be just who she is and be given the dignity and respect of retaining her own individuality and identity? If her mate were mentally deficient would she be codeficient? If he developed a disease such as epilepsy or diabetes would she be a coepileptic or codiabetic? Is it not enough that a woman married to an alcoholic share the agony and grief of his disease? Must we also make her share the disease in name?

Codependency and Sickness

Wives of alcoholics are emotionally affected in numerous ways—but are they really sick? The answer is almost unequivocally no. In feeling the way she does and in attempting to cope in the way she does, the wife shows signs of health, not sickness. It is natural and healthy to feel bitter about a man who is destroying one's life and one's family.

It is also understandable that a wife feels worried and even pities her mate, because this is a man she certainly once loved a great deal and perhaps still does. If alcoholism were considered to be willful misconduct, then we might legitimately ask ourselves how she can feel pity for such a man. But if we say that alcoholism is an illness, then it makes little sense to criticize the woman who loves him for being concerned about what is happening to her sick husband. It is as if certain professionals are looking for any way in which to interpret the wife's behavior as illness.

We speak about emotional and mental disturbance when an individual does not behave in a manner appropriate to a given circumstance. Here we have an entire population of women who are behaving in a manner most appropriate to their circumstances, and their actions are defined as indicative of disturbance and a need for psychiatry. Why?

Part of the answer is that we are living in a sickness-oriented rather than a health-oriented society. In other words, by virtue of our training and diagnostic ability, we are often so busy looking for the telltale flaw, the hidden hint of sickness, that we fail to recognize signs of health. In short, for health we can do nothing, so we look for sickness, because we have remedies for that.

Many people who are quite normal suffer from problems in living, and wives of alcoholics suffer from a very specific problem—they are living with an alcoholic. There is no question that the experience may bring on a wide range of negative emotions. But this is surely a most appropriate reaction to a very painful and frightening problem in life. How, therefore, does this translate into codependence and thus sickness?

"Wives of alcoholics are emotionally affected in numerous ways—but are they really sick? The answer is almost unequivocally no."

According to at least one author, codependence is a disease because it has a clearly identifiable onset (the point at which the individual's life is not working), it has a definable course (the continued deterioration of the individual, emotionally and mentally), and if it is not treated, there is a predictable outcome (death).

If this is the basis for determining that so-called codependency is a disease, then almost anything in life is a disease—in fact, life itself is a disease. It has a clear onset (birth) and a definable course (the human being after initially growing and developing begins to deteriorate physically and mentally), and whether it is treated or not, the outcome is predictable—in fact, guaranteed. It is death.

The logic of such arguments defies comprehension.

Alternatives

The time is well overdue to stop accusing wives of alcoholics for everything and anything they do or fail to do. The name-calling should stop—they are *not* codependent, coalcoholic, coaddicted, near-alcoholic, or enablers, they are just human beings living in a tremendously difficult situation that requires immediate, urgent attention. They need proper information, education, and support. They need professional services that will treat them in an understanding, sensitive manner and help highlight how well they have actually done in their efforts to keep themselves and their families bonded together against spectacular odds.

Tragically, this is unlikely to happen. There are those who will not be satisfied until they have "pathologized" the behavior of these women—in other words, until they have identified their behavior as a form of disease. There is even a suggestion that codependency not only be retained as an appropriate term, but be adopted into the official psychiatric handbook, *Diagnostic and Statistical Manual of Mental Disorders*, as a legitimate personality disorder. I, for one, hope that this idea will be carefully reconsidered. The additional harm that this would do to wives of alcoholics is unconscionable.

"Codependency," just like its predecessors "coalcoholic" and "coaddiction" and its contemporary "enabler," is an absolutely unsatisfactory and insidious term. Granting it further status as a disease only adds to the damage already done by the alcoholic and his bottle.

Similarly, when attempts to cope are defined as enabling, the responsibility for drinking or not drinking is turned over to the wife. My understanding has always been that alcoholics do not need to be enabled to drink. They are quite adept at enabling themselves whatever the circumstances, if that is what they choose to do.

"The time is well overdue to stop accusing wives of alcoholics for everything and anything they do or fail to do."

The alcoholic needs to assume responsibility for his disease and for doing something about it. Instead, well-intentioned theorists too often pass the buck and point the finger at the wife. Where the wife needs understanding, she receives negative labels. The unfortunate result is that all too often she is condemned even before she enters the specialist's office.

Morris Kokin is a clinical psychologist and associate director at the Foster Clinic, an alcohol and drug treatment center in Montreal, Canada. Ian Walker is a writer and former senior editor at Reader's Digest.

"Except for my brother's drinking, we all look reasonably good on the surface. But, beneath the surface, I see the same self-hatred, self-abuse . . . that I know so well within myself."

viewpoint 3

Alcoholic Parents Harm Their Children

Regina Gray

For many years I struggled for some sense of understanding and detachment, some beginning of forgiveness. I thought that I had done much of my work by learning about alcoholism and by healing, as much as possible, my relationship with my mother. But three years ago, in graduate school, I heard the term "adult child of an alcoholic" for the first time and discovered that I—my entire self—had been affected by my mother's alcoholism. It wasn't just a matter of dealing with Mom, but of looking into and dealing with myself. Listening to that teacher, I could feel everything she said sink in. It was kind of like thinking that you had to paint your house and then discovering that all the wood had been destroyed by termites and needed to be replaced—the task felt huge. It was too deep. I felt as if I just wanted to chuck the whole process and move somewhere else.

However, it was comforting to discover that many of my personal quirks were common to ACOAs. That made me feel much less screwed-up somehow, because there was a reason for the way I felt about myself and the world. I had learned to be a certain way, and there was hope that I could unlearn it. This meant going back into the craziness of my family again, opening up wounds I thought I was finished with. But the hope of changing, of finding out that there was another way to be, was irresistible. I could do more than make peace with my life. I could learn another way to live.

Restarting the Healing Process

So, the process began again: therapy, reading, workshops to discover what I had taken in as a child, to investigate the alcoholic distortion I'd known as reality. I have been expanding my world, learning new choices, new meanings. I don't believe that anyone ever heals completely, but I am a lot better.

Regina Gray, "Daughters." Copyright © 1989 by E. Nelson Hayes. Reprinted from *Adult Children of Alcoholics Remember*, edited by E. Nelson Hayes, by permission of Harmony Books.

This, then, is not only about what it was like, but also who I am. I am writing it under a pseudonym, a contradiction I suppose, but I am unwilling to unmask the family that still lives so much in denial, a model family in a model community. This comes less from a desire to protect them than from my unwillingness to take on the role of family savior. I don't want to try to fix my family anymore. So I step out, love them, hope they will find their own paths to healing while I get on with my life.

I hope that I may touch the memories of others who grew up as I did, not knowing that there was anything else. We may not be able to save our families, but we can help and support each other. That is almost enough.

First Memories

The first memory, always, is that of coming home, tense and scared, furtively looking for someone to ask, "How is she?" All six of us did it, and I remember it clearly back to first grade.

If the answer was OK, my shoulders came down, my throat opened, I could breathe. Those were moments of safety, of being able to look forward to some happiness, some fun. If the answer was bad, my body stayed tense, stomach lurching with nausea, and I'd tiptoe into the house and head upstairs, avoiding any noise that might catch her attention.

Frequently, there were terrifying rides home from grammar school. Once a week or so Mom would arrive there late, very drunk, and drive us home at ten miles an hour, through stop signs and red lights. The six of us would sit rigidly in the back seats, not looking at each other. We made no sound of fear, afraid of increasing her anger. I knew clearly that we could have been killed. We never had an accident, and my mother has never been arrested for drunk driving. I used to pray on those rides, promising novenas, promising perfection, if only we would make it home safely. Once there we would sit in our rooms, listening to her noises, the crashing of pots in the kitchen, the loud muttering in her thickened voice. And I would dread her call. As the oldest and a daughter, I knew I would eventually have to go down into the kitchen to set the table. It was better to go voluntarily rather than to wait to be called. But sometimes I would hide, unable to force myself downstairs. I always entered that kitchen hoping that if I did it right and fast and quietly, maybe she wouldn't notice me, wouldn't attack. She rarely hit me, but I felt as though I was always waiting for a blow.

As children, we didn't know we were dealing with alcohol, but thought it was some mysterious, unpredictable mood. My family was ruled by these "moods." We all developed finely tuned antennae that were sensitive not to our own thoughts, feelings, and needs, but to hers. If we could read her, we might be able to figure out what she wanted and avoid an outburst. I don't remember that it ever worked, but we kept on trying.

We went through these dreadful experiences together and yet we never talked about them among ourselves. However, we would warn each other when Mom needed to be avoided. And there was an unspoken agreement to protect each other from being too much the focus of her abuse. If she was on one of us for too long, someone would do something like spill a glass of milk to draw her fire. As the oldest I was most frequently the buffer, but I remember being rescued often myself. The strangest part is that it was not even conscious. We have only become aware of it as we have begun to talk together in the last year. We agreed that we shared some sense of trying to take care of each other by parceling Mom's anger out among us, and that we knew when she was going too far and needed to be redirected.

The Two Mothers

Most confusing for us kids was that my mother was like two persons. One was an all-loving, playful, perfect Mom who baked her own cakes, gave wonderful parties and hugs, and told us how much she loved us. She was never angry or impatient, and she taught us that anger was bad. She told us how much she loved having us and recounted long romantic stories about how she and Dad had met. The other person was someone filled with hatred who told us she wished we'd never been born to ruin her life. She screamed at us and hit us. She said that Dad had forced her to have sex with him, and we were all unwanted and resented pregnancies. So we thought of her as two people and were always wary about which one was home on any given day. It was bewildering and terrifying .

I remember how silent we all were with each other. Maybe we were afraid to stir up trouble, but I think also it was because we'd been robbed of the capacity to name our experience. We did not have the permission, the courage, or the words to do so. We were focused on my mother's responses, not our own. As children we were allowed to be happy, even rambunctious when Mom was okay. Dad is a reserved, rational, nonexpressive man, and he would show irritation or bemusement, but was most often impassive behind a book. Anger, and to a lesser extent sadness, belonged to my mother.

"As children, we didn't know we were dealing with alcohol, but thought it was some mysterious, unpredictable mood."

Of course we fought as kids, sometimes bitterly, but always quietly, so as not to draw Mom's attention. We did not ask for help or intervention from our parents. We were both isolated from each other and bonded to each other. We protected one another, lied for one another, but did not know one another.

As I got older I continued to try to put the two mothers together, but I was never very successful. When she was in a warm and loving mood, I rushed to be with her, to tell her my adolescent secrets. Later, she would spill them out viciously to my family or friends, her contempt for me apparent. And always beneath my rage and humiliation there was a feeling of surprise, as though I'd forgotten that one Mom would know what I'd confided to the other. It took me years to learn finally to shut her out and look for intimacy elsewhere. Still, those brief moments of closeness were, somehow, worth the later betrayal.

Sometimes I think that my mother's dislike of me comes partially from my refusal to leave her alone, my persistent expectations of love, my demands that she give me what I now know she could not give. I tried to make her love me in a way that my siblings never did. I was a drain on her energies and a reminder of her inadequacies and self-doubts. I wanted her to give to me what she had never received for herself.

Revulsion of the Body

One time in my early adolescence, I heard a strange sound in the bathroom. I went to investigate and found my mother dazed, sitting on the toilet, vomiting down her chin and onto her chest. Cleaning up the vomit, wiping her, dragging and pushing her upstairs to her bedroom, I choked with wanting to cry out to someone to stop it—this was my mother! Seeing her that way was more than I could bear. The sense of something gone terribly wrong was overwhelming. Her degradation became my most secret shame. I needed her to be someone I could want to be like, someone who would show me that it was good to be a woman. But I could see only danger. At that moment I wanted to disown her. I hated her, and I hated everything about her.

I looked at her body, fouled with vomit and shit, and felt a self-disgust that translated itself into years of confused and angry feelings about my own female body. The more my body became like hers, the more I fought any identification with her. I retreated into rigid rationality and undermined my physical attractiveness in order to strangle my sexual feelings, which threatened me with loss of control and a female's fate.

It was brutal, growing into adulthood while trying to fight my womanhood at the same time. I am still discovering what my efforts to exorcise my mother cost me. I am still learning to inhabit and enjoy my female body. Sexuality is now more about connection than about violation, although I am still frightened by sexually aggressive men. I am still learning that appetite does not have to be addiction. I have been lucky. I have found other mothers, women who have been mentors and friends to me and who have helped me deal with the social sexism that also diminishes all women's lives.

I now know that my mother's disease is alcoholism, not gender, and that I can be a woman without being alcoholic. Today I can identify with my mother's body and sense the similarities and the differences. Her body speaks to me now of our mortality, but with tones of poignancy rather than disgust.

The Father's Role

When I was about twenty, I stood in the hallway and watched a scene between my parents that typified how they behaved toward each other. Dad was sitting in his favorite chair, reading, and Mom was standing in front of him, yelling about something. He ignored her, calmly turning the pages of his book. She became so enraged that her voice escalated into a screech and she began to jump up and down like Rumplestiltskin in the fairy tale. I began to laugh, filled with contempt for her and proud of my father's disdain of her childishness. She heard me, turned, and ran toward me, tears streaming down her cheeks. She hit me hard across the face. We began fighting with each other, hurling insults until she ran upstairs and I slammed out the front door. My father never stopped reading.

It took me years to discover the fury I harbor toward my father. He was always the rock I huddled against in order to escape Mom's stormy presence. I mistook his indifference for calm. I modeled myself after him as a way to avoid Mom's scary craziness. I tried to be like him and thought that we had a relationship.

It was my husband who first got angry about Dad. I remember my surprise the first time he asked why my father hadn't protected us from her. It had never entered my head that he could protect us. Mom was like a natural disaster, a hurricane, whose outbursts we all tried to live through. I was just grateful that his detachment balanced her ragings. I didn't notice his lack of input because it was such a relief that he wasn't contributing to the destructiveness. I didn't think about whether or not there was anything he could do to make things different. I didn't know it could be any different. My father did not grow up in an alcoholic home, yet he made no effort either to confront his wife about her drinking, or to protect his children from her random violence.

"It took me years to discover the fury I harbor toward my father."

When I look back, I feel incredible compassion for this woman who was so abandoned by her spouse. Nothing Mom did could penetrate his calm. She must have felt his contempt for her, his sense of moral superiority and self-sufficiency. My father, a well-known lawyer in a university town, was married to his work, and Mom was married to her bottle. I think that Dad reacted to Mom's drinking by retreating from her, looking on her as a weak and distasteful person. I think Mom believed that husbands were supposed to work hard to achieve money and acclaim, but then felt abandoned by Dad's preoccupation with his career. She did not have a husband, and we didn't have a father. Somehow, this marriage of workaholism and alcoholism has survived for thirty-five years.

Once I invited Dad to go to Al-Anon with me, but he said he was too busy. When my angry sister accused him of allowing us to be abused by Mom and challenged him to accept some responsibility, he told her that many children are abused and survive to live healthy, useful lives. So he knew and was, typically, concerned only that we not try to hold him accountable for our personal failures. I still can't believe that he didn't say he was sorry.

I feel ashamed now of laughing at my mother and of sharing my father's contempt for her. Today I have a better understanding of her unhappiness, and I know that she was ill, not bad. My mother came from a long line of alcoholics, so she might have become addicted in the happiest of relationships. But I sometimes think that if my father had confronted her, had taken more responsibility for the well-being of his children, we might have been in treatment many years ago.

How Brothers and Sisters Coped

Each of us has reacted differently to the past. One brother still speaks of our childhood like something out of the children's stories he wants to write. Having created a fantasy of the past, he lives in one in the present. I watch how he drinks. He abuses alcohol now, and I fear he is heading for alcoholism. I hate talking to him. It makes me feel scared and sad and helpless.

One sister is furious, holding on to her anger through years of therapy and Al-Anon. She goes home frequently, then storms out when she does not find what she wants there, leaving my parents bewildered and defensive. They talk periodically about hospitalizing her.

"I hated her drinking, but I worshiped her. Only through therapy and learning about alcoholism was I finally able to put those two sides of Mom together."

Another sister detached herself from Mom in her early teens and began her addiction to men. She has just broken off a relationship with her third alcoholic lover. She earns a lot of money and makes everyone around her laugh. I don't think anyone in the world knows who she is.

Another brother is a sexy womanizer with a cocaine habit. He works at a boring job for fast money and has no plans for the future. He was the most affectionate one of us as a child. I remember him crying for hours after he had tried to kiss Mom and she'd pushed him away. It sounds trite, but I think that in his promiscuity he is looking for the love and reassurance he never got. Underneath the macho bullshit, I see that little boy.

And the youngest, my little brother, is a determined go-getter who wants to have a lot of money so that he doesn't have to be dependent on anybody. He kicked cocaine because he didn't like needing anything. He is upset that he becomes periodically impotent when he falls in love with a woman. He is twenty-five and still lives with my parents, waiting until he has enough money to move out. Sounds like a soap opera.

The hardest part about getting to know my sibs has been finding out about their pain and their compromises with life. Except for my brother's drinking, we all look reasonably good on the surface. But, beneath the surface, I see the same self-hatred, self-abuse, anger, incapacity for love, and lack of trust inextricably mingled with the desperate hope for redemption yet fear of life that I know so well within myself. We look very different from each other, but we are truly brothers and sisters under the skin.

Several Themes

It's been hard for me to look at what I learned about myself and the world by being the daughter of an alcoholic mother. Thinking over my memories of her, I can uncover several themes operating within myself these past thirty-four years.

The first is about trust. I learned that people cannot be trusted, that professions of love are wonderful but fleeting moments that feel good but aren't real. I love people easily; I trust very few. It was a revelation when I slowly discovered another kind of love with the man who is my husband, a love that can be tested, that continues even as I hesitantly reveal myself. My first, very positive experience with therapy helped me get to the point where I could recognize the uniqueness and reality of this man's caring for me. There are now several more people whom I love and trust. It is still very hard for me to ask for help as I am still afraid of being a burden, of asking for too much, of being rejected. But so far I've been lucky in my choice of intimates and have not been harmed by them. They have taught me that I don't have to be perfect to be loved.

I also have trouble trusting myself and my ability to influence something in a positive way. I can be very ingratiating, so I struggle to learn a healthy assertiveness. I am more often aware of what another person wants than I am of my own requirements. I am learning to identify what I want and how to try to create it in a positive way. I want to stop feeling so impotent, so convinced that I will always make a fool of myself or that my impertinence will spread disaster. I need to know that I am not destructive, nor will I be destroyed.

I am preoccupied with death. If my husband is late coming home from work, I'm sure he has been in an accident. I am afraid of cars, and when I buy one my first concern is how it will survive an accident. An early morning phone ringing means a death. Life feels tenuous to me. I am sure that the world is a dangerous place, with disaster waiting in the wings to catch the unwary. I worry myself sick. It is a form of control. I still do not trust the universe.

Controlling Her Life

My mother's moods ran my life for years, and I found it extraordinarily difficult to separate from her. I lived at home until I was twenty-five, locked in a battle to force her to love me and to force her to stop drinking. They seemed somehow connected. When I finally left, at the urging of my therapist, I felt as though I was abandoning her to increasingly worse bouts of drinking. And I thought I was giving up any chance for love. Her drinking has progressed over the years to the point where it's hard to believe that her body still functions. But it does, without me. And I found love instead of losing it when I left.

I hated her drinking, but I worshiped her. Only through therapy and learning about alcoholism was I finally able to put those two sides of Mom together. Having to accept the fact that my perfect mother did not exist initiated a lengthy mourning process in which I began to know who she really was and what she could never be for me. It's been a coming to terms with her limitations and knowing that she was incapable of giving the unconditional love I longed for. It was letting go of the angel and the witch, and allowing her to be an imperfect human being. That helps me accept my own humanity and makes me more able to love.

My mother's love was scary when she was drunk. I felt—and she sometimes acted—as though she was out of control. We children were afraid of physical attack. Even now when someone gets angry with me I can still feel inside me a cowering three-year-old child who is scared to death. I am afraid of my own anger, too, afraid that it will kill or provoke an attack. When she was angry, Mom said she wanted to kill us. Sometimes anger still feels as though it can kill.

Anger is still a problem. My husband and I sometimes do fight. We talk in angry voices but never yell. A couple of friends help me by being willing to be reassuring even as they risk being angry and risk my being angry. It's slowly getting better, but I doubt I'll ever be at ease about it.

Carrying Guilt

I almost have my body back. By learning how to relax and how to breathe, I'm recovering from years of physical tension, from the tensed shoulders holding fear, the constricted throat stopping words, and the old, old anger that is locked away somewhere, invisible—almost. I used to shrivel up, to make myself small so that Mom would not notice me, so I would not offend her. My body carries the guilty conviction that I harmed her, ruined her life. By shutting myself down, I tried to apologize for being alive.

The saddest part for her daughters is what my mother taught us about being a woman. When she was sober, she lived and preached a life of selfless devotion to others—the worst thing she could call us was selfish. I was taught that I was supposed to marry a man I adored, have his children, and feel fulfilled and happy being a wife and mother. That would provide me with peace and satisfaction. When Mom was drunk, I saw her loneliness, anger, boredom, guilt, and self-hatred. It came pouring out, the alcohol giving voice to what was otherwise denied. I learned about dutiful sex and unwanted pregnancies. I heard that she made herself always available, yet saw herself as a doormat that the world could walk on—and did. I saw, hidden within the rage, the things she longed for but had forbidden herself: companionship and respect, her own money, the freedom to say no, to put herself first sometimes.

Like many women of her generation, Mom believed in an image of womanhood that strangled who she was as a person. All the "bad" parts of herself that she could not otherwise acknowledge came out when she was drunk. Some of the things she said were the secret, horrible truths of women's lives. And some were the alcoholic's lies.

In joining the women's movement, I learned about the lives of other women and placed my mother among them. I believe her unhappiness is real. I know how trapped she was. For years I refused to consider marriage and children, I was so afraid of following in her footsteps. But in pulling apart the sexism and the

alcoholism, I discovered what I can truly and effectively fight and what I must let go. I work to help make women's lives better. I do not try to cure Mom's alcoholism.

I do not drink, but that doesn't matter. Alcohol has affected every area of my life. This is true of every ACOA whose parent's or parents' most important relationship was with the contents of a bottle.

One Year Later

This might take a lifetime. Last year was frightening. My husband got very drunk at several parties, and I had to admit to myself that something was wrong. He was drinking alcoholically. He told me I was being oversensitive and exaggerating because of my history. In couples counseling to deal with another issue, he finally did admit to the therapist that he knew he was abusing alcohol and had a potential drinking problem. As relieved as I was that he recognized that, after his admission I was on an emotional roller coaster for days. I was frightened, furious; I felt trapped. All my sibs had either developed a personal problem with drugs and alcohol, or been involved with lovers who were addicts. I had felt blessed that I had somehow managed to escape. But when I looked into my dear husband's slack face and watched his personality change, I knew I hadn't escaped.

"I do not drink, but that doesn't matter. Alcohol has affected every area of my life."

We have agreements now. He has only three drinks at any party. When we go out, I have the car keys and he carries money for a taxi. I don't want to be a policeman, so if I get uncomfortable with his drinking and he does not want to leave, I can go home knowing he will get home safely.

Several months ago he got very sick in the middle of the night after drinking, and I made myself go downstairs and sleep on the couch while he cleaned up after himself. It took a lot of self-control not to take care of him. I will not participate; I will not be a coalcoholic. Maybe that will help us both. He has been fine lately, I think shaken by what he saw inside himself. But I don't relax around alcohol with him the way I used to. There is a part of me that watches, that is scared.

Last year we decided to move to the West Coast. Soon after the announcement my family went into action. My parents decided to redecorate their house, and the turmoil has given Mom the excuse for a lengthy binge. One of my brothers had a serious accident while driving drunk. One sister thought she was pregnant by her alcoholic ex-boyfriend. The other sister terminated a lengthy therapy and became suicidal. One brother is dealing cocaine to support his habit. Only the youngest and my ever-unflappable father were able to tell me that they would miss me. The others were all busy with their crises. This whole mess shows me both how woven I am into this family and how we hold together through crises and guilt. I felt like a traitor, abandoning them by refusing to help.

Detachment

Al-Anon has taught me about detachment. What a hard concept to understand as humane. I have had to learn to lovingly detach not only from my parents, but also from the siblings who try to pull me into their lives to fix them. I was supposed to sympathize with my brother because he was "tired" when he had an automobile accident. The pact in the family was that his exhaustion, not drunkenness, was the cause. At first I went along with the game; it made us feel close. Then I began to confront the denial. That was fine, but I took a further, fatal step. I thought it was my responsibility to make each one of them see what was happening. I drained myself trying to change them. I have had to learn not to do that anymore. I listen. I am interested. I confront. But I no longer make it my task to change them. The hardest part for me in being a part of an alcoholic family is this helpless loving, the heartbreaking realization that I cannot stop their denial, cannot live their lives. I wish I could.

This year I have learned that I must monitor the relationship I have with my brothers and sisters just as I do with my parents. We are closer than we used to be, but I have discovered with sadness that our interactions are also governed by denial. I know them better—for that I'm grateful. I cannot be as real with them as I can with my friends—for that I grieve. This process of understanding and healing seems like an archaeological dig: I keep going down through layers, each discovery a piece of healing in itself. I rest for a while, then I begin to dig again, not because I enjoy it, but because something new and upsetting has just thrust up through the surface.

I don't know where this will end, but I've made a commitment to go as far as I can with it. I have recently begun thinking seriously about having a child, which brings up in a new way my mother and her mothering. And I know that more than anything else in the world I want my daughter to have a mother who can love her. I want to spare her the grief of the daughters in my family.

Regina Gray is a pseudonym. She contributed this piece to Adult Children of Alcoholics Remember, *a collection of memoirs.*

"Although my childhood was certainly not pretty or conventional, it was a challenge, and I am a firm believer in the positive power of challenging situations."

Alcoholic Parents May Benefit Their Children

Tamela Beth

The greater the difficulty, the greater the glory.
Cicero

Adult children of alcoholics—that phrase has very recently become both part of our popular psychology and public property. Dozens of books and long lists of specialty counselors and therapy groups are all shouting, "You need help! Let us help you!" And many seem to be buying the words, sympathetic ears and therapy sessions—buying into the popular modern myth that says if we can understand and name a problem, it is no longer a problem; buying into the assumption that because we grew up in alcoholic homes, we are automatically in need of psychological help. Self-pity rears its ugly head here; it's lovely for some to get the attention, to be sure—and it's long overdue attention at that—but it all leaves a very sour taste in my mouth. It's just too hard to assume and generalize where human beings and their emotions are concerned, especially since there will always be at least one person who adamantly refuses to run with the pack or follow the popular or easier path. That person absolutely will not be a victim of her own life and circumstances.

I'll take hard-won integrity over cheap self-pity every time. No contest!

Yes, my mother is an alcoholic. Yes, it is nearly certain that both my father and stepfather are undiagnosed alcoholics. Yes, things were certainly difficult growing up. One might assume I would be dissatisfied with my childhood and upbringing. On the contrary. I'm actually rather pleased. Although my childhood was certainly not pretty or conventional, it was a challenge, and I am a firm believer in the positive power of challenging situations.

I am the eldest of four children, the others being a half brother and two half sisters. During my childhood I was often involved in caring for them,

whether I was willing or not. But children are great teachers of responsibility if one chooses to learn the lessons. Being the eldest, I was exhorted by my parents to set a good example for my younger siblings. In reality, I did more than that. At various times, I acted as caretaker, advisor, shelter from the neighborhood bullies and the creature under the bed, even the port in the storm. This meant that I learned to deal with my own fears privately, a capability that has certainly come in handy.

Self-Reliance

The faith my younger brother and sisters invested in me was particularly clear during several stressful situations. One was a blizzard—not a small one, but a major whiteout. We were living on a remote ranch in Colorado. For three days, the two youngest children were stranded with me, alone, miles from the nearest help. The children were calm and trusting, and even seemed disappointed when the rest of the family made it home.

Several months later, when our stepfather, William, made an insane but fake attempt at suicide, their faith in me really paid off. Not only did it help them through the crisis, but it was rather like a reward for me—it made me feel that the years of care had been well invested, and it reinforced my ability to be calm in a crisis.

William was feeling sorry for himself because my mother had finally decided to divorce him. One sunny afternoon he claimed he was upset enough to kill himself. Just the two of us and his three children were there that day, isolated on that ranch in the middle of nowhere. Drunk and full of self-pity, he declared he was going to end it all then and there. I tried to talk him out of it, told him he had a responsibility to his children that he couldn't just disregard, but I was unable to dissuade him. His bedroom had a balcony, and he walked out onto it and told me he was going to jump. I was disgusted with him by this point, and I didn't think he had even enough courage to commit the cowardly act of suicide, so I said, "Do what you want to do."

I then hurried downstairs to comfort my brother and sisters, who were understandably confused. We looked out the window of the family room together; we could see William on the balcony. Then we watched in astonishment as he climbed carefully (he was drunk) down the post and laid himself on the ground so his children would think he was dead. Feeling nothing but contempt for him now, I gathered his children to me and reassured them that everything would be all right somehow, and then we walked outside together so I could inform him that we'd seen him climb down and knew he wasn't injured. The fool continued to play dead, however, and after a few minutes I took his children back inside with me, made them some dinner, and life went on. That was another very important lesson: life goes on.

Other Benefits

Other indirect benefits of my childhood were the development of comfort in solitude and a passion for reading. They grew simultaneously, as I was housebound caring for my siblings much of the time. I became a voracious reader, consuming book after book—even reading through our encyclopedias. I read for escape, for entertainment and adventure, for the sheer pleasure of learning, and for the information I could glean from the volumes, especially about how others experienced life. I wanted perspectives other than my own, views I could never get from where I stood. Reading became my one compulsion, a comparatively harmless one, really, and one that has given me immeasurable rewards: knowledge of myself through reflection and introspection, knowledge of the world around and beyond me, and introduction to flights of fancy and imagination that gave license to my own.

"It is undoubtedly from watching my mother display the extremes of dependency that I have made myself as independent as I am."

My sense of reality is yet another advantage. I'll never try to change the world through wishful thinking, since I already know quite well that that simply doesn't work. Reality is what is, not what we want or wish it to be. When one is realistic enough to depend primarily on oneself and to see one's own conscience as the ultimate authority, one is never without guidance or courage, no matter the various hazards of life. I believe self-sufficiency is good for people, especially for women. All too often we are taught to rely on others as the focus and purpose of

our lives; of course, this is unfair to the people around us as well as to ourselves. It is undoubtedly from watching my mother display the extremes of dependency that I have made myself as independent as I am: she is utterly convinced that she cannot make it, cannot be a whole person, without a man. Fortunately for me, I have seen where belief like hers can lead. I can only trust others to a certain extent, probably because of my untrustworthy alcoholic parents, but at least I will never lay myself down, body and soul, at another's feet and expect them to take responsibility from my hands and do what must be done.

Obviously, during my childhood there were exceptionally ugly experiences directly or indirectly attributable to alcoholism. My mother was involved in two of the most memorable, not because she was necessarily my worst parent, but because I simply spent more time with her.

The first was relatively minor: she unexpectedly showed up at an elementary-school field day. It would have been fine, enjoyable even, except that she was a mess: unflattering old clothes, no stockings, wild hair, no makeup, and she seemed to be staggering. My teachers were politely horrified, and my classmates giggled. This was one of the very few times in my life that I was socially sensitive. I quit the various games and contests and dragged her to the top of the hill overlooking the field. For the next few days I was aware of pitying looks and gossip about the incident, but it was also my first conscious experience with hardening against the opinions of others.

The other episode was much worse. My mother and stepfather had separated by this point, and she had an apartment of her own. I was staying with her for the summer, and I got my first experience of the sordidness both of severe alcoholism and of a woman, my mother, entirely wrapped up in a sick relationship with a heartless married man I'll call Robert. She would wait by the front window of the apartment on nights he was expected, watching for him with a bottle of tequila in her hand, all night long. Some mornings when I awakened she would still be out in the living room, asleep or passed out, awaiting her faithless lover with a now-empty bottle in hand.

Her lover had a good friend, also married, whom I'll call Andy. My mother claimed Andy was her best friend, although like many drinking buddies, all they ever did together was drink or sometimes smoke dope and take downers or painkillers. There were occasional trips to country-western bars and the like, but since Robert and Andy were, after all, married men, they didn't have much discretionary time.

One Evening

I had turned fifteen that spring; an experienced and cynical fifteen, to be sure, but fifteen just the same. My mother and Andy decided to party one evening. It started with margaritas and beer and progressed to downers and dope smoking. Eventually my mother passed out on her bed. I suspected Andy had intended for this to happen as he'd brought the drugs and booze and encouraged my mother to "loosen up and have a good time."

"No experience, no matter how humiliating, painful, or devastating, can be entirely negative if we learn something from it."

At any rate, as soon as she was out of it, I wanted Andy to leave. I'd never liked or trusted him. Although I'd tolerated him for the sake of my mother's dubious friendship with him, I always felt very uneasy around him and had always taken care never to be alone with him. I walked to the front door to let Andy out, but when I turned around he was still back in the living room. "You know, I've always been attracted to you," he said, grinning, obviously not intending to go anywhere.

My heart sank. "I need to get some sleep," I replied, unable to keep the nervous fear from my voice. "Mom and I are going to Cheyenne tomorrow for the rodeo, and I'm pretty tired, and—"

"Aw, come on baby doll, don't make excuses. You want me, I can feel it." With that he grabbed me and kissed me hard, grinding his rough beard into my face.

"Oh, no, please don't, please," I cried again and again, but he wouldn't stop, and wouldn't stop, and wouldn't stop. . . .

It was useless to scream; my mother was beyond hearing my screams, drugged to unconsciousness in the next room. I had never felt so alone, so beyond help, so dirty and used, so degraded.

And I never looked at men the same way again.

No Ideal Home

My point is not to cause shock or to evoke pity with ugly stories. I could tell several more, and most people could probably tell at least a few. There are indeed ugly things in the world like rape, abuse, incest, and neglect. They happen to real people like you and me, which is what makes them so horrible. After all, how many of us come from truly ideal homes? For that matter, what is an ideal home? No parent or home can be perfect, and children from a perfect home, if such a place and such parents could exist, would hardly be prepared to deal with the real world of occasional failure, heartache, and certain death. Everyone has a sad story to tell—the important thing is what we do with our experiences, our feelings, and ourselves. No experience, no matter how humiliating, painful, or devastating, can be entirely negative if we learn something from it. And that in

turn, makes it easier to say to the world, "Go ahead. Take your best shot!"

Such an attitude gives a certain set to the shoulders, a special jauntiness to the walk. It creates a rock-solid self-confidence that has been through flame and acid tests until one can be sure that not only is it indestructible, it is unalterably and undeniably one's own. An identity and security that are not at all mysterious because one has literally given them birth and nurtured them through years of despair to final triumph. A soul that one is well acquainted with because it is self-made and cherished.

Of course, social structure can make an individual identity difficult to create and keep. Social norms are like cookie cutters in that their products are all the same shape, but to carry the analogy further, is a cookie any less a cookie because it's a star rather than a circle like the rest? Is a human being any less valuable, any less a person, if she refuses to be the same as everyone who's declared normal? What is normal, anyway? Who decides? Even psychologists can't seem to agree, and definitions of normal vary widely between cultures and eras. I know that I wouldn't feel unique or an individual if I wasted my life trying to be just like everyone else. Society encourages us to play follow the leader, to preserve the status quo. Is it worth the sacrifice of self?

True Freedom

Naturally, it's easier to do what everyone else does. One always knows just what to do, what the proper reaction is, what the proper goal is, and one can bask in the complacent and easy comfort of conformity and general, impersonal social approval. But true freedom is taking responsibility for oneself and telling the Mr. and Mrs. Grundys of the world to go fly the famous kite. Once that freedom has been tasted and savored, going back to the status quo seems insane. It looks like walking into a prison voluntarily, locking the door behind oneself, and handing the key to an anonymous authority figure.

In the difficulty of individualism lies the challenge, and therefore the attraction, for those of us not satisfied with the average, the normal, the easy, the known. Of course, it takes courage, but courage is the complement to fear and the use of fear, not the absence of it. Like anything else one wishes to master, it also takes desire and practice.

The wildest scenery is off the beaten track. It demands courage to strike off on one's own to find it and glory in its very wildness. In its very wildness lies its haunting beauty. It is like the difference between a caged, semitame lion at the zoo and an utterly wild lion roaming the savanna, free and proud, living as it was meant to live. The same animal, yet not the same animal at all.

None of these attitudes and beliefs would probably have occurred to me, much less become an intrinsic part of me, had I not been raised in an alcoholic home. My life has always been a challenge. I chose to take the challenge rather than buckle under in weakness and self-pity. The choice, like all choices, was mine alone. I continue to challenge myself. I am a single mother by choice; I'm also putting myself through college, self-supporting, independent, and a radical feminist. I'm convinced that life would be boring and unrewarding if it were too easy.

"My life has made me strong and reliable, honest and individual, and I don't regret a minute of it."

And what an exhilarating challenge my life is! I'll never settle for the easy answer or the easy way out, and I continually test myself, my strengths and weaknesses, and thus expand and improve my abilities. I'm quite outspoken, highly curious, and very self-confident. My upbringing and its difficulties have taught me many valuable lessons. The most important were to trust and respect myself. I'm proud of my abilities, my attitudes, my courage in the face of adversity, and my calm during crises, for I know I build my better qualities alone. Certainly there are disadvantages, including, in all honesty, a seeming aloofness, a lack of trust in others, and occasional recklessness. But to me the benefits of my personality far outweigh the few drawbacks. After all, nobody is perfect, including myself.

No Regrets

My life has made me strong and reliable, honest and individual, and I don't regret a minute of it. The alcoholism of my parents stole my childhood, my trust and innocence. But I don't blame my parents for being alcoholics—victims of a disease that robbed them of as much as it robbed me. Neither do I blame myself. At my first and last session with an Al-Anon counselor, I was told that I was at least partially responsible for my mother's alcoholism because I was an enabler. To the contrary, I did what had to be done and found myself in the process. I don't wish it had been different, for it was as it was, and I rather like the way things turned out.

I wouldn't change a thing.

Tamela Beth is a single mother and college student. She contributed this piece to Adult Children of Alcoholics Remember, *a collection of memoirs.*

"Thousands of children are . . . identifying parental alcoholism as a primary influence on their families and on development."

Adult Children of Alcoholics Face Emotional Problems

Stephanie Brown

"My name is Brad, and I am the child of an alcoholic. My father has been an alcoholic for as long as I can remember, but I never knew it until now."

Brad knew his father drank every night, and that he frequently exploded into fits of rage and terrorized the family. But Brad believed, like everyone else, that his father drank to deal with a demanding boss and a high-pressure job. Drinking was not the problem, but the solution to cope with these stresses.

Alcoholism and Denial

The family becomes dominated by the presence of alcoholism and its denial. The double bind produces the three rules of the alcoholic family noted by author and therapist Claudia Black: "Don't talk, don't trust and don't feel." Reality cannot be known or felt; what is true today will not be true tomorrow. There can be no trust. The family's stability rests on maintaining a lie.

Cindy, a young adult in a therapy group for adult children of alcoholics (ACAs), illustrated the strength of denial: "There were two rules in our family. The first was that there is no alcoholism, and the second was that we don't talk about it."

Today, thousands of children and adults are talking about it, identifying parental alcoholism as a primary influence on their families and on development.

Cindy recalled: "There was always an atmosphere of fear—overwhelming fear. My parents drank a lot every day, but we never knew when the fighting would start. Sometimes they just drank, and things went on in a tense, guarded way, and other times they could've killed each other. I tried to stay out of the way, but always got pulled in to rescue my brother or take a side. That was horrible. It usually ended up with both parents yelling at me for starting the whole mess. I grew up knowing that I would cause some

awful problem today, but I didn't know what or how."

The alcoholic family is characterized by chaos, inconsistency, unpredictability, unclear roles, arbitrariness, changing limits, arguments, repetition and illogical thinking, and perhaps by violence and incest. There is an atmosphere of tension, hostility, fear, shame, guilt and futility.

Inconsistency may become a predictable, stable feature of the family environment. A permission granted by an alcoholic father on one day is rescinded arbitrarily on the next. The complex pattern of rationalizations necessary to sustain family denial of alcoholism leads to very inconsistent explanations for behavior and events. What explains behavior one day is contradicted the next. Inconsistency also manifests itself in unclear parental roles. One parent may take over the role of both mother and father, or a child may substitute for one or both. This pattern may be stable, or it may be constantly affected by the drinking behavior of the alcoholic or the inconsistent, unpredictable response of the partner.

Damaging Consequences

ACAs—estimated to total 28 million in the U.S.—emphasize the damaging consequences of their parents' behavior and logic. Many trace their lack of trust and their hypervigilance as adults to this early environment, in which a catastrophe was always imminent. Children growing up in this kind of home are robbed of critically important experiences and relationships necessary for healthy development. As a result, they reach adulthood unable and unprepared to cope with the demands of maturity.

Many ACAs suffer from depression, anxiety and chronic fear. They are terrified of becoming like their parents—alcoholic or addictive, abusive, emotionally unavailable, and destructive to themselves and to their own spouses and children. Indeed, the fear is warranted. It's estimated that more than 50 percent of children of alcoholics become alcoholics themselves.

Stephanie Brown, "Adult Children of Alcoholics," *The American Legion Magazine,* January 1989. Reprinted by permission, The American Legion Magazine, copyright © 1990.

Yet most ACAs cannot recognize or name these fears, or accept the reality of parental alcoholism. Instead, they enter adulthood with four major defenses, or character traits, that provide an illusion of safety and, unfortunately, a guarantee of severe problems in building and maintaining close intimate relationships:

A strong need for control. ACAs exert an enormous amount of energy and attention to be in control. Being out of control is equated with being weak, needy, dependent and abused, or alcoholic and destructive. They believe that the only way to protect themselves and others is to maintain control, which means they cannot permit themselves to experience any need or vulnerability. These people are often anxious and hypervigilant. As Brad explained, "I determined early on that I must be prepared for all things. I lived my childhood and teen years standing guard, vigilant and ready to respond. I swore that I'd never let myself lose control."

An inability to trust. Children learn that parental needs come first. They must constantly adjust their own wishes and needs to fit. They learn early not to trust, not to build up expectations and not to depend on anyone to come through for them. They can't trust themselves, either. They doubt the validity of their own perceptions, wondering constantly whether what they see is real.

Cindy shared her experience: "I have a hard time knowing what I think. It's even hard for me to have opinions. I was always told that what I saw—my parents' drinking—was not what I saw."

A tendency to suppress needs and feelings. As children, ACAs learned that their needs and feelings were not acceptable, or weren't the right ones. This left them feeling frightened and out of control. These feelings are intolerable, in Cindy's view. "I know I had feelings as a child," she said. "I can see it in family pictures. There's no doubt that I was afraid, sad and lonely. But I was always told that what I felt wasn't what I felt, or it was wrong or my fault. There were no prizes given for being a feeling kid."

A sense of personal responsibility for all of life's problems. All children need to believe that their parents will take care of them. When this doesn't happen, children automatically assume it is their fault. This belief provides a sense of control. Said Brad: "If it was my fault, I could fix it. All my efforts went into trying to be better or figuring out what was wrong with me that I could cause so much damage and be so unlovable."

Hope

There is hope for ACAs if they can remember what happened, and challenge the old beliefs and defenses that were so necessary to their survival. Countless children and adults of all ages are seeking help to undo the damage. ACA self-help groups affiliated with Al-Anon, the autonomous arm of Alcoholics Anonymous, are available all over the country. Large and small, these groups offer support and education through the sharing of personal experience. The Al-Anon ACA group is an excellent choice for anyone who is just starting to look at the painful reality. . . .

Many books also detail this childhood reality and the path to recovery.

"Many ACAs suffer from depression, anxiety and chronic fear."

Although it has gained national prominence just recently, the children-of-alcoholics movement has helped unlock the inner doors for millions of children and adults who must confront the ravages of alcoholism. As Brad said after seeking help: "By learning that I am the child of an alcoholic, I can open up the secrets. My life makes sense when I can know the truth."

Stephanie Brown is a clinical psychologist and author of Treating the Alcoholic *and* Treating Adult Children of Alcoholics.

viewpoint 6

The Problems of Adult Children of Alcoholics Are Exaggerated

Denise Grady

We seem to be everywhere lately: written up in popular books and *People* magazine, comparing our sad stories in church basements, on radio and TV talk shows. We even have our own magazine. "We"—twenty-two million strong—are the adult children of alcoholics. We have taken on the trappings of a cultural movement, and I, for one, am sick of us.

According to the books and the shrinks and the social workers, we supposedly suffer from inexplicable guilt, deep insecurity, isolation, helplessness, lack of self-esteem and intense sadness. If we don't feel terrible, that's a symptom right there: We should—and, in fact, we probably do and just don't know it. We're repressing our emotions—another part of the syndrome. Whether we want it or not, we need help. If we don't get it, we're at high risk of becoming alcoholics ourselves or of marrying them. Even if we escape those fates, we're more likely than others to raise children who become alcoholics: all due to "alcoholic family dynamics" handed down from generation to generation, even if nobody drinks. We can't win.

There is some sensible advice in these books, and they're on statistically solid ground—a lot of today's alcoholics did have alcoholic parents. But there are too many tales like the one of the thirty-three-year-old woman who, supposedly because one of her parents drank, was so undone when her car got a flat tire she called a suicide hot line instead of a garage. Give me a break.

My father drank. He was a smart, gentle, funny man who ruined himself with alcohol and wasted his life. His binges and my mother's rages were the salient facts of my childhood, and one of the most painful aspects of my life has been the pity and disgust I've felt for him. I'd not deny that having an alcoholic parent can be devastating. That it can batter

the ego and leave behind a lifelong residue of sadness. That it can be dangerous indeed to avoid coming to grips with those realities. Or that kids growing up with parents who drink should have counseling.

Not a Syndrome

Why, then, should I bristle at the books and the groups springing up to help us? Because, in spite of all I've said of such a childhood, I still think too much is being made of it. I draw the line at calling it a syndrome—which, apparently, has become fashionable. The fact is, people do get over hardships. It can take a lot of thought and a lot of conversation. But there's a point when sorting out bad memories can deteriorate into dwelling on them, and I think the children-of-alcoholics movement has the potential to lure people over the line into emotional hypochondria. Everyone has problems, garden-variety neuroses, things about themselves that they hate. It is only human nature to look for an explanation, but that can go too far. I have a friend who has read the books and gone to the meetings and who, it seems to me, blames every mistake he's ever made on his father's drinking. "I acted just like what I am," he has said on several occasions, blaming his "child of" status when some minor thing went wrong. The "what I am" is what gets me. A certain period of anger or self-pity may be expected, but I find myself thinking that my friend's now well past the age at which he should have worked out that part of his childhood and started accepting both credit *and* blame for what he does.

Making Excuses

Books for children of alcoholics tend to encourage that kind of excuse-making with laundry lists of psychic woes: Do you lack trust? Feel lonely? Guilty or sad? Do you overreact to criticism? Who doesn't, at one time or another?

What is most offensive about the books is that despite their purported messages of hope and recovery, they are actually grim and humorless. The general theme: If a parent drank, you must be damaged goods, and only professional help or this book can save you. One author, for instance, states, "ACoAs [trend-speak for adult children of alcoholics] are bound by the four rules of the alcoholic family. They really have little choice in the matter."

"The general theme: If a parent drank, you must be damaged goods, and only professional help or this book can save you."

Surely people are more resilient than that, more spirited, intelligent and creative. We do have choices; we can change if we want to; and we don't always need therapists to lead the way. The will to live, emotionally as well as physically, is a powerful force. I also think there is something to the notion that one can be strengthened by adversity and even enriched by sadness.

Putting the Past Behind

Maybe I'm getting soft because I'm past thirty-five, or because my parents are dead and I miss them. Maybe it's because I'm a parent myself now. I didn't realize until I had my own children how all-consuming parental love can be, how it leads to an impossible wish to do everything right. Nor was I braced for the wave of self-reproach when you blow it. Suddenly, I appreciate how dear and fragile a child's trust and respect can be, and I know I would be devastated by their loss. When I imagine the perpetual shame my father must have felt before his children, it becomes clear that he suffered even more than I realized. And it seems to me that the ability to forgive and, finally, to put the past behind us is an essential part of growing up and getting on with life.

Denise Grady is a writer on health issues who has written articles for American Health *and* Ladies' Home Journal.

Drugs' Effects on the Fetus: An Overview

Andrew C. Revkin

Call him Timothy. He's a robust baby boy, about to have his first birthday. Lying in a stainless steel crib, he giggles and reaches for a blue plastic hose dangling nearby. He puts it to his mouth and sucks some of the misty gases coming from the end. "Good boy, you're taking your inhaler yourself," says Kathryn Crowley, a neonatologist at New York's Harlem Hospital. Timothy has lived the first year of his life in the sunny west wing of the hospital's fourth floor, the neonatal intensive care unit. On one side is a room full of extremely sick premature infants, encased in clear plastic incubators; on the other is a room full of not-so-sick babies—intermediate care, they call it.

Timothy doesn't need to be in the hospital. Although his lungs were underdeveloped at the time of his premature birth—after only 29 weeks of gestation—he has now caught up to the point where he could easily be cared for at home. He spends much of his time like any healthy one-year-old, suspended in a walker, feet just touching the floor, scooting across the linoleum. "Everybody here loves him," Crowley says. "Everybody wants to take him home." Everybody except Timothy's mother.

No one seems to know where she is. She was too busy for prenatal care. The first time she saw a doctor was when she entered the delivery room. She was high on cocaine throughout the pregnancy, she had cocaine in her system when she walked into the hospital in labor, and when last seen she was spending all her time trying to score another five-dollar rock of the pure, crystallized, fast-food form of cocaine called crack.

It's almost certain that Timothy was born prematurely because cocaine caused his mother's uterus to contract spasmodically; the connection is understood even on the streets, where the word is that a crack binge is a surefire way to give yourself a no-fuss abortion. It's almost certain too that when Timothy was a fetus, cocaine stanched the flow of nutrients and oxygen to his developing body and brain. And it's almost certain that cocaine has denied Timothy any chance he might have had for a normal family life.

Devastating Impact

Cocaine is having a devastating impact on the lives of a booming generation of babies born to addicted women. The effects include strokes while the baby is still in the womb, physical malformations, and an increased risk of death during infancy. And the number of cocaine-exposed babies is growing explosively, doubling each year in many major cities; estimates put the number in the United States as high as 200,000. And the problem, although at its worst in crack-infested inner-city neighborhoods, cuts across lines of race and class and the borders of geography to infest not just the cities but the suburbs and rural towns.

Cocaine is not only destroying individual lives but overburdening obstetric and pediatric wards around the country and adding to the ever-mounting cost of health care. If cocaine use during pregnancy were a disease, its impact on infants would be considered a national health-care crisis. And the effect will ripple onward as these children grow up and enter the school system.

One can get a quick reading of the scope of the problem by walking around the corridors at Harlem Hospital. On this day there are ten preemies in the intensive care nursery. Four were born steeped in cocaine. One of them, over in the corner, is noticed only because there's a slight movement beneath a nest of tubes and wires as his leg, just a little bigger than a man's index finger, gives a kick. This baby is six days old and shouldn't have been born for another three and a half months.

In intensive care a newborn's weight is measured

Andrew C. Revkin, "Crack in the Cradle," *Discover*, September 1989. Andrew C. Revkin/© 1989 Discover Publications.

in grams. This infant tips the scale at 890 grams—just under two pounds. He's kept warm by bright lights similar to the heat lamps that keep burgers warm in a take-out restaurant. A tube that runs beneath a bandage on his chest drains air that's leaking from a tear in his fluid-clogged lungs. Two of the other cocaine babies are "thousand-gramers" who lie in incubators across the room. The fourth, just down the row, is now a solid 1,500 grams, but he was born just above the line technology draws between life and death—500 grams.

Small Babies, Big Expense

According to David Bateman, the hospital's chief of neonatology, in a typical week 50 to 70 percent of the babies in the unit had cocaine in their urine when they were born. These high numbers are most likely the result of cocaine's tendency to trigger uterine contractions and raise blood pressure. The latter effect often leads to a condition called abruptio placentae, in which the capillary-rich placenta rips away from the lining of the uterus, causing bleeding and early labor. Big-city hospitals report that in recent years the number of abruptions has increased dramatically. The number of emergency calls for which ambulance teams find a mother deep in sudden labor has also risen sharply. The preemies that result tend to be extreme preemies—24, 25, 26 weeks—and very small infants require a vastly greater amount of care and cost far more to treat.

Just down the hall there's a room designated convalescent care. Most of the ten babies in this room are being treated for syphilis they contracted from their mothers. And most also had cocaine in their bodies at birth. "Five years ago we never really saw syphilis," Crowley says. The rampant trade in sex for crack has apparently contributed to the sudden resurgence of this disease.

"As recently as 1982 there were still textbooks . . . stating that cocaine had no harmful effects on a fetus."

Crowley walks toward the floor's other wing, where the "boarder babies" live. In New York and a handful of other states, when it has been determined that a newborn infant has drugs in its system, the case must be investigated. At hospitals in places like New York City, Los Angeles, and Washington, D.C., babies are piling up by the dozen as case workers arrange home inspections and decide which babies must go to foster homes or grandparents and which stay with the mother. (A nurse at Howard University Hospital in the nation's capital says, "We've got storage rooms that can't be used for storage anymore because they're storing babies.")

Crowley peeks into three boarder nurseries. There are ten steel carts to a room, each with a plastic bassinet on top. Each bassinet holds a baby. The typical stay for the boarder babies at Harlem Hospital is one to two months, and a stay of three or four months is far from uncommon.

Repeating the Cycle

Only in some of the communities where the crack problem originated are neonatologists seeing a leveling off of the flood of cocaine babies—and not for any encouraging reasons. "It's reached a saturation point," says Bateman. "There's a certain group of people who are going to be susceptible to this, and that group has been used up." What he's seeing more frequently now are repeats: mothers who year after year come in to deliver babies—and who still have cocaine in their systems. "They almost always look much worse each time," he says. "We've got some mothers coming in now on their third try."

Hospitals in Dallas, San Francisco, and Gainesville, Florida, have found that about 10 percent of all births show signs of cocaine. A study conducted in 1988 confirmed that such numbers do not vary significantly nationwide. And because the urine tests can only detect cocaine use by the mother within the last 24 to 48 hours, physicians say that this is just the tip of the iceberg. Undoubtedly, many more women used the drug during pregnancy.

A basic understanding of how cocaine affects the adult brain and body has begun to develop only over the past decade, as the level of urgency has risen along with the drug's popularity. Even now little is known about the mechanism by which cocaine exerts its addictive pull—a pull so powerful that monkeys in laboratories have been known to inject themselves with the drug for days, until they convulse and die. There is even less understanding of how the drug affects a fetus. As recently as 1982 there were still textbooks on high-risk obstetrics stating that cocaine had no harmful effects on a fetus. . . .

Just how addictive is crack? Alicia is 25 years old and pregnant. She lives in the Bushwick section of Brooklyn, in a forgotten wasteland of poverty across the East River from the sparkle of Manhattan. Alicia started shooting heroin after dropping out of high school at age 17. She switched to crack in 1987 and wasn't able to stop until she was brought to an emergency room in September 1988, naked and comatose. She doesn't remember how she got there.

The pull of crack far exceeds the pull of heroin, she says. "When I was shooting, I'd like do two or three bags and I was all right. Crack is much worse. The high isn't good at all. When you inhale it, you feel it, but as soon as you exhale it, it's gone. You go out and do things you never felt you'd do for just a few dollars."

Only her coma pulled her out of crack's grip; until then, she ignored the starkest warnings: "A friend just passed away about a year and a half ago," Alicia recalls. "They found him in his house. His brains were beat open. But that didn't stop me from getting high. You know, my brother, they beat him up with an ax and busted his mouth. That didn't stop me. I've been in jail. That didn't stop me."

Alicia now attends a clinic for addicts at Kings County Hospital in Brooklyn. She often catches herself thinking about the fetus growing in her womb. "I worry a lot. I've got this feeling that something's going to happen because of the things I used to do. They're going to backfire on me."

Open Door to Cocaine

A fetus is particularly vulnerable to cocaine for several reasons. First, although the placenta does shield the womb from many large, complex molecules—particularly those that can't diffuse across fatty cell membranes—it is an open door to cocaine. Because the cocaine molecule "likes" fatty compounds, the drug readily crosses the placental barrier. Once cocaine enters the fetus's blood and tissues, it lingers there much longer than in adults: the liver has not yet developed into the powerful detoxifying agent it will become, and cocaine is broken down much more slowly.

The fetus is not only exposed to the direct effects of cocaine but also subjected to abuses brought on by the drug's effect on the mother-to-be. When a woman on crack gets pregnant, the last thing she is thinking about is the care of the developing fetus, let alone care of herself. The result is an explosion in the number of pregnancies taking place with absolutely no health care. Eighteen percent of all mothers who gave birth at Harlem Hospital in 1988 had no prenatal care. That number was double what it had been in 1987. Almost all of that rise is because of crack.

The hospital estimates that between 40 and 50 percent of these so-called unregistered pregnant women have been exposed to the AIDS virus. Neonatologist Leonard Glass of the Children's Medical Center of Brooklyn says, "We have reason to believe that as much AIDS or more AIDS is being transmitted in the crack houses of 1989 as in the bathhouses of 1980." Between 30 and 50 percent of the babies born to these infected women will themselves develop AIDS. Asked how the situation is in his intensive care nursery, Glass says, "We may be a little slow today. We're down to one hundred percent occupancy."

Consequences of Cocaine

No one has more single-mindedly absorbed himself in the direct consequences of fetal exposure to cocaine than pediatrician Ira Chasnoff of Northwestern Memorial Hospital in Chicago. He has published more than a dozen frequently cited studies of the effects of cocaine on some 200 pregnant women who have sought drug treatment or prenatal care at Northwestern Memorial since 1985. Many of the studies have traced the progress of individual babies for two years or more.

Chasnoff is rarely at his home base these days. He is on the road constantly, lecturing on fetal problems caused by drug use. "Two years ago," he says, "I was giving maybe one or two lectures a month on this. Now I'm up to fifteen or more." On this day Chasnoff finds himself at Howard University Hospital, in the middle of one of Washington's crack zones. He's there to speak at a conference called "Perinatal Substance Abuse—the Cry of the City," which has attracted about 200 nurses, doctors, and social workers from as far away as California.

He quickly paints a portrait of the consequences of cocaine exposure in the womb, based on his most recent study. His research team compared the outcomes of pregnancies in three groups: women who used cocaine throughout pregnancy, women who stopped using cocaine after the first three months of pregnancy, and a control group who never used drugs.

"An explosive situation is bound to develop when a difficult baby is placed in the care of a woman on cocaine."

The numbers tell the story. Ten pregnancies out of the 75 in the cocaine-exposed groups ended in abruptions; there were none in the control group. The average reduction of head circumference in the babies exposed to cocaine throughout pregnancy was about three-quarters of an inch. The reduction in birth weight was about 21 ounces. These differences are significant: obviously many small babies or babies with small heads live perfectly normal lives; statistically, however, these characteristics have been clearly linked to later learning problems and an increased risk of infant mortality. The prevailing theory is that this group of relatively subtle effects have a common cause—the tendency of cocaine to restrict the flow of blood to the uterus and placenta.

Chasnoff and others have also often noted a period of extremely disturbed behavior in cocaine-exposed babies that lasts eight to ten weeks after delivery. In some cases it may continue for as long as four months. The tragedy of this, Chasnoff says, is "that's exactly when the newborn infant begins to interact with its mother, begins to bond, to have a relationship with its environment." During this time cocaine babies are often hypersensitive. Just picking up the baby can unleash a torrent of tremors and crying.

Avoiding Intimate Contact

"Cocaine-exposed infants spend all their time either crying and irritable or in deep sleep," Chasnoff tells his audience. "They don't go in between." On top of that, the babies tend to shun intimate contact, even the stare of a mother simply trying to catch her child's eye. "If you try to make eye contact with a cocaine-exposed infant," Chasnoff says, "you see a specific behavior called gaze aversion. If you do make eye contact with the infant, you overpower him. He gets so overloaded that he shuts down; he closes his eyes."

It is this kind of behavioral profile that has sociologists and pediatricians convinced that cocaine is contributing to a sharp rise in child abuse in cities around the United States. One of the researchers looking into this is neo-natologist Loretta Finnegan, who since 1970 has run a drug-treatment program for pregnant addicts at Jefferson Medical College in Philadelphia. An explosive situation is bound to develop when a difficult baby is placed in the care of a woman on cocaine. "It's not too good to have a child in front of you," she says, "when you're irritable or depressed and you have a drive for cocaine. What are you going to do with that baby? Certainly not what you're supposed to do."

In the study at Northwestern Memorial, Chasnoff and several psychologists assessed the behavioral development of the cocaine-exposed babies and controls. The findings were startling: "At one month, the cocaine-exposed babies still have not reached the functional level of a two-day-old drug-free infant," Chasnoff says. There are indications that in a good environment cocaine-exposed babies can catch up developmentally. But these babies are rarely in a good environment.

"It may be the subtlest aspects of the epidemic of cocaine babies that create the biggest problems for society."

Chasnoff goes on to tell his audience about rarer but much more dramatic effects of fetal exposure to cocaine. He unreels a case study he often uses to illustrate one of the most devastating effects of cocaine (and to remind everyone that cocaine babies aren't restricted to poor, black communities). He describes a 32-year-old white housewife from a prosperous suburb of Chicago. She was near the end of her pregnancy and, although she'd used cocaine quite a bit in the past, had held off during most of the nine months.

On their wedding anniversary, her husband, who worked at the Chicago Board of Trade, forgot until the last minute to get a present. So he bought five grams of cocaine on the trading floor and brought it home. Chasnoff continues in a sing-songy, story-telling style: "Her husband said, 'Dear, I wanted to give you something special.' The woman snorted most of the cocaine over the next three days and noticed that her baby began to get extremely active." The next day, the woman began to have contractions. "During the

thirty-minute drive to the hospital, she used the last gram." Sixteen hours after delivery, the baby boy stopped breathing and turned blue several times. His right arm, shoulder, and hip became limp. He had several seizures and his heart stopped.

The baby was resuscitated. A CT scan of his skull showed the problem. Chasnoff flicks on a slide. There is a white ovoid ring, the skull, surrounding a gray lacy area, denoting brain tissue. Pointing to the image, Chasnoff says, "If you look right here, you can see an area where this baby had an acute cerebral infarction, a stroke, in utero." The region he indicates is a dark blotch, shaped like South America. He flicks to the next slide—a CT scan taken three months later. The infarcted area has coalesced into a kidney-shaped cyst of functionless tissue. Chasnoff's voice hardens. "It's been three years now and this boy is microcephalic"—he has a small head for his size, a condition leading almost invariably to some degree of developmental disability.

Loss of Blood Flow

Such strokes may be caused by high blood pressure brought on by cocaine's tendency to raise levels of the vessel-constricting neurotransmitter norepinephrine. "We've now collected cases from all over the country of babies having strokes," Chasnoff says. "They're usually referred to us by lawyers in cases where an obstetrician is being sued for malpractice. It turns out that the stroke was not caused by forceps, but by cocaine."

Chasnoff reviews some other cases of damage wrought by cocaine used during pregnancy. The common feature to all of them is that they seem to have resulted from a reduction in the flow of blood to some particular organ or tissue. In his last study, 15 of the cocaine-exposed babies developed malformed or malfunctioning kidneys or genitals. He and other researchers have found numerous cases in cocaine-exposed babies of a condition called ileal atresia, or dead bowel—in which part of the intestine fails to develop for lack of blood. An infant must quickly undergo surgery to make the digestive tract intact. In several instances, Chasnoff notes, cocaine babies have been born without the two middle fingers of a hand. This is probably caused not by some genetic defect, but rather by the loss of blood flow into those digits. . . .

Threat Continues

Laboratory research also hints that the threat to infants from cocaine may not end at birth. Cocaine users who breast-feed may pass along a strong hit of the drug to the suckling infant. Neuroscientist Richard Wiggins of West Virginia University Medical School has fed radioactively labeled cocaine to lactating female rats, then measured levels of the drug in the rats' blood and milk. "The bottom line," says Wiggins, "was that the concentration of cocaine was eight times higher in their milk than in their blood."

In the long run, he says—although the strokes and missing bowels and the like are terrible—it may be the subtlest aspects of the epidemic of cocaine babies that create the biggest problems for society. Even a 5 percent drop in scores of learning ability, for instance, is important. "A child doesn't have to be in a wheelchair to have a birth defect," says Wiggins. "Whenever you limit a child's full potential, even by a small amount, that's going to have an effect on society—particularly when you multiply that by the thousands of women who are addicted to cocaine."

He and many other researchers studying the problem predict that the most dramatic impact won't really be registered until today's cocaine babies grow up to become tomorrow's school-age children. Judy Howard, a pediatrician at the UCLA [University of California at Los Angeles] School of Medicine, agrees. "What I'm concerned about is, these children are going to hit school age and the teachers aren't going to know what to do with them," she says. Efforts are under way to follow the progress of children who were exposed to cocaine in the womb as they enter the Los Angeles school system. Preliminary findings show that there may indeed be lasting effects of drug exposure, says Howard. "They're socially not real initiators. They need a lot of direction. They have short attention spans, exhibit short-term memory loss, and are uncomfortable in new situations."

Bright Notes

There are a few bright notes in this otherwise grim scenario. Chasnoff's group has classes for mothers to teach them how to swaddle and hold the difficult babies to minimize their crying and foster a mother-child bond. In several cities, progress has been made in reaching out to cocaine-using women before they become pregnant, or at least early in pregnancy. The Commission of Public Health in Washington has a "Mom Van" cruising the district's most desolate neighborhoods, driven by a zealous outreach worker named Tawana Fortune. When Fortune hears of a women in a crack neighborhood who is pregnant, she will go up to the house and knock on windows until she gets someone's attention. She has successfully gotten dozens of women into treatment.

At Harlem Hospital, perinatologist Janet Mitchell runs a clinic for pregnant addicts that has such high ratings from patients that several have volunteered to go out and recruit other young crack-using mothers. "Our goal is not only to keep them off drugs but to keep them in care," says Mitchell. "They know that they can come in with dirty urines. We'll talk about it. They can bring in the father. We let him listen to the baby's heartbeat."

In St. Petersburg, Florida, Shirley Coletti, president of a program called Operation Parental Awareness and Responsibility, was given 16 houses that the county had removed from their foundations to make way for a highway. The houses will provide shelter for pregnant addicts, away from the drugs in their neighborhoods.

"That's just the way it is when you're on crack. You just don't care about nothing."

The problem remains that these outreach programs are treating only dozens of women in a nation where Florida alone conservatively estimates that its hospitals delivered 10,000 cocaine babies in 1988. Also, the mothers are extremely difficult to work with. In some cases the only way to get them to participate is to threaten to place their other children in foster care, on the grounds that an addicted mother poses a threat to her children. Most of these outreach programs have drop-out rates of 50 percent or more. Says Coletti, "We've worked with women with alcohol and heroin problems. Often the maternal instinct of those women has overpowered the drug. They've stayed clean through pregnancy. But with crack, they're unable to do that. It's the nature of the drug; it's so potent and powerfully addictive. Crack always wins."

The most discouraging fact of life for those attempting to solve the problems posed by crack-using mothers is that, ultimately, the only solution to the cocaine-baby problem would be to eliminate the conditions that lead a young woman, in the prime of life, to use cocaine. That is a daunting challenge.

No one adequately describes the environment that is causing America's epidemic of crack use better than Alicia, the young addict who narrowly escaped crack's hold once, sought help at Kings County Hospital last fall, and is expecting her baby this month. She reflects on the situation that nearly killed her and that she and her child will go home to: "My brother is on drugs. I've got three cousins, they're on crack. One is nine months pregnant. She's got three other kids. She stays out like three or four days at a time. I used to do the same thing. Didn't care about nothing or nobody. That's just the way it is when you're on crack. You just don't care about nothing. It's got you stuck in a place that you don't want to be, like a black hole, you know. Basically, I didn't really want to get high. I just wanted something better for myself. And then they all came knocking on my door with the crack and saying this is the cure."

Andrew C. Revkin is a senior editor for Discover, *a monthly science magazine.*

"A mother who knowingly . . . endangers her baby's life . . . during pregnancy is no less guilty of neglect than one who abandons her child on the street."

Pregnant Women Who Abuse Drugs Should Be Prosecuted

Alan Dershowitz and Jacob Sullum

Editor's note: The following viewpoint is in two parts. Part I is by Alan Dershowitz and Part II is by Jacob Sullum.

I

There is a dangerous implication in some pro-choice arguments that may frighten the Supreme Court into restricting or even overruling Roe vs. Wade, the 1973 decision that established women's right to abortion. The implication is that the right to abortion also precludes the state from requiring women to take any degree of prenatal care after they make the decision not to abort.

Syndicated columnist Ellen Goodman recently suggested this in criticizing the Bush Administration's efforts to overrule Roe vs. Wade. She wrote: "There are suggestions among those who talk of fetal rights that the government could constrain a pregnant woman's diet and physical activities, stamp out her cigarettes, empty her wine glass . . . or else." Goodman also invoked the specter of mandatory testing and treatment for the fetus.

Now, I am not a "fetal-rights" advocate. I favor Roe vs. Wade. I believe that a pregnant woman should have the right to choose between giving birth or having an abortion. But I am a human-rights advocate, and I believe that no woman who has chosen to give birth should have the right to neglect or injure that child by abusing their collective body during pregnancy.

Lasting Consequences

Once a woman has made the decision to bear a child, the rights of that child should be taken into consideration. What happens to the child in the womb may have significant impact on his or her entire life. One example is the woman who drank half a bottle of

Alan Dershowitz, "Drawing the Line on Prenatal Rights," *Los Angeles Times,* May 14, 1989. © 1989, Los Angeles Times. Reprinted with permission. Jacob Sullum, "The Suffering of Innocents." Reprinted, with permission, from the December 1989 issue of REASON magazine. © 1989 by the Reason Foundation, 2716 Ocean Park Blvd., Suite 1062, Santa Monica, CA 90405.

whiskey a day while pregnant and gave birth to a mentally retarded child. She is now suing the whiskey company for not warning her about the relationship between heavy drinking during pregnancy and birth defects. Anyone who has spoken to an inner-city obstetrician is aware of the near epidemic of birth defects among babies born to heavy drug users.

This is not to argue for intrusive governmental rules on occasional drinking or smoking. But at the extremes, there is a compelling argument in favor of some protection for the future child against maternal excesses that threaten to cause enduring damage. Once a woman decides to give birth, a balance must be struck between her rights during the nine months of pregnancy and the equally real rights of her child during its life span. I believe that the balance should generally be struck in favor of the woman's privacy and against the power of state compulsion. But a balance, nonetheless, must be struck.

The Limits of Privacy

My colleague, Prof. Laurence Tribe agrees with Goodman and argues as follows: "There's no principled way to say that the government can use women's bodies against their will to nurture the unborn without accepting the other serious and totalitarian implications about privacy." With respect, I disagree.

There is a principled distinction between totalitarian intrusions into the way a woman treats her body, and civil-libertarian concerns for the way a woman treats the body of the child she has decided to bear. That principled distinction goes back to the philosophy of John Stuart Mill and is reflected in the creed that "your right to swing your fist ends at the tip of my nose." In the context of a pregnant woman's rights and responsibilities in relation to the child she has decided to bear, the expression might be: "Your right to abuse your own body stops at the border of your womb."

Of course, any recognition that a future child may have rights—even limited ones—in relation to its mother, may be grist for the "right to life" mill. Antiabortionists will argue that if a future child has the right not to be damaged during pregnancy, then it follows that the fetus has the even more important right not to be killed—i.e., aborted.

"The state should begin by making prenatal care available to every pregnant woman."

But the second conclusion does not necessarily follow from the first. Under Roe vs. Wade, a fertilized egg, or even a biologically more advanced fetus, has no right to be born unless the mother chooses to give birth. But it does not follow, as a matter of constitutionality, principle or common sense, that a woman has the right to inflict a lifetime of suffering on her future child, simply in order to satisfy a momentary whim for a quick fix.

A principled person can fully support a woman's right to choose between abortion or birth, without supporting the very different view that the state should have no power to protect the health of a future child. The state should begin by making prenatal care available to every pregnant woman. But we need not be frightened, by the specter of totalitarianism, from considering reasonable regulations designed to reduce the serious long-term problems caused by pregnant women who abuse their future children.

Proponents of a woman's right to abortion should not weaken their powerful argument in favor of a woman's right to control her body.

And, in the eyes of many who support choice, they do weaken it when they link it to the far weaker argument denying the state the power to protect babies who are to be born.

II

One of the most troubling challenges to proponents of drug legalization is summed up in the simple question: "What about the crack babies?" We see them on television, their tiny bodies ravaged by the effects of their mothers' drug habits. Their piercing wails seem to express outrage at their predicament. Here are the most innocent of bystanders, harmed beyond repair by another person's carelessness. Here is a problem that would not be mitigated—indeed, could very well be worsened—by the repeal of prohibition.

But here also is evidence of the drug war's assault on individual responsibility. Until recently, the notion of holding the mothers of crack (or heroin or methamphetamine) babies accountable for their actions was virtually unthinkable. Indeed, the prevailing view remains that they, like their children,

are victims. The drugs made them do it.

Rarely is it asked, Who made them do the drugs? Not only is that initial choice treated as a *fait accompli*, but the addict is portrayed as someone who has lost all volition. In this light, crack babies are an inevitable result of drug use.

It is dangerous, you see, for a drug warrior to acknowledge the distinction between merely taking cocaine and forcing it on a third party. People might start wondering why the government should bother to prohibit the former. Still, a few prosecutors have implicitly recognized the difference, and one has obtained the conviction of a Florida woman who endangered two babies by smoking crack throughout her pregnancies.

Unfortunately, the charge in that case, delivering cocaine to a minor, obscures the fundamental issue. In previous cases, judges or grand juries have thrown out more appropriate charges—such as manslaughter, felony injury to a child, and failure to provide medical care—against mothers whose babies died or suffered injury as a result of prenatal neglect. Critics of treating such neglect as a crime rightly point out that users of illegal drugs are not the only ones who might be found guilty of harming a baby through negligence during pregnancy.

Take the Seattle woman who drank half a fifth of whiskey virtually every day of her pregnancy and consequently gave birth to a baby suffering from fetal alcohol syndrome [FAS]. She certainly did not consider herself a criminal. In fact, she turned around and sued Jim Beam. In one of those periodic miracles of civil justice, a federal jury found that the liquor company could not be held liable. But wait a minute—what about the mother?

An odd thought, perhaps—in what other crime does the perpetrator injure the victim by doing something perfectly legal to her own body? Moreover, unlike the effects of a robbery or an assault, the consequences of prenatal negligence are not immediate. The mother is not to be punished for harming a fetus—this would, after all, cover abortion—but for the delayed effect of threatening, injuring, or killing a baby. Then again, ordinary child neglect or abuse can also have a cumulative impact, but this does not absolve parents who starve their kids or feed them lead.

Mother's Awareness

The key question is whether the mother is aware of the harm she is doing. It is obviously unjust to punish a woman who falls down the stairs during pregnancy for the damage such an accident might do to her baby. But a mother who knowingly and repeatedly endangers her baby's life through reckless action during pregnancy is no less guilty of neglect than one who abandons her child on the street, heedless of the consequences. Indeed, she is arguably more culpable: A crack baby or an FAS infant is the product of not one decision but a whole string of them—the decision to engage in a potentially dangerous activity, the decision to have a child or to have sex without contraception, the decision to continue the hazardous behavior, the decision to carry the fetus to term.

It seems plausible to suggest that the threat of a criminal penalty would, in at least some instances, break one of the links in this chain. But regardless of deterrent value, the state has a legitimate role in punishing a mother who knowingly hurts her child, just as it should punish anyone who violates another person's rights. That, in short, is one answer to "What about the crack babies?" If we want government to mind its own business, we must clearly define what that business is.

Alan Dershowitz is a professor of law at Harvard University in Cambridge, Massachusetts. Jacob Sullum is an assistant editor of Reason, *a monthly magazine.*

"In jail . . . 'the mother won't get drug treatment, she won't get parenting classes and she won't get off the self-destructive cycle she's on.' "

Pregnant Women Who Abuse Drugs Should Not Be Prosecuted

Susan LaCroix

Butte County, California, seems an unlikely place for babies to be born already exposed to cocaine and heroin. The quiet agricultural region three hours' drive northeast of San Francisco is noted for its almonds and olives, not the problems of the inner city, where the estimated rates of drug-exposed newborns have reached as high as 25 percent. But with the hospitals in this county of 175,000 people delivering a growing number of infants with symptoms of drug exposure, Michael Ramsey, the local District Attorney, decided something had to be done.

In October 1988, after consulting with area hospital administrators, mental health workers and law enforcement officials, Ramsey announced that county hospitals would start screening all newborns exhibiting symptoms of exposure to a controlled substance. Any positive test results might then be used as evidence to prosecute the mothers for illegal drug use—a misdemeanor that, unless the offender enters a drug treatment program, carries a mandatory sentence of ninety days in jail. The plan, believed to be the first of its kind in the nation, has drawn harsh criticism from attorneys, health care workers and civil rights activists across the country, who question the legality and ethics of inviting criminal-justice authorities into the delivery room. Judith Rosen, a founder of California Advocates for Pregnant Women, offers the following scenario.

What Might Happen

A woman has just given birth and in walks someone from the Child Protective Services who wants the mother to be candid about her drug habits so that C.P.S. can help her and the infant. An Assistant District Attorney enters and begins, "You have the right to remain silent. . . ." The mother takes advantage of her constitutional rights and refuses to say anything. She then might be labeled "uncooperative" by social service agencies and would risk having her baby taken away.

Rosen knows this terrain well. In 1986, as a volunteer attorney for the American Civil Liberties Union in San Diego, she criticized the treatment of Pamela Rae Stewart. The 27-year-old mother had been arrested, jailed and prosecuted on a charge of criminally contributing to her baby's death by using illicit drugs and ignoring doctors' advice to stay off her feet and abstain from sexual intercourse during her pregnancy. Rosen argued that it was no crime to disobey a doctor's orders and asked, "Are we, as women, to have perfect babies and be subject to prosecution if we don't?"

The case against Stewart was dismissed in 1987, when San Diego municipal court Judge E. Mac Amos Jr. ruled in a pretrial motion that the District Attorney's office erred in invoking a 1925 child-support law to prosecute her. Although this California statute makes it a crime for a parent willfully to withhold medical care from a child, and specifically includes the fetus in its definition of the word "child," it generally applies to situations in which pregnant women seek support payments from estranged husbands.

Were it not for the Stewart dismissal, Butte County's District Attorney Ramsey might have attempted to apply the same statute to drug users in his jurisdiction. The mothers of the county's drug-exposed infants "certainly appear to be abusing children," Ramsey says. But the courts have not recognized drug abuse by pregnant women as child abuse. So, says the D.A., he devised a "creative way of using the law": prosecuting for illegal drug use rather than for child abuse or "fetal neglect." This way, Butte County would be able to circumvent some of the legal issues raised in the Stewart case, such as whether a woman's basic right to privacy can be sacrificed to the

Susan LaCroix, "Jailing Mothers for Drug Abuse," *The Nation,* May 1, 1989. © 1989 The Nation Company, Inc. Reprinted with permission.

state's interest in the health of her fetus. Also at stake is whether she can be branded a criminal for not following a doctor's orders despite court rulings that patients have the right to refuse medical care.

Such issues lie at the heart of a growing conflict between maternal autonomy and the extent of fetal rights, a conflict involving pregnant women's control over their behavior as well as their medical treatment during pregnancy. The Butte County controversy addresses only one behavior issue—drug use—in what conceivably includes any activity or environmental hazard that may harm the fetus, such as smoking, alcohol consumption and hazards in the workplace. Feminists and civil rights advocates worry that the trend, if unchecked, could lead to the prosecution of pregnant women for even poor eating and exercise habits.

Making Mothers Liable

How far will the law go in enforcing a doctor's judgment that conflicts with the mother's wishes? In a survey published in the May 1987 *New England Journal of Medicine*, medical institutions in eighteen states and the District of Columbia reported thirty-six attempts over a five-year period to override through law a pregnant woman's refusal of therapy. In the interest of the fetus, hospitals have sought and obtained court orders for Caesarean sections, intrauterine transfusions and hospital detention of pregnant women against their will. Court orders for Caesareans were granted in all but one of fifteen instances. A Gallup poll commissioned by *Hippocrates* magazine showed that support for intervention extends beyond the medical community to the general public. Nearly half those surveyed agreed that a woman who smokes cigarettes or drinks alcohol while pregnant—or refuses to have a Caesarean birth as recommended by her doctor—should be held legally liable for any related harm done to the fetus. Such findings are particularly puzzling in light of the general legal trend toward honoring patients' control over medical decisions. Recent court rulings have sharply restricted forced medication of psychiatric patients and have allowed mentally competent adults to refuse drug treatment, surgery and blood transfusions.

"The trend, if unchecked, could lead to the prosecution of pregnant women for even poor eating and exercise habits."

While acknowledging that pregnancy complicates the issue, advocates of reproductive freedom argue that forcing women to assume medical risks and forfeit their legal autonomy in a manner not required of men and nonpregnant women treads on the generally accepted privileges of medical patients: the common-law rights to bodily integrity and the constitutional rights of liberty, privacy and religious freedom. The courts have generally interpreted these rights to allow patients to refuse medical treatment when they disagree with a doctor's advice or object on religious grounds, such as in cases where Jehovah's Witnesses refuse blood transfusions. Many rulings, however, have denied pregnant women these rights, even forcing them to undergo major surgery when their religion forbids it.

Ramsey says he simply wants to prevent Butte County's women from harming their unborn children, by controlling their abusive behavior. He may be unable to change most of their behavior—smoking, drinking and other potentially harmful activities—but targeting illicit drug users is within his power. However, the plan Ramsey calls creative, critics call draconian. "A lot of people are very upset because they think it's punitive and not productive," says Lucy Quacinella, an attorney with Legal Services of Northern California in Butte County. Citing a severe lack of county drug programs and treatment services, she says, "The real issue is that women are not getting the treatment they need before the baby is born." Ramsey counters that the prospect of a jail sentence will work as an incentive for drug-addicted women to enroll in "diversion" programs that allow some such women to avoid incarceration. "People with substance abuse problems do not voluntarily get into these treatment programs," he says. He is confident that, faced with a choice between the drug diversion program or jail, women will choose treatment.

Frightening Women Away

This argument is profoundly misleading, charges Judith Rosen, the advocate for pregnant women. "First of all, it's not up to the D.A. whether or not a woman gets into treatment" through diversion, she says. Only the courts determine eligibility, and the criteria for diversion are so narrow that it's very likely most of the women will be ineligible. Under the California penal code, a woman does not qualify if she has previously been convicted of illegal drug use or of any felony in the past five years, if she has previously been diverted to treatment or if she has ever had probation or parole revoked. Furthermore, a movement in California seeks to repeal the diversion law in hope of sending more drug users to jail. "We don't know that diversion will even be in effect a year from now," Rosen says.

Whether or not the law is repealed, Rosen predicts that most women prosecuted for illegal drug use will end up in jail, and that their babies will flood the state's already overburdened foster care programs. In jail, Rosen warns, "the mother won't get drug treatment, she won't get parenting classes and she won't get off the self-destructive cycle she's on." Meanwhile, the separation of mother and child could destroy what psychologists and social workers agree is a critical bonding period, causing emotional and psychological damage to the infant and feelings of overwhelming guilt and depression in the mother.

"Jail sentences for pregnant drug users [is] a quick fix that makes it appear that something fundamental is being done about this public-health crisis."

Perhaps the most widespread concern, voiced by obstetricians, lawyers and health care workers, is that the threat of drug testing and prosecution will frighten women away from seeking medical aid. The result may be a greater number of what San Francisco deputy city attorney Lori Giorgi calls "toilet-bowl babies"—babies born at home, in toilets and bathtubs and on kitchen floors, without medical attention. "We're seeing more and more of them because their mothers are too scared to go to the hospital," Giorgi says. "They're afraid their babies will be taken away."

Drug Use Increasing

Drug use among expectant mothers is a growing problem nationwide. While few studies have been completed on drug-exposed infants, a cross-section sampling of thirty-six U.S. hospitals compiled by the National Association for Perinatal Addiction Research and Education in Chicago revealed that 11 percent of the women in those hospitals had used illegal drugs during pregnancy, including cocaine, marijuana, heroin, amphetamines and PCP. The effects of these drugs on fetuses and newborns include prematurity or stillbirth, prenatal strokes, tremors, deficient motor reflexes and learning disabilities.

As pressure grows to deal with the problem of drug babies, other states are considering punitive measures against substance-abusing pregnant women and new mothers. In Pennsylvania, for example, State Senator Jim Greenwood sponsored legislation to amend the civil child abuse law to include penalties for the presence of drugs or symptoms of fetal alcohol syndrome in newborns. Several other states, including Florida, Massachusetts and New Jersey, already have child abuse and neglect statutes designed to protect any infant harmed prenatally by its mother's drug abuse. Related punitive actions have also been taken by the courts. In Washington, D.C., a Superior Court judge sentenced a woman convicted of second-degree theft to 180 days in jail—an unusually harsh punishment for a first-time offender—because she was pregnant and tested positive for cocaine.

But such punitive action is not the answer—in Washington, Butte County or elsewhere. "If these mothers were walking away from treatment, I might feel differently," says Ann O'Rielly, director of family and children's services for the San Francisco Department of Social Services. "But they're not walking away from treatment—they're walking away from waiting lists."

Although Federal spending on drug treatment and prevention has increased substantially in the past several years, public clinics are still financially strapped and not equipped to deal with the crisis. Butte County is one of many in the United States that offers little or no treatment or support services for pregnant drug users. Women in the county addicted to heroin, for example, must travel eighty-five miles for treatment, to a private outpatient clinic in Sacramento, which charges $200 a month for a methadone maintenance program. Without methadone, sudden withdrawal from heroin can be deadly to both mother and baby, but in Butte County the treatment price is out of reach even for many middle-income women.

What is not out of reach is jail sentences for pregnant drug users—a quick fix that makes it appear that something fundamental is being done about this public-health crisis. Butte County has yet to prosecute a mother under the new plan, but the A.C.L.U. vows to oppose District Attorney Ramsey's actions—in court, if necessary. Meanwhile, other organizations, including the American College of Obstetricians and Gynecologists, are speaking out against the trend toward forced medical treatment of pregnant women.

Susan LaCroix is an associate at the Center for Investigative Reporting in San Francisco, California. The Center is a nonprofit organization that is involved in and promotes investigative reporting.

"Alcoholism is the oldest disease known to mankind. It is the most complex and the most devastating."

Alcoholism Is a Serious Disease

Joseph C. Martin

Every single one of us has very, very definite attitudes toward every facet of alcohol: alcoholics, alcoholism, drinking and drunkenness—in fact, toward alcohol itself. Our attitudes come from our parents, from our religious background, and our cultural background, but above all else, from our contact with an alcoholic. Every one of us knows an alcoholic, and many of us live with someone who is actively drinking.

Number One Problem

Alcoholism is the number one health problem in the United States. Every alcoholic seriously affects a minimum of six other people. So let's examine some of the background sources of our attitudes.

Some of us were raised with the notion that alcohol is evil. This is very intimately wrapped up with our religious background. Go to a football or baseball game and watch the reactions to a drunk. There is no single reaction. Some people laugh nervously. Others say, "Isn't that funny?" (Dean Martin says "whiskey" and an entire audience cracks up!) But again, above all else, our attitudes are formed basically by our contact with some alcoholic.

Alcoholism is the oldest disease known to mankind. It is the most complex and the most devastating. It affects every single facet of the human person—body, mind, emotions and soul. And it is the illness about which we know the least. What you know is what you see, and what you see is alcoholic behavior. And let's face it, it's obnoxious. What we don't see is what we don't see of an iceberg—what's hidden. Our reasoning says that if an alcoholic knows *why* he or she drinks, the problem will disappear. Not so. Knowing why he or she drinks doesn't make the alcoholic stop drinking.

Of the 18 million alcoholics in this country there

are about a half million sober ones. In fact, one out of thirty-six gets well and the other thirty-five die. So what I will try to do here is tell you a bit about alcohol and then about alcoholism. . . .

An Escape

Alcohol is drunk for escape. Forget all the ins and outs of psychiatric reasoning. I'm talking about normal people with normal problems who want to get away from them for awhile, and so they drink three or four martinis. Their problems are still there, but they won't bother them as much, and there is a biochemical reason why that is so. For those who can take it, it is marvelous, but here in the United States about one out of eight of them will become an alcoholic. The other seven can drink until their death enjoying it. In fact, Scripture refers to wine as "the gift of God that gladdens the hearts of men." Tensions, frustrations, anxieties about the job or the marriage—take three drinks and just settle back. The relaxation is wonderful. Some give pain as their reason for drinking. In fact, when whiskey, gin, and all the so-called hard stuff came into being, it was used for medication only. Euphoria—a sense of well being—is mainly what the human animal wants to achieve by drinking alcohol. It makes us feel good.

Alcohol is a chemical; it is not a food and has no food properties. There are no minerals in it, no vitamins, no proteins. In fact, the stomach can't digest it. Beer, for example, is about 5% alcohol—the rest of it is foodstuff. The alcohol itself is not digested; it is oxidized by the liver. Basically it's a solvent—it will remove stains from tables, stomachs, bank rolls, marriages, jobs, friendships, and lives. It is erroneously looked upon as a stimulant because of the wacky things people do when they drink it. It is an antiseptic, and for centuries it was the only anesthetic that mankind had. Basically, in its drinkable form, alcohol is a sedative drug and alcoholism is addiction to it. I maintain firmly and strongly that we know

Joseph C. Martin, "Alcoholism: What You See and What You Don't," *Catholic World,* July/August 1989. Reprinted with permission of Kelly Productions.

nothing of addiction. Nothing. The only thing we can do is describe it. And treat it. All addiction is characterized by compulsive use of an addictive substance. That's why the drinker that you know drinks the way he does. He doesn't will it—he drinks that way against his will. Would that he could handle it, but he can't. Addiction is progressive and, once contracted, progresses until death, even though it can be arrested. The addiction is always still there, and it worsens when it is gone back to.

To parents let me say that you cannot teach your children how to drink. And if they are teenagers, your capacity to teach them is gone anyway. The number one thing you have to give your children is a sense of values and proper attitudes, and then you hope to God that when they hit their teen years they will choose responsibly. Alcohol is a drug—in beverage form. But you can't scare kids with that information. It will not work. They know that most people who drink do not become alcoholics, and they find out soon enough that it makes them feel good.

Functioning Better?

Why does alcohol make us feel good? What is not oxidized by the liver gets into the blood stream and the blood ultimately brings it to the brain and begins to sedate it. And we feel good when we drink because alcohol knocks out of the picture what may be making us feel bad. It's an escape from problems. You can see it. We may even feel we function better after a couple of drinks. But because we *feel* we function better doesn't mean that we do. Watch someone that has had a few drinks—the slow blinking of the eyelids, the tongue getting a little bit thick. M-o-t-o-r a-c-t-i-v-i-t-y i-s a-f-f-e-c-t-e-d.

Here's a fellow who comes home from work three hours late. The dinner is ruined and his wife is furious. When she accuses him of being drunk, he's affronted. After all, he thinks he is functioning perfectly. So do you when you drink. After a few drinks even the most intelligent people say real nutty things and keep repeating themselves. If you want to know what I mean, the next time you go to a cocktail party, don't drink. After about three-quarters of an hour you either want to go home or get drunk yourself, just to be able to put up with it. After four or five drinks inhibitions are gone and people talk freely. Then after a few more, the emotions come out—and they come out drug-affected.

How many of us have looked at a problem drinker and said, "He needs a psychiatrist"? What would you think of a psychiatrist who would never dream of trying to treat somebody under the influence of ether, but tries to treat actively practicing alcoholics? I am not saying that psychiatric therapy isn't necessary. What I'm saying is that the alcoholic needs sobriety first. He needs to get sober in order to find out if he needs a psychiatrist for his emotional problems. Some alcoholics do. In fact, everyone who has ever done a

study on it has found that the percentage of alcoholics who do need psychiatric attention is exactly the same percentage as the non-alcoholic population. So the conclusion is that in the initial stages of recovery, psychiatry is contraindicated.

How does alcoholism kill? Through cirrhosis and through malnutrition, and all that these give birth to. And by accidents. Millions, literally millions of dollars are now being spent trying to reduce alcohol-related highway accidents. Over fifty percent of the carnage is caused by alcoholics, and over fifty percent of the pedestrians killed are alcoholics.

Symptoms of Alcoholism

What is an alcoholic? I will go into some of the symptoms. Everybody has a definition of alcoholism they can bring to mind. And usually everyone's definition of alcoholism will be descriptive and will be based on past knowledge. I'd be willing to bet that those who are having trouble with their own drinking will describe a drinking pattern that does not include theirs. Some are weekend drinkers, some drink all day, some get drunk only occasionally. An alcoholic is someone whose drinking causes serious life problems. It is just that simple. Let me ask you this seemingly stupid question: Have you ever heard of a man or woman who wrecked an automobile and nearly killed himself or herself, or someone else, as a result of eating string beans? No. But you've all known people who have wrecked their car because they were drunk. They can wreck a car for many reasons, but if alcohol is the reason, then alcohol is a problem.

How many of us have looked at someone in our family, someone we work for or works for us, and said this totally insane thing: "Well, yes, he drinks too much, but he's not that bad yet." He's not *what* bad yet? You wait till he's dead, and when he's dead conclude that yes, perhaps he did have trouble with his drinking? This is the insanity behind misinformation in this field. There is no field on earth in which the half truth results in more tragedy than this one. If you believe that alcoholism is a disease, then it is diagnosable and treatable.

"An alcoholic is someone whose drinking causes serious life problems."

All alcoholics drink too much. You might say, "Well, good heavens, I know that!" But let me ask you this: How much is too much? It doesn't have to do with any set amount. It is purely relevant. Too much is however much is too much for you.

All people who drink alcohol are going to be affected by it. Both alcoholics and non-alcoholics can experience blackouts, but if you tell a non-alcoholic who can't remember last night and has a dent in his right front fender that he may have hit somebody, he'll never drink and drive again. But the alcoholic drinks and drives all the time. A blackout is present inability to remember something done recently under the influence of alcohol. He can remember graduating from grammar school umpteen years ago, but he can't remember last night. I know a woman who, from 4:00 p.m. on every afternoon of her life, has no recollection at all of the evening. This no more phases her than the man in the moon. She blacks out every evening. She is sick. She has lost control. And there's the man who sneaks into the bathroom, lifts the lid off the toilet tank, pulls out a bottle and drinks three shots. It never dawns on him that this is different behavior than that of normal people. He was drunk at his daughter's graduation. He only meant to have three drinks, but he drank *twenty*-three. He is more baffled than you why he does it, so when you ask him why, he comes up with alibis. He has an alibi system: it's the people he works with; it's his wife; his dog died; his team won; his team lost—whatever. I don't mean to ridicule him. His reasons for drinking are somewhat valid because they did play a part in his contracting the disease. But not in why he's drunk today.

Antisocial Behavior

Often the alcoholic drinks alone, to hide the frequency and the amount. Alcoholics don't want anyone to know they drink as much as they do, or as often. They're usually embarrassed when they are caught drinking. Are normal drinkers embarrassed if you see them taking a drink of whiskey? Hiding to drink is not a normal way to drink.

An actively drinking alcoholic often exhibits antisocial behavior. Have you ever said of someone you know, "He's a wonderful person—when he's sober"? Antisocial behavior can result in loss of friends, jobs, and families. These same things can happen as a result of many other things, but if they result from one's drinking, then that's alcoholism. And if you remember nothing else, please remember that alcoholism is a family disease, and those who live with it get as sick or sicker than the alcoholic, and they need treatment as well. Let me give you an example of what I mean. A bunch of high school kids are down in the cafeteria eating lunch and talking about something they saw on TV last night, or some lesson they just had in class, but there's going to be one kid down at the end of the table who is staring into his soup. He's saying nothing. At 2:30 this morning he was shaking to pieces, listening to his dad calling his mother names in the midst of a drunken rage. And this happens on your block. What happens in the heart of a little eight-year-old girl who comes home from school with a classmate to find her mother passed out in the middle of the dining room floor, drunk? They don't get over these things. They can't ventilate them with anyone. Most recovering alcoholics in A.A. [Alcoholics Anonymous] are

children of alcoholics and I don't think it's because they inherit it. I think they inherit attitudes caused by their experience with an alcoholic.

Many Causes

Alcoholism is, indeed, a result of a combination of causative factors. It is not purely biochemical; it's not purely psychological; it's not purely emotional. It's a combination of all these things and they differ with the individual. Alcoholism is a symptom, but it's not just a symptom. That is a half-truth. With the word "symptom" in mind we have focused on the cause and not the problem. Two men, one a New York stockbroker and the other a physician-surgeon from Akron, Ohio said, "Let's treat the alcoholism." And they did. How many of us have discussed the drug problem with a drink in our hand? The most overused drug on earth is alcohol. A doctor might say to an alcoholic, "You've got cirrhosis. If you drink again, you'll die." So he stays sober out of fear. But if he drinks again, even after a prolonged period of sobriety, he'll wind up on a binge and wonder what happened. Remember, I said in the beginning that addiction is characterized by compulsive use, and once contracted it progresses till death. If an alcoholic drinks again, no matter how long he's been sober, he does not begin at the beginning and he does not pick up where he left off. He picks up where he would have been if he had been drinking all that while. Why is this? Nobody knows: it is simply a fact.

"An actively drinking alcoholic often exhibits antisocial behavior."

The inner shakes, tremors, screaming for a drink—this is indicative of a positive cellular craving for the drug without which the alcoholic cannot operate normally. This is an infallible sign of addiction. Alcoholics drink because they are alcoholics. It is the nature of alcoholism to use alcohol compulsively. In other words, alcoholics drink because they can't *not* drink. It is perfectly true that an alcoholic's freedom is going between drinks ten and eleven, but I maintain that he is not free before the first drink. Do you know anybody who hides bottles? You know an alcoholic. People don't hide milk.

The alcoholic is unreasonable and full of resentments. He may run out of alibis, but he needs a reason to drink. Alcoholism teaches one thing to its victims—how to be scared. They eventually come to the end of the line—the collapse of the alibi system. "I didn't get drunk because the Colts lost; I didn't get drunk because of my wife; it's not the people I work with. I drank because I couldn't help it." He has reached his moment of truth.

Is it true to say you can't help an alcoholic until he

wants it? Yes. He will not respond to treatment until he wants to. But get him into treatment. Try to make him want to. Don't wait till he asks for help. You can't ask a person with a sick mind to make a major decision about his life. You're presuming the health of mind that he needs and doesn't have. You can lead a horse to water and not make him drink. I know that. But you can lead him there and make him thirsty. Get him into treatment and see if he will respond. If he surrenders to his addiction he'll wind up incarcerated, insane or dead—or he can surrender to help. There are clinics, treatment centers, psychiatry, psychology—and I beg you, don't undersell the virtue and the value and the place of a return to religious faith as a component of complete recovery.

"Alcoholics drink because they can't not drink."

But above all else, what works best for most is A.A. There's nothing on God's green earth that succeeds like success. It is twelve principles to live by, based on the first three: "I can't handle it." "God can." "I believe I'll let him." It has worked for a half million people.

Father Joseph C. Martin is a Catholic priest who has written and lectured extensively on alcoholism. He founded Ashley, Inc., a chemical dependency treatment center in Havre de Grace, Maryland.

Alcoholism May Not Be a Disease

Richard E. Vatz and Lee S. Weinberg

What does "alcoholism" mean? Almost no one agrees—not even in the medical or legal communities. Yet, decisions on the meaning and determinations as to whether alcoholism is a disease have profound consequences for legal and social policy in America. If we believe medicine can define alcoholism and identify alcoholics, we can justify the expenditures on employee assistance programs currently being made by over 10,000 firms and public agencies; the spending of millions of dollars for alcoholic services provided by health insurance policies; and the extending of financial and legal protections accorded to handicapped individuals to millions of Americans.

The costs of identifying and treating "alcoholics" plus the expense of paying for the damage done by excessive drinking in this country exceed $120,000,000,000, according to the National Institute on Alcohol Abuse and Alcoholism (NIAAA). Such estimates assume the ability to define alcoholism and identify what drinkers are "alcoholics" and not just willful drinkers. Moreover, the estimates are based on the assumption that alcohol is the cause of the actions of people who drink heavily, including those not diagnosed as "alcoholic."

A Common Belief

It is easy to understand why the public assumes such a causal connection. Statistically, alcohol consumption is highly correlated with a wide variety of anti-social and socially disvalued behaviors. About one-half of all fatal driving accidents involve intoxicated drivers. Up to 70% of 4,000 drowning deaths last year involved victims who had been drinking. According to the Department of Justice, nearly one-third of the nation's 523,000 state prison inmates drank heavily before committing rapes, burglaries, and assaults. About 45% of over 250,000

homeless are substantial drinkers. Significantly, when the NIAAA and other alcohol-interested parties present such statistics, they imply that the alcohol consumption is the *cause* of the incidents. However, the unending message bombardment of the public by medical and alcohol-interest groups, often citing "alcoholism" as the underlying problem, does not reflect the actual confusion in the medical and legal communities over the definition and diagnosis of "alcoholism."

The persuading of the public that alcoholism is a disease (79% in a 1982 Gallup poll)—well-defined, identifiable, and rendering its victims out of control—has been so successful that even those who should least accept it often do so. Mothers Against Drunk Driving (MADD), whom one would expect to be among the first to challenge the notion that alcoholism is a disease, takes no consistent position. Dr. Donald Harting, chairman of the State Coordinating Committee of MADD in Maryland, told us repeatedly that the organization "has no quarrel" with the assumption that alcoholism is a disease.

Although the public may not feel confused about alcoholism, the medical community certainly does. There is even a debate in medicine as to what "disease" means. As one medical journal survey found, the public usually conceptualizes disease in a simple, straightforward way as meaning a biologically unhealthy condition with a clear medical cause, such as infections. However, the "disease" of alcoholism is diagnosed mostly by criteria of behavior. Indeed, it might surprise much of the public to know that there are no laboratory tests which are specific for alcoholism.

If the medical community is divided on what constitutes disease, they are in near anarchy as to what alcoholism is. The well-received 1987 work, *The Medical Basis of Psychiatry*, argues that research on "alcoholism" hopelessly is confused by conceptual inconsistency: "Epidemiological studies of alcohol use

Richard E. Vatz and Lee S. Weinberg, "Confusion over Alcoholism: Psychiatry, Medicine, and the Law Disagree." Reprinted from USA TODAY MAGAZINE, September 1989. Copyright © 1989 by the Society for the Advancement of Education.

and abuse are bedeviled by the uncertainties of what to measure and how to measure it. The terms alcoholism, alcohol dependence, alcohol abuse, problem drinking, and drinking problems continue to be used by different researchers in different ways."

"The search for biological markers for alcoholism has been unsuccessful."

Partially due to these definitional difficulties, the search for biological markers for alcoholism has been unsuccessful. Researcher Donald Goodwin points out that "Almost without exception, whenever a report of an association between a marker and alcoholism is followed by attempts to replicate the finding, the findings are contradictory." In sum, as he points out, "we are not certain that *anything* is inherited."

Most researchers agree that the behaviors we call alcoholism are a result of a complex combination of innate influences, simple learned behavior, and freedom of choice. The suspicion that there is some genetic component to uncontrolled heavy drinking rests on the finding that alcoholism, however defined, tends to run in families, even though the vast majority of children of biological parents diagnosed as alcoholics do not become alcoholics (in fact, a disproportionate number become lifelong teetotalers), and most alcoholics have no such family history. Still, studies of twins, even when they are separated at birth and adopted by non-alcoholic parents, do show significantly higher rates of alcoholism (again, even with varying definitions) than children whose biological parents were non-alcoholic.

Goodwin asks the key question that goes to the root of all the confusion—even if there is a heredity factor, "what is inherited?" Speculations include, most prominently, an increased euphoria from alcohol and the *lack* of intolerance to alcohol. Interestingly, the strongest evidence of the effect of innate influences on alcoholism is the inability of some segments of the population to tolerate liquor physiologically, such as large numbers of Orientals. Therefore, the surest thing scientific studies can tell us is who genetically is undisposed to become alcoholic.

Volition

In addition, no study can measure the most important criteria of most notions of alcoholism—volition, or whether the drinker can control whether he or she drinks. The question of volition is the critical one in the diagnosis of alcoholism, particularly with respect to the formulation of legal and social policies concerning how we deal with the drinking and behavior of so-called alcoholics. Despite all the confusion over the meaning of alcoholism, almost all medical experts see the loss of control as a defining hallmark. Alcoholism researcher Sheila Blume notes

that, as early as E.M. Jellinek's seminal work on alcoholism a generation ago, "the impaired ability of the individual to control his or her drinking [was considered] to be one of the central aspects of alcoholism as a disease." However, the concept of volition, like that of alcoholism itself, is more complicated than generally acknowledged. In addition to control of drinking is the crucial question of whether and to what extent the drinker can control his or her behavior when drinking.

The component of volition is supremely important, since the assumption that alcoholics can not control their drinking or behavior is the justification for providing free help, as well as excusing some people for their actions. Yet, that key symptom of alcoholism can not be measured, since willfulness only can be assumed and not tested. Even the American Psychiatric Association states that psychiatrists can not measure volition, in response to attacks on the insanity plea several years ago.

Alcoholism and the Law

It is not surprising that the medical community's confusion and uncertainty are reflected in the law's posture as well. In a 1962 case involving drugs, the Supreme Court held that California could not punish narcotics addicts merely for being addicts—*i.e.*, to criminalize the "status or condition" of being an addict amounted to cruel and unusual punishment. Yet, in 1968, the Court held that Texas could punish public drunkenness despite the offender's being a chronic alcoholic. The divided Court ruled that, while punishing an individual based on his status as an alcoholic is impermissible and that punishment of the mere act of drinking might be similarly impermissible, the further act of being drunk in public is punishable.

The 1988 Supreme Court decision in *Traynor v. Turnage* and *McKelvey v. Turnage* and the publication of Herbert Fingarette's 1988 book, *Heavy Drinking: The Myth of Alcoholism as a Disease*, together mark a new phase and sophistication in the debate over the definition and nature of alcoholism.

It is ironic that the Court and a philosopher—non-medical authorities—should have so great an impact on public perception of alcoholism, when the medical and scientific communities in recent years have had so little. Moreover, it is ironic that a court decision that specifically does not answer the question of whether it is a disease should cast so much doubt on the medical authenticity of alcoholism.

The actual Court ruling involved only a decision as to whether the refusal by the Veterans Administration (VA) to grant extensions of benefits to two "alcoholic" veterans—on the ground that their "alcoholism" resulted from "willful misconduct"—was inconsistent with Section 504 of the Rehabilitation Act. Under the law governing veterans' benefits, Congress has provided for extensions to "any eligible veteran who was prevented from initiating or completing such veteran's chosen program of education within such time period because of a physical or mental disability which was not the result of such veteran's willful misconduct." The VA's refusal was based on its conclusion that alcoholism and the resulting inability of the claimants to complete their education during the allotted time resulted from their "willful misconduct." The VA took the view that some people simply choose to drink too much (primary alcoholism), while others drink too much as a "manifestation of an acquired psychiatric disorder" (secondary alcoholism). The former are denied time extensions for benefits because their conditions presumably result from "willful misconduct," while the latter are granted extensions because it is believed that they do not contract these psychiatric disorders willfully.

The 1988 Supreme Court decision upheld the VA position. However, it did more than provide an interpretation of Section 504, which prohibits the denial of benefits to anyone "solely by reason of his handicap." Protestations by the Court to the contrary notwithstanding, this decision implies an official recognition that, except for those suffering from an identifiable underlying mental illness, all other alcoholics conclusively may be presumed to have a willfully incurred disability. While noting the lack of agreement in the medical literature on the nature of "alcoholism" and explicitly refusing to address whether or not it is a disease, the logic of the majority opinion necessarily leads to the following conclusions: "primary alcoholics" drink too much by choice; and volitional conduct itself logically can not constitute disease, though it may, of course, *cause* disease.

Fingarette's Argument

Fingarette, in his lucid and tightly reasoned book, examines the scientific evidence underlying the widely held public belief that excessive drinking meaningfully may be thought of as a disease and shows all the major assumptions of the alcoholism-as-disease ideology to be without scientific validity. What makes his contribution most noteworthy is his reliance on conventional medical sources and respected establishment "alcoholism" researchers for proof of his contentions. His work on alcoholism brilliantly illustrates a common phenomenon—the gap between actual scientific knowledge and public beliefs about such conclusions. Long after scientists have gathered new evidence and altered their views, the public—frequently with the unintentional support of the media and always with the encouragement of those who benefit from the outdated state of knowledge—may continue to believe in ideas which have been discredited.

Yet, Fingarette uses conventional science to debunk alcoholism myths (*e.g.*, the alcoholics' lack of control, the inexorable fall after an alcoholic takes one drink,

and the medical nature of alcoholic treatment) including the seminal myth that the scientific community consensually recognizes alcoholism as a disease.

None of this is new. For decades, Fingarette has addressed the question of legal responsibility of those labeled as alcoholic. Similarly, for over 20 years, psychiatrist and psychiatric critic Thomas Szasz has written on the myth of alcoholism as a disease. In 1972, in *Lancet*, for example, Szasz questioned the same myths addressed by Fingarette, including how the problems and failures of alcoholics—such as criminality, homelessness, job difficulties, and divorces—are assumed to be caused by drinking, and not vice-versa.

"The medical community's confusion and uncertainty are reflected in the law's posture as well."

The new threat to the public's unquestioned acceptance of the disease model of alcoholism presages a new emphasis in research, seeking out genetic markers which will "prove" there is a "disease" of heavy drinking. For, if "crises are a necessary precondition for the emergence of novel theories," as Thomas Kuhn argued, then alcohol interests soon must find a mystifying escape from the growing realization that science simply is not on their side. Thus, it is likely that there will be more frequent announcements of scientific "discoveries" to authenticate alcoholism as a disease once again. . . .

It is too early to say whether the one-two punch of the *Traynor* decision coupled with Fingarette's book will change our notion of whether people who drink too much are "sick" or irresponsible. Still, with the costs of studying, identifying, and treating alcoholism running into the billions of dollars, the possible consequences of a change in public perception are mind-boggling.

Most of the private and public support, sympathy, and spending on alcohol-related problems are grounded in the alcohol-as-disease concept. Adoption of the view that heavy drinking is controllable behavior might result in the bottom dropping out of the support systems (medical, familial, business, and government). These support systems lessen the penalties society exacts from irresponsible drinkers.

Richard E. Vatz is a professor of rhetoric and communication at Towson State University in Maryland. Lee S. Weinberg is an associate professor in the Graduate School of Public and International Affairs at the University of Pittsburgh.

"Alcohol companies deliberately devise ads designed to appeal to heavy drinkers."

Liquor Advertising Contributes to Alcoholism

Jean Kilbourne

Alcohol is the most commonly used drug in the United States. It is also one of the most heavily advertised products in the United States. The alcohol industry generates more than $65 billion a year in revenue and spends more than $1 billion a year on advertising. The advertising budget for one beer—Budweiser—is more than the entire federal budget for research on alcoholism and alcohol abuse. Unfortunately, young people and heavy drinkers are the primary targets of the advertisers.

What Does Advertising Do?

There is no conclusive proof that advertising increases alcohol consumption. Research does indicate, however, that alcohol advertising contributes to increases in consumption by young people and serves as a significant source of negative socialization for young people. Those who argue that peer pressure is the major influence on young people strangely overlook the role of advertising.

The alcoholic beverage companies claim that they are not trying to create more or heavier drinkers. They say that they only want people who already drink to switch to another brand and to drink it in moderation. But this industry-wide claim does not hold up under scrutiny. An editorial in *Advertising Age* concluded: "A strange world it is, in which people spending millions on advertising must do their best to prove that advertising doesn't do very much!"

About a third of all Americans choose not to drink at all, a third drink moderately, and about a third drink regularly. Ten percent of the drinking-age population consumes over 60 percent of the alcohol. This figure corresponds closely to the percentage of alcoholics in society. If alcoholics were to recover (i.e. to stop drinking entirely),the alcohol industry's gross revenues would be cut in half. Recognizing this

important marketing fact, alcohol companies deliberately devise ads designed to appeal to heavy drinkers. Advertising is usually directed toward promoting loyalty and increasing usage, and heavy users of any product are the best customers but, in the case of alcohol, the heavy user is usually an addict.

Another perspective on the industry's claim that it encourages only moderate drinking is provided by Robert Hammond, director of the Alcohol Research Information Service. He estimates that if all 105 million drinkers of legal age consumed the official maximum "moderate" amount of alcohol—.99 ounces per day, the equivalent of about two drinks—the industry would suffer "a whopping 40 percent decrease in the sale of beer, wine and distilled spirits, based on 1981 sales figures."

Such statistics show the role heavy drinkers play in maintaining the large profit margins of the alcohol industry. Modern research techniques allow the producers of print and electronic media to provide advertisers with detailed information about their readers, listeners and viewers. Target audiences are sold to the alcohol industry on a cost per drinker basis.

Target Audiences

One example of how magazines sell target audiences appeared in *Advertising Age*: *Good Housekeeping* advertised itself to the alcohol industry as a good place to reach women drinkers, proclaiming, "You'll catch more women with wine than with vinegar. She's a tougher customer than ever.You never needed *Good Housekeeping* more."

The young audience is also worth a great deal to the alcohol industry. *Sport* magazine promoted itself to the alcohol industry as a conduit to young drinkers with an ad in *Advertising Age* stating, "What young money spends on drink is a real eye-opener." Budweiser's Spuds MacKenzie campaign is clearly designed to appeal to young people. Miller has a new television

Jean Kilbourne, "Advertising Addiction." Reprinted with permission from the June 1989 issue of *Multinational Monitor,* a monthly news magazine published by Essential Information, Inc.

commercial featuring animated clay figures of a monkey, an elephant and a lion, with a voice that says "three out of four party animals preferred the taste of Miller Lite." Wine coolers are often marketed as soft drinks with ads featuring puppets, animated characters, Santa Claus and other figures that appeal especially to young people. Even in supposedly commercial-free movies, showing in theaters, viewers are targeted. Many films, especially those appealing to young people, include paid placements of cigarettes and alcohol.

The college market is particularly important to the alcohol industry not only because of the money the students will spend on beer today, but because they will develop drinking habits and brand allegiances that may be with them for life. As one marketing executive said, "Let's not forget that getting a freshman to choose a certain brand of beer may mean that he will maintain his brand loyalty for the next 20 to 35 years. If he turns out to be a big drinker, the beer company has bought itself an annuity." This statement undercuts the industry's claim that it does not target advertising campaigns at underage drinkers since today almost every state prohibits the sale of alcohol to people under 21 years old and the vast majority of college freshman are below that age.

The alcohol industry's efforts to promote responsible drinking must also be evaluated carefully. Much of its advertising promotes irresponsible and dangerous drinking. For example, a poster for Pabst Blue Ribbon features a young woman speeding along on a bicycle with a bottle of beer where the water bottle is supposed to be. Obviously biking and drinking beer are not safely complementary activities.

Even some of the programs designed by the alcohol industry to educate students about responsible drinking subtly promote myths and damaging attitudes. Budweiser has a program called "The Buddy System" designed to encourage young people not to let their friends drive drunk. Although this is a laudable goal, it is interesting to note that none of the alcohol industry programs discourage or even question drunkenness per se. The implicit message is that it is alright to get drunk as long as you don't drive; abuse is acceptable, even encouraged.

Linking Alcohol and Power

The industry often targets relatively disempowered groups in society, primarily women and minority groups, and associates alcohol with power. For example, a Cutty Sark Whiskey ad features a retired Black baseball player, Curt Flood, promoting its drink. The ad shows Flood holding forth a glass of whiskey with the text "Some people think you can't beat the system. Here's to those who show the way." This ad associates Flood and his successful athletic performance with his drinking Cutty Sark whiskey.

The link between advertising and alcoholism is unproven. Alcoholism is a complex illness and its etiology is uncertain. But alcohol advertising does create a climate in which abusive attitudes toward alcohol are presented as normal, appropriate and innocuous. One of the chief symptoms of alcoholism is denial that there is a problem. It is often not only the alcoholic who denies the illness but also his or her family, employer, doctor, etc. Alcohol advertising often encourages denial by creating a world in which myths about alcohol are presented as true and in which signs of trouble are erased or transformed into positive attributes.

"Alcohol advertising does create a climate in which abusive attitudes toward alcohol are presented as normal."

One of the primary means of creating this distortion is through advertising. Most advertising is essentially myth-making. Instead of providing information about a product, such as its taste or quality, advertisements create an image of the product, linking the item with a particular lifestyle which may have little or nothing to do with the product itself. According to an article on beer marketing in *Advertising Age*, "Advertising is as important to selling beer as the bottle opener is to drinking it. . . . Beer advertising is mainly an exercise in building images." Another article a few months later on liquor marketing stated that "product image is probably the most important element in selling liquor. The trick for marketers is to project the right message in their advertisements to motivate those motionless consumers to march down to the liquor store or bar and exchange their money for a sip of image."

False Links

The links are generally false and arbitrary but we are so surrounded by them that we come to accept them: the jeans will make you look sexy, the car will give you confidence, the detergent will save your marriage. Advertising spuriously links alcohol with precisely those attributes and qualities—happiness, wealth, prestige, sophistication, success, maturity, athletic ability, virility, creativity, sexual satisfaction and others—that the misuse of alcohol destroys. For example, alcohol is often linked with romance and sexual fulfillment, yet it is common knowledge that alcohol misuse often leads to sexual dysfunction. Less well known is the fact that people with drinking problems are seven times more likely than the general population to be separated or divorced.

Image advertising is especially appealing to young people who are more likely than adults to be insecure about the image they are projecting. Sexual and athletic prowess are two of the themes that dominate advertising aimed at young people. A television commercial for Miller beer featured Danny Sullivan, the race car driver, speeding around a track with the Miller logo emblazoned everywhere. The ad implies that Miller beer and fast driving go hand in hand. A study of beer commercials, funded by the American Automobile Association, found that they often linked beer with images of speed, including speeding cars.

The Magic Transformation

"It separates the exceptional from the merely ordinary." This advertising slogan for Piper champagne illustrates the major premise of the mythology that alcohol is magic. It is a magic potion that can make you successful, sophisticated and sexy; without it, you are dull, mediocre and ordinary. The people who are not drinking champagne are lifeless replicas of the happy couple who are imbibing. The alcohol has rescued the couple, resurrected them, restored them to life. At the heart of the alcoholic's dilemma and denial is this belief, this certainty, that alcohol is essential for life, that without it he or she will literally die—or at best suffer. This ad and many others like it present the nightmare as true, thus affirming and even glorifying one of the symptoms of the illness.

Glorifying Alcoholism

Such glorification of the symptoms is common in alcohol advertising. "Your own special island," proclaims an ad for St. Croix rum. Another ad offers Busch beer as "Your mountain hide-a-way." Almost all alcoholics experience intense feelings of isolation, alienation and loneliness. Most make the tragic mistake of believing that the alcohol alleviates these feelings rather than exacerbating them. The two examples above distort reality in much the same way as the alcoholic does. Instead of being isolated and alienated, the people in the ad are in their own special places.

The rum ad also seems to be encouraging solitary drinking, a sign of trouble with alcohol. There is one drink on the tray and no room for another. Although it is unusual for solitary drinking to be shown (most alcohol ads feature groups or happy couples), it is not unusual for unhealthy attitudes toward alcohol to be presented as normal and acceptable.

The most obvious example is obsession with alcohol. Alcohol is at the center of the ads just as it is at the center of the alcoholic's life. The ads imply that alcohol is an appropriate adjunct to almost every activity from lovemaking to white-water canoeing. An ad for Puerto Rican rums says, "You know how to make every day special. You're a white rum drinker." In fact, less than 10 percent of the adult population makes drinking a part of their daily routine.

There is also an emphasis on quantity in the ads. A Johnnie Walker ad features 16 bottles of scotch and the copy, "Bob really knows how to throw a party. He never runs out of Johnnie Walker Red." Light beer has been developed and heavily promoted not for the dieter but for the heavy drinker. The ads imply that because it is less filling, one can drink more of it.

Thus the ads tell the alcoholic and everyone around him that it is all right to consume large quantities of alcohol on a daily basis and to have it be a part of all of one's activities. At the same time, all signs of trouble and any hint of addiction are conspicuously avoided. The daily drinking takes place in glorious and unique settings, such as yachts at sunset, not at the more mundane but realistic kitchen tables in the morning. There is no unpleasant drunkenness, only high spirits. There are never any negative consequences. Of course, one would not expect there to be. The advertisers are selling their product and it is their job to erase any negative aspects as well as to enhance the positive ones. When the product is a drug that is addictive to one out of 10 users, however, there are consequences that go far beyond product sales.

Glorifying Alcohol

The U.S. culture as a whole, not just the advertising and alcohol industry, tends to glorify alcohol and dismiss the problems associated with it. The "war on drugs," as covered by newspapers and magazines in this country, rarely includes the two major killers, alcohol and nicotine. It is no coincidence that these are two of the most heavily advertised products. In 1987, the use of all illegal drugs combined accounted for about 3,400 deaths. Alcohol is linked with over 100,000 deaths annually. Cigarettes kill a thousand people every day.

"Alcohol is often linked with romance and sexual fulfillment."

A comprehensive effort is needed to prevent alcohol-related problems. Such an effort must include education, media campaigns, increased availability of treatment programs and more effective deterrence policies. It must also include public policy changes that would include raising taxes on alcohol, putting clearly legible warning labels on the bottles and regulating the advertising.

Jean Kilbourne is on the board of directors of the National Council on Alcoholism. Two award-winning films, "Still Killing Us Softly: Advertising's Image of Women" and "Calling the Shots: The Advertising of Alcohol," have been made of her lectures.

"Nobody has been able to demonstrate that advertising does anything more than shift brand preferences."

Liquor Advertising Does Not Contribute to Alcoholism

Jacob Sullum

More than half a century after repeal, the spirit of Prohibition lives on in the form of numerous restrictions that reflect America's fundamental ambivalence toward alcohol. (Although most Americans drink, a 1988 Gallup poll found that majorities also favor a variety of control measures, including excise taxes and warning labels.) In addition to the legacy of post-repeal fears, Americans face a set of recently enacted and proposed control measures that observers identify with a neoprohibitionist trend in public policy.

"There's been a tremendous anti-alcohol upsurge," says Washington University sociologist David J. Pittman, who has studied alcohol issues for more than three decades. Pittman, a prominent critic of neoprohibitionism, says we are in the midst of the third major temperance movement since 1820.

Unlike its predecessors, the third wave is not primarily moral or religious in tone. Rather, like so many other statist movements in this risk-averse age, the New Temperance focuses on health and safety. Its proponents—which include the World Health Organization and the U.S. Department of Health and Human Services as well as such private advocacy groups as the Center for Science in the Public Interest [CSPI]—argue that drinkers must be saved from themselves, lest their health suffer as a result of excessive consumption. Further, pointing to the role played by alcohol in violence and traffic accidents, they maintain that drinking endangers public safety.

New Temperance advocates, both in and out of government, have set as their goal a reduction in per capita alcohol consumption. They seek to achieve this goal both directly, by restricting the availability of alcoholic beverages, and indirectly, by stigmatizing beer, wine, and liquor as inherently bad. For example, Loren Archer, deputy director of the National

Institute on Alcohol Abuse and Alcoholism, has declared there is no such thing as responsible drinking.

Although the 21st Amendment left alcohol control in the hands of the states, New Temperance lobbyists have been focusing their efforts on the federal government in an attempt to develop a national alcohol policy. The movement's most conspicuous successes illustrate its two-track approach. A 1984 law has restricted availability by threatening to withhold federal highway funds from any state that did not raise its legal purchase age to 21 by July 1987. A 1988 law has helped to delegitimize alcohol by requiring health-and-safety warning labels on every bottle of beer, wine, and liquor. Yet to come, if the neoprohibitionists have their way, are federal excise-tax increases and further advertising restrictions. . . .

Push For Warning Labels

Although the neoprohibitionists tend to ignore the role of individual choice in drunk driving, they recognize that it plays a part in alcohol consumption. In fact, they are eager to help consumers make up their minds. At least, that is the ostensible motivation for the warning labels that were required on all alcoholic beverages as of November 18, 1989. Ironically championed by Mr. Tobacco, Sen. Strom Thurmond, the labels were promoted as a simple educational device. "Consumers have a right to know about the health and safety risks of a product," says Pat Taylor, director of the alcohol project at the Center for Science in the Public Interest (CSPI). "It's a very standard consumer-information strategy."

Standard it may be, but the warnings are not terribly helpful. For example: "Consumption of alcoholic beverages impairs your ability to drive a car or operate machinery, and may cause health problems." This is not exactly news.

The other warning on the label is more misleading than gratuitous: "According to the Surgeon General, women should not drink alcoholic beverages during pregnancy because of the risk of birth defects." Medical experts say fetal alcohol syndrome has been observed only in the children of heavy drinkers, and there is no evidence that light consumption harms the fetus.

Dr. Henry Rosett and Lyn Weiner, of Boston University, conclude in *Alcohol and the Fetus* that "the recommendation that all women should abstain from drinking during pregnancy is not based on scientific evidence, since no risks have been observed from small quantities." Indeed, according to Dr. Jack Mendelson of Harvard University, "it is possible that some doses of alcohol, low or moderate, may improve the probability for healthy pregnancies and healthy offspring."

Is Drinking Safe?

Christine Lubinski defends the Department of Health and Human Services' absolutist stand on drinking during pregnancy. "It's important to stress that there is no known safe level of alcohol during pregnancy," she says. "The correct course is not to drink at all."

But this position requires the alcohol industry to prove a negative. No matter how many studies fail to find a risk from moderate consumption, drinking during pregnancy remains suspect. In any case, especially given the controversy, "consulting one's physician would be more appropriate than consulting a label on a beer can," says Jeff Becker, a spokesperson for the Beer Institute.

Gene Ford, a Seattle author and editor of his own *Moderate Drinking Journal*, has led a virtual one-man crusade to change the wording of the warning labels. Not only does the warning about drinking during pregnancy misrepresent the scientific research, Ford says, but the label taken as a whole gives the impression that drinking *per se* is bad, because the message makes no distinction between moderate and excessive consumption. And, unlike government-mandated labels on other products, it makes no mention of alcohol's health benefits—in reducing the chances of coronary disease, for example.

"For the neoprohibitionists, alcohol advertising is different because it involves a clear evil."

Pittman agrees that the failure to make any reference to dosage is glaring. "It's such a general, vague statement that it has no meaning," he says. "Basically, it says drinking is hazardous to your health. That's a false statement. . . . Alcohol in small quantities is not injurious."

Pittman, who testified against warning labels

during congressional hearings in 1979, says research shows that people don't read such messages until after they buy the product, anyway. "I think they will have no effect whatsoever in terms of changing the behavior of individuals," he says. Pittman acknowledges that some supporters of warning labels may genuinely believe they are doing consumers a service, but he says many are motivated by a desire to stigmatize the product.

Despite such objections, industry groups were remarkably quiet during the debate over warning labels. . . .

One reason for the reticence may have been the hope that warning labels would do for the alcohol industry what they did for the tobacco industry— provide a virtual blanket of protection from legal liability. Pittman notes that the industry decided not to fight the warning labels shortly after parents of fetal alcohol syndrome babies filed multi-million-dollar lawsuits against liquor companies. . . .

But the industry may not need the warning labels to help it win suits. On May 17, 1989 a federal jury absolved Jim Beam of responsibility for the birth defects suffered by the child of a Seattle woman who had drunk about half a fifth of bourbon virtually every day during her pregnancy. The woman's attorneys argued that a warning label could have deterred her from drinking.

That is the neoprohibitionist position writ small. People cannot be trusted to make their own decisions about alcohol; they must be nudged, discouraged, and coerced. From this perspective, alcohol problems can best be solved by reducing alcohol consumption. Excise taxes are a favored method. . . .

Alcohol Advertising

While excise taxes make sense if you believe that reducing consumption is the best way to control alcohol abuse, the neoprohibitionist obsession with advertising is harder to understand. Former Surgeon General C. Everett Koop has been particularly vocal in this area. A workshop that he convened in December 1988, ostensibly to study drunk driving, issued a report that recommended mandatory warnings on alcohol ads, anti-alcohol messages for which the industry would have to pay, and elimination of the tax deduction for alcohol advertising expenses. In May 1989 Koop called a press conference to criticize beer companies' use of celebrity representatives who appeal to young people and their sponsorship of rock concerts and sporting events.

Both the CSPI and the NCA [National Council on Alcoholism] support a law that would require radio and television broadcasters to air one health-and-safety message for every beer or wine commercial. The CSPI's Taylor says it would be up to the stations to decide how to pass the cost along. The Beer Institute's Becker is understandably appalled at the idea. "Who's going to pay for it?" he asks, wondering if an auto-safety message for every car commercial will be next. "Where do you draw the line? What product is 100 percent safe?"

"Although advertising expenditures have increased dramatically during the past decade, drinking has declined."

For the neoprohibitionists, alcohol advertising is different because it involves a clear evil. "We need to scrutinize $1 billion of glitzy drug pushing on TV," Lubinski says. The NCA doesn't just want to scrutinize beer and wine ads—it wants to ban them from shows with audiences that include a substantial number of people under the age of 21. Lubinski isn't sure just how many underage viewers it would take to make a program's commercial time off-limits to beer and wine companies.

The CSPI also objects to billboards using black celebrities to advertise alcoholic beverages in poor neighborhoods. "We think that type of targeting should not be allowed," Taylor says.

The advertising restrictions pushed by HHS, the CSPI, and the NCA would be in addition to existing requirements imposed by industry standards and federal regulations. Liquor, for example, has never been advertised on radio or television. In view of lingering prohibitionist hostility following repeal, the industry refrained from using these media, a stance that was incorporated into its Code of Good Practice. Similarly, although no law prohibits it, beer and wine commercials never show people actually drinking. Federal restrictions on alcohol advertising include a ban on statements about health benefits or nutritional properties.

Why all this concern about advertising? The CSPI argues that "alcohol advertising tends to glamorize alcohol use and presents a one-sided view without information about the risks of drinking." Is this so appalling? One is hard pressed to think of advertisers who try to sell their products by denigrating them, associating them with negative images, and warning about the dangers of misusing them. But, say Koop and others, the $2 billion spent each year on advertising alcoholic beverages *encourages drinking*. Aside from the fact that this is troubling only if one thinks of drinking as inherently bad, there is no evidence that it is true.

For one thing, although advertising expenditures have increased dramatically during the past decade, drinking has declined, a trend that is expected to continue through the end of the century. Between 1980 and 1987, beer consumption dropped 7 percent, wine consumption fell 14 percent, and liquor consumption declined 23 percent, according to the

industry publication *Impact*. Control advocates see such figures as a sign of their success—a result of education, excise taxes, and purchase restrictions. Were it not for alcohol advertising, Lubinski says, consumption probably would have declined further. But pressed for evidence that advertising increases consumption, she can only cite research suggesting it encourages attitude changes. As any social psychologist can tell you, the connection between attitudes and behavior is tenuous at best.

"Nobody has been able to demonstrate that advertising does anything more than shift brand preferences," Pittman says. "It surely doesn't increase consumption." A 1985 research survey by the Senate Subcommittee on Alcohol and Drug Abuse came to a similar conclusion.

A Positive Role

Ford suggests that people who oppose alcohol advertising simply reject the possibility that beer, wine, and liquor have a positive role to play in society. Emblematic of that attitude are activists such as Dr. Trisha Roth, a pediatrician known as the Carry Nation of Beverly Hills. Roth, a teetotaler, has reported about 40 restaurants and institutions, including her own synagogue, for violating a state law that imposes a $2,500-a-day penalty on establishments that serve alcohol and fail to post signs warning about birth defects and cancer. She has campaigned against the serving of alcohol at city events and fundraisers for charitable organizations. She convinced the Beverly Hills Unified School District to cancel a wine-tasting class for adults, and she called in a vice-squad officer to investigate plans for an after-prom party in West Hollywood.

On the national level, Ford cites expurgation of references to responsible drinking from government publications, the repeated association of alcohol with illegal drugs, and the refusal to consider research showing health benefits from moderate use as evidence of a systematic effort by health officials and advocacy groups to brand alcohol with a skull-and-crossbones. A former salesman for Christian Brothers winery, Ford criticizes the industry for yielding to control measures and failing to defend itself vigorously. . . .

Ambivalent Attitudes

Why is the alcohol industry so bullied in a nation where a majority of adults use its products? "America is a very ambivalent country," psychologist Stanton Peele says. "We tend to want to influence people not to drink at all. We don't do a very good job at encouraging sensible consumption."

There is strong evidence that such an attitude breeds abuse. For example, a survey reported in *The Journal on Alcohol Studies* in 1986 found that states with the most restrictive alcohol laws—the top three are Utah, Kentucky, and Mississippi—have the most alcohol problems. Similarly, dry towns in Tennessee tend to have greater problems with alcohol than wet towns. One explanation for this phenomenon is the "forbidden fruit syndrome"—prohibiting something makes it more attractive. More important, a prohibitionist approach encourages people to drink large quantities surreptitiously and makes teaching responsible drinking difficult or impossible. Peele points out that alcohol problems are less common in countries, such as Italy and Greece, where good drinking habits are inculcated from an early age. Alcohol is an accepted part of the culture, and it does not have the same mystique as in the United States.

"People who oppose alcohol advertising simply reject the possibility that beer, wine, and liquor have a positive role to play in society."

Peele says the notion of alcohol addiction encourages an all-or-nothing attitude toward drinking, a belief that moderation is impossible. For example, Dr. Ernest F. Noble, former director of the National Institute on Alcoholism and Alcohol Abuse, has said that everyone is a potential alcoholic.

Alcoholics, of course, can't help themselves, so government must step in. Ford's answer to that paternalistic attitude is typically combative: "I think we should tell the prohibitionists to stick it up their ass. I'm tired of their sanctimonious poop." He says the key to fighting further restrictions is to mobilize all the groups that benefit from the alcohol industry.

Pittman takes the long view. "The last [temperance] surge went on for about 30 years," he says. "We're just at the beginning of this surge. The real battle will be in the 1990s."

Jacob Sullum is an assistant editor of Reason, *a libertarian magazine.*

"The gravest domestic threat facing our nation today is drugs."

The War on Drugs Is Necessary

George Bush

Editor's note: The following viewpoint is an excerpt from a nationally televised speech given by President Bush on September 5, 1989.

This is the first time since taking the oath of office that I felt an issue was so important, so threatening, that it warranted talking directly with you, the American people. All of us agree that the gravest domestic threat facing our nation today is drugs.

Drugs have strained our faith in our system of justice. Our courts, our prisons, our legal system are stretched to the breaking point. The social costs of drugs are mounting. In short, drugs are sapping our strength as a nation.

Turn on the evening news, or pick up the morning paper and you'll see what some Americans know just by stepping out their front door: Our most serious problem today is cocaine, and in particular, crack.

Who's responsible?—Let me tell you straight out.

Everyone who uses drugs.

Everyone who sells drugs.

And everyone who looks the other way.

I will tell you how many Americans are using illegal drugs. I will present to you our national strategy to deal with every aspect of this threat. And I will ask you to get involved in what promises to be a very difficult fight.

Crack cocaine [is] . . . as innocent-looking as candy, but it is turning our cities into battle zones, and it is murdering our children. Let there be no mistake, this stuff is poison.

Some used to call drugs harmless recreation. They're not. Drugs are real and a terribly dangerous threat to our neighborhoods, our friends and our families.

No one among us is out of harm's way. When 4-year-olds play in playgrounds strewn with discarded hypodermic needles and crack vials—it breaks my

George Bush, "National Drug Control Strategy," *Vital Speeches of the Day,* October 1, 1989.

heart. When cocaine—one of the most deadly and addictive illegal drugs—is available to school kids—school kids—it's an outrage. And when hundreds of thousands of babies are born each year to mothers who use drugs—premature babies born desperately sick—then even the most defenseless among us are at risk.

These are the tragedies behind the statistics. But the numbers also have quite a story to tell. Let me share with you the results of the recently completed household survey of the National Institute on Drug Abuse. . . .

Fewer Casual Users

In 1985, the Government estimated that 23 million Americans were using drugs on a "current" basis—that is, at least once in the preceding month. In 1988, that number fell by more than a third. That means almost nine million fewer Americans are casual drug users. Good news.

Because we changed our national attitude toward drugs, casual drug use has declined. We have many to thank: our brave law-enforcement officers, religious leaders, teachers, community activists, and leaders of business and labor. We should also thank the media for their exhaustive news and editorial coverage; and advertisers for running anti-drug messages.

Finally, I want to thank President and Mrs. Reagan for their leadership. All of these good people told the truth—that drug use is wrong and dangerous.

But, as much comfort as we can draw from these dramatic reductions, there is also bad news—very bad news. Roughly eight million people have used cocaine in 1989, almost one million of them used it frequently, once a week or more.

What this means is that, in spite of the fact that overall cocaine use is down, frequent use has almost doubled in the last few years. And that's why habitual cocaine users—especially crack users—are the most pressing, immediate drug problem involving every family.

I sent our first such national strategy to the Congress. It was developed with the hard work of our nation's first drug policy director, Bill Bennett. In preparing this plan, we talked with state, local and community leaders, law-enforcement officials, and experts in education, drug prevention, and rehabilitation. We talked with parents and kids. We took a long hard look at all that the Federal Government has done about drugs in the past: what's worked, and—let's be honest—what hasn't. Too often, people in government acted as if their part of the problem—whether fighting drug production, or drug smuggling, or drug demand—was the only problem. But turf battles won't win this war. Teamwork will.

"If you sell drugs, you will be caught. And when you're caught, you will be prosecuted. And once you're convicted, you will do time. Caught. Prosecuted. Punished."

I'm announcing a strategy that reflects the coordinated, cooperative commitment of all Federal agencies. In short, this plan is as comprehensive as the problem. With this strategy, we now finally have a plan that coordinates our resources, our programs and the people who run them.

Our weapons in this strategy are: the law and criminal justice system, our foreign policy; our treatment systems, and our schools and drug prevention programs. So the basic weapons we need are the ones we already have, what has been lacking is a strategy to effectively use them.

Let me address four of the major elements of our strategy.

First, we are determined to enforce the law, to make our streets and neighborhoods safe. So to start, I'm proposing that we more than double Federal assistance to state and local law enforcement. Americans have a right to safety in and around their homes.

And we won't have safe neighborhoods unless we are tough on drug criminals—much tougher than we are now. Sometimes that means tougher penalties. But more often it just means punishment that is swift and certain. We've all heard stories about drug dealers who are caught and arrested—again and again—but never punished. Well, here the rules have changed: If you sell drugs, you will be caught. And when you're caught, you will be prosecuted. And once you're convicted, you will do time. Caught. Prosecuted. Punished.

More Prisons

I am also proposing that we enlarge our criminal justice system across the board—at the local, state and Federal levels alike. We need more prisons, more jails, more courts, more prosecutors. So I'm requesting—altogether—an almost billion-and-a-half dollar increase in drug-related Federal spending on law enforcement.

And while illegal drug use is found in every community, nowhere is it worse than in our public housing projects. You know, the poor have never had it easy in this world. But in the past, they weren't mugged on the way home from work by crack gangs. And their children didn't have to dodge bullets on the way to school. That is why I'm targeting $50 million to fight crime in public housing projects—to help restore order, and to kick out the dealers for good.

The second element of our strategy looks beyond our borders, where the cocaine and crack, bought on America's streets, is grown and processed. In Colombia alone, cocaine killers have gunned down a leading statesman, murdered almost 200 judges and seven members of their Supreme Court. The besieged governments of the drug-producing countries are fighting back, fighting to break the international drug rings. But you and I agree with the courageous President of Colombia, Virgilio Barco, who said that if Americans use cocaine then Americans are paying for murder. American cocaine users need to understand that our nation has zero tolerance for casual drug use. We have a responsibility not to leave our brave friends in Colombia to fight alone.

The $65 million emergency assistance was just our first step in assisting the Andean nations in their fight against the cocaine cartels. Colombia has already arrested suppliers, seized tons of cocaine and confiscated palatial homes of drug lords. But Colombia faces a long, uphill battle, so we must be ready to do more.

Military Assistance

Our strategy allocates more than a quarter of a billion dollars for 1990 in military and law enforcement assistance for the three Andean nations of Colombia, Bolivia and Peru. This will be the first part of a five-year, $2 billion program to counter the producers, the traffickers and the smugglers.

I spoke with President Barco, and we hope to meet with the leaders of affected countries in an unprecedented drug summit, all to coordinate an inter-American strategy against the cartels. We will work with our allies and friends—especially our economic summit partners—to do more in the fight against drugs. I'm also asking the Senate to ratify the United Nations anti-drug convention concluded in December 1988.

To stop those drugs on the way to America, I propose that we spend more than a billion-and-a-half dollars on interdiction. Greater interagency cooperation, combined with Defense Department technology, can help stop drugs at our borders.

Our message to the drug cartels is this: The rules have changed. We will help any government that wants our help. When requested, we will for the first time make available the appropriate resources of America's armed forces. We will intensify our efforts against drug smugglers on the high seas, in international airspace and at our borders. We will stop the flow of chemicals from the United States used to process drugs. We will pursue and enforce international agreements to track drug money to the front men and financiers. And then we will handcuff these money launderers, and jail them—just like any street dealer. And for drug kingpins, the death penalty.

The third part of our strategy concerns drug treatment. Experts believe that there are two million American drug users who may be able to get off drugs with proper treatment. But right now, only 40 percent of them are actually getting help. This is simply not good enough.

Drug Treatment

Many people who need treatment won't seek it on their own. And some who do seek it are put on a waiting list. Most programs were set up to deal with heroin addicts. But today, the major problem is cocaine users. It's time we expand our treatment systems and do a better job of providing services to those who need them.

I'm proposing an increase of $322 million in Federal spending on drug treatment.

With this strategy, we will do more. We will work with the states. We will encourage employers to establish employee assistance programs to cope with drug use. And, because addiction is such a cruel inheritance, we will intensify our search for ways to help expectant mothers who use drugs.

Fourth, we must stop illegal drug use before it starts. Unfortunately, it begins early—for many kids, before their teens. But it doesn't start the way you might think, from a dealer or an addict hanging around a school playground. More often, our kids first get their drugs free, from friends, or even from older brothers or sisters. Peer pressure spreads drug use. Peer pressure can help stop it.

Prevention Programs

I am proposing a quarter-of-a-billion-dollar increase in Federal funds for school and community prevention programs that help young people and adults reject enticements to try drugs. And I'm proposing something else. Every school, college and university—and every workplace—must adopt tough but fair policies about drug use by students and employees. Those that will not adopt such policies will not get Federal funds. Period.

The private sector also has a role to play. I spoke with a businessman named Jim Burke who said he was haunted by the thought—a nightmare really—that somewhere in America, at any given moment, there is a teen-age girl who should be in school, instead of giving birth to a child addicted to cocaine. So Jim did

something. He led an anti-drug partnership, financed by private funds, to work with advertisers and media firms. Their partnership is now determined to work with our strategy by generating a million dollars worth of air time every day for the next three years—a billion dollars total. Think of it, a billion dollars of television time, all to promote the anti-drug message.

As President, one of my first missions is to keep the national focus on our offensive against drugs. So I will take the anti-drug message to the classrooms of America . . . one that I hope will reach every school, every young American. But drug education doesn't begin in class or on TV. It must begin at home and in the neighborhood. Parents and families must set the first example of a drug-free life. And when families are broken, caring friends and neighbors must step in.

These are the most important elements in our strategy to fight drugs. They are all designed to reinforce one another, to mesh into a powerful whole. To mount an aggressive attack on the problem from every angle. This is the first time in the history of our country that we truly have a comprehensive strategy.

As you can tell, such an approach will not come cheaply. In February 1989, I asked for a $700 million increase in the drug budget for 1990. We have found an immediate need for another billion-and-a-half dollars. With this added $2.2 billion, our 1990 drug budget totals almost $8 billion—the largest increase in history.

"One of my first missions is to keep the national focus on our offensive against drugs."

We need this program fully implemented—right away. . . . So I'm asking the Congress—which has helped us formulate this strategy—to help us move it forward immediately.

We can pay for this fight against drugs without raising our taxes or adding to the budget deficit. We have submitted our plan to Congress that shows just how to fund it within the limits of our bipartisan budget agreement.

I know some will still say we are not spending enough money. But those who judge our strategy only by its price tag, simply don't understand the problem. Let's face it, we've all seen in the past that money alone won't solve our toughest problems.

To be strong and efficient, our strategy needs these funds. But there is no match for a united America, a determined America, an angry America. Our outrage against drugs unites us, brings us together behind this one plan of action, an assault on every front.

This is the toughest domestic challenge we've faced in decades. And it is a challenge we must face—not as Democrats or Republicans, liberals or conservatives—

but as Americans. The key is a coordinated, united effort. We have responded faithfully to the request of the Congress to produce our nation's first national drug strategy. I'll be looking to the Democratic majority and our Republicans in Congress for leadership and bipartisan support. And our citizens deserve cooperation, not competition; a national effort, not a partisan bidding war.

Toughen Sentences

To start, Congress needs not only to act on this national drug strategy, but also to act on our crime package announced in May 1989; a package to toughen sentences, beef up law enforcement and build new prison space for 24,000 inmates.

You and I both know the Federal Government can't do it alone. The states need to match tougher Federal laws with tougher laws of their own—stiffer bail, probation, parole and sentencing.

And we need your help. If people you know are users, help them get off drugs. If you are a parent, talk to your children about drugs—tonight.

Call your local drug prevention program. Be a big brother or sister to a child in need. Pitch in with your local neighborhood watch program. Whether you give your time or talent, everyone counts.

Every employer who bans drugs from the workplace.

Every school that's tough on drug use.

Every neighborhood in which drugs are not welcome.

And most important, every one of you who refuses to look the other way. Every one of you counts.

"The war on drugs will be hard-won, neighborhood by neighborhood, block by block, child by child."

Of course, victory will take hard work and time. But together we will win—too many young lives are at stake.

Not long ago, I read a newspaper story about a little boy named Dooney, who, until recently, lived in a crack house in a suburb of Washington, D.C. In Dooney's neighborhood, children don't flinch at the sound of gunfire. And when they play, they pretend to sell to each other small white rocks they call crack.

Life at home was so cruel that Dooney begged his teachers to let him sleep on the floor at school. And, when asked about his future, 6-year-old Dooney answered: "I don't want to sell drugs, but I will probably have to."

Well, Dooney does not have to sell drugs. No child in America should have to live like this. Together, as a people, we can save these kids. We have already transformed a national attitude of tolerance into one of condemnation. But the war on drugs will be hard-won, neighborhood by neighborhood, block by block, child by child.

If we fight this war as a divided nation, then the war is lost. But, if we face this evil as a nation united, this will be nothing but a handful of useless chemicals.

Victory. Victory over drugs is our cause, a just cause, and with your help, we are going to win.

George Bush was elected president of the United States on November 7, 1988. He served as the vice president from 1980 to 1988 under Ronald Reagan.

viewpoint 15

The War on Drugs Is Unnecessary

Lewis H. Lapham

If President Bush's September 1989 address to the nation on the topic of drugs can be taken as an example of either his honesty or his courage, I see no reason why I can't look forward to hearing him declare a war against cripples, or one-eyed people, or red geraniums. It was a genuinely awful speech, rooted at the beginning in a lie, directed at an imaginary enemy, sustained by false argument, proposing a policy that already had failed, playing to the galleries of prejudice and fear. The first several sentences of the speech established its credentials as a fraud. "Drugs," said Bush, "are sapping our strength as a nation." "The gravest domestic threat facing our nation," said Bush, "is drugs." "Our most serious problem today," said Bush, "is cocaine." None of the statements meets the standards either of minimal analysis or casual observation. The government's own figures show that the addiction to illegal drugs troubles a relatively small number of Americans, and the current generation of American youth is the strongest and healthiest in the nation's history.

Crack Cocaine

In the sixth paragraph of his speech, the President elaborated his fraud by holding up a small plastic bag, as distastefully as if he were holding a urine specimen. "This is crack cocaine," he said, "seized a few days ago by Drug Enforcement Administration agents in a park just across the street from the White House. It could easily have been heroin or PCP." But since nobody, ever, has been known to sell any kind of drug in Lafayette Park, it couldn't possibly have been heroin or PCP. The bag of cocaine wasn't anything other than a stage prop: The DEA was put to considerable trouble and expense to tempt a dealer into the park in order to make the arrest at a time and place convenient to the President's little dramatic effect.

Bush's speechwriters ordered the staging of the "buy" because they wanted to make a rhetorical point about the dark and terrible sea of drugs washing up on the innocent, sun-dappled lawns of the White House. The sale was difficult to arrange because the drug dealer in question had never heard of Lafayette Park, didn't know how to find the place on a map, and couldn't imagine why anybody would want to make such complicated travel arrangements in order to buy rocks of low-grade crack.

A Safe Topic

Two days later, confronted by the press with the mechanics of his sleight of hand, Bush said, "I don't understand. I mean, has somebody got some advocates here for this drug guy?" The surprised and petulant tone of his question gave away the nature of the political game that he was playing, playing on what he assumed was the home field of the nation's best-loved superstitions. After seven months in office, he had chosen to make his first televised address on a topic that he thought was as safe as mother and the undesecrated flag. He had politely avoided any and all of the "serious problems facing our nation today" (the deficit, say, or the environment, or the question of race) and he had done what he could to animate a noncontroversial platitude with a good visual. He expected people to be supportive and nice.

Apparently it never occurred to him that anybody would complain about his taking a few minor liberties with the facts. Nor did he seem to notice that he had seized upon the human suffering implicit in the drug trade as an occasion for a shabby political trick. He had exploited exactly the same device in his election campaign by transforming the image of Willie Horton, a black convict who committed violent crimes after being released on furlough from a Massachusetts prison, into a metaphor for all the world's wickedness. I can imagine his speechwriters explaining to him that the war on drugs was nothing more than Willie Horton writ large.

The premise of the war is so patently false, and the hope for victory so obviously futile, that I can make sense of it only by asking the rhetorical question *cui bono?* Who stands to gain by virtue of Bush's lovely little war, and what must the rest of us pay as tribute?

A Political War

The question is a political one. But, then, the war on drugs is a political war, waged not by scientists and doctors but by police officers and politicians. Under more fortunate circumstances, the prevalence of drugs in American society—not only cocaine and heroin and marijuana but also alcohol and tobacco and sleeping pills—would be properly addressed as a public-health question. The American Medical Association classifies drug addiction as a disease, not as a crime or a moral defeat. Nor is addiction contagious, like measles and the flu. Given the folly and expense of the war on drugs (comparable to the folly and expense of the war in Vietnam), I expect that the United States eventually will arrive at some method of decriminalizing the use of all drugs. The arguments in favor of decriminalization seem to me irrefutable, as do the lessons of experience taught by the failed attempt at the prohibition of alcohol.

But for the time being, as long as the question remains primarily political, the war on drugs serves the purposes of the more reactionary interests within our society (i. e., the defenders of the imagined innocence of a nonexistent past) and transfers the costs of the war to precisely those individuals whom the promoters of the war say they wish to protect. I find it difficult to believe that the joke, although bitter, is unintended.

"The drug war, like all wars, sells papers, and the media, like the politicians, ask for nothing better than a safe and profitable menace."

To politicians in search of sound opinions and sustained applause, the war on drugs presents itself as a gift from heaven. Because the human craving for intoxicants cannot be suppressed—not by priests or jailers or acts of Congress—the politicians can bravely confront an allegorical enemy rather than an enemy that takes the corporeal form of the tobacco industry, say, or the Chinese, or the oil and banking lobbies. The war against drugs provides them with something to say that offends nobody, requires them to do nothing difficult, and allows them to postpone, perhaps indefinitely, the more urgent and specific questions about the state of the nation's schools, housing, employment opportunities for young black men—i.e., the conditions to which drug addiction

speaks as a tragic symptom, not a cause. They remain safe in the knowledge that they might as well be denouncing Satan or the rain, and so they can direct the voices of prerecorded blame at metaphors and apparitions who, unlike Senator Jesse Helms and his friends at the North Carolina tobacco auctions, can be transformed into demonic spirits riding north across the Caribbean on an evil wind. The war on drugs thus becomes the perfect war for people who would rather not fight a war, a war in which the politicians who stand so fearlessly on the side of the good, the true, and the beautiful need do nothing else but strike noble poses as protectors of the people and defenders of the public trust. . . .

A Safe and Profitable Menace

The drug war, like all wars, sells papers, and the media, like the politicians, ask for nothing better than a safe and profitable menace. The campaign against drugs involves most of the theatrical devices employed by *Miami Vice*—scenes of crimes in progress (almost always dressed up, for salacious effect, with the cameo appearances of one or two prostitutes), melodramatic villains in the Andes, a vocabulary of high-tech military jargon as reassuring as the acronyms in a Tom Clancy novel, the specter of a crazed lumpenproletariat rising in revolt in the nation's cities.

Like camp followers trudging after an army of crusader knights on its way to Jerusalem, the media have displayed all the garish colors of the profession. Everybody who was anybody set up a booth and offered his or her tears for sale—not only Geraldo and Maury Povich but also, in much the same garish language, Dan Rather (on *48 Hours*), Ted Koppel (on *Nightline*), and Sam Donaldson (on *Prime Time Live*). In the six weeks between August 1 and September 13, 1989, the three television networks combined with the *New York Times* and the *Washington Post* to produce 347 reports from the frontiers of the apocalypse—crack in the cities, cocaine in the suburbs, customs agents seizing pickup trucks on the Mexican border, smugglers named Julio arriving every hour on the hour at Key West. . . .

The story of the drug war plays to the prejudices of an audience only too eager to believe the worst that can be said about people whom they would rather not know. Because most of the killing allied with the drug trade takes place in the inner cities, and because most of the people arrested for selling drugs prove to be either black or Hispanic, it becomes relatively easy for white people living in safe neighborhoods to blur the distinction between crime and race. Few of them have ever seen an addict or witnessed a drug deal, but the newspapers and television networks keep showing them photographs that convey the impression of a class war, and those among them who always worried about driving through Harlem (for fear of being seized by gangs of armed black men) or who always wished that they didn't feel quite so guilty about the socioeconomic distance between East 72nd Street and West 126th Street can comfort themselves, finally, at long last, and with a clear conscience, with the thought that poverty is another word for sin, that their BMW is a proof of their virtue, and that they or, more likely, their mothers were always right to fear the lower classes and the darker races.

As conditions in the slums deteriorate, which they inevitably must because the government subtracts money from the juvenile-justice and housing programs to finance its war on drugs, the slums come to look just the way they are supposed to look in the suburban imagination, confirming the fondest suspicions of the governing and possessing classes, justifying the further uses of force and repression. The people who pay the price for the official portrait turn out to be (wonder of wonders) not the members of the prosperous middle class—not the journalists or the academic theorists, not the politicians and government functionaries living behind hedges in Maryland and Virginia—but (mirabile dictu) the law-abiding residents of the inner cities living in the only neighborhoods that they can afford.

It is in the slums of New York that three people, on average, get killed every day—which, over the course of a year, adds up to a higher casualty rate than pertains in Gaza and the West Bank; it is in the slums that the drug trade recruits children to sell narcotics, which is not the result of indigenous villainy but of the nature of the law; it is in the slums that the drug trade has become the exemplary model of finance capitalism for children aspiring to the success of Donald Trump and Samuel Pierce; and it is in the slums that the police experiment with the practice of apartheid, obliging residents of housing projects to carry identity cards and summarily evicting the residents of apartment houses tainted by the presence of drug dealers.

Someone Else's Problem

To the extent that the slums can be seen as the locus of the nation's wickedness (i.e., a desolate mise-en-scène not unlike the Evil Empire that Ronald Reagan found in the Soviet Union), the crimes allied with the drug traffic can be classified as somebody else's moral problem rather than one's own social or political problem. The slums become foreign, alien nations on the other side of the economic and cultural frontiers. The deliberate confusion of geography with metaphysics turns out, again to nobody's surprise, to be wonderfully convenient for the sponsors of the war on drugs. The politicians get their names in the papers, the media have a story to tell, and the rest of us get off the hooks that otherwise might impale us on the questions of conscience or the obligation of higher taxes. In New York, I overheard a woman in an expensive restaurant say that she didn't understand why the government didn't arrange to put "arsenic or

something" in a seized shipment of cocaine. If the government (or "the CIA [Central Intelligence Agency] or the FBI [Federal Bureau of Investigation] or whoever does that sort of thing") allowed the poisoned cocaine to find its way back onto the streets, then "pretty soon we'd be rid of the whole damn thing."

If the folly of the war on drugs could be understood merely as a lesson in political cynicism, or simply as an example of the aplomb with which the venal media can play upon the sentiments of a mob, maybe I would rest content with a few last jokes about the foolishness of the age. But the war on drugs also serves the interests of the state, which, under the pretext of rescuing people from incalculable peril, claims for itself enormously enhanced powers of repression and control.

"The war on drugs becomes a useful surrogate for the obsolescent Cold War, now fading into the realm of warm and nostalgic memory."

An opinion poll conducted during the week following President Bush's September address showed 62 percent of the respondents "willing to give up some freedoms" in order to hold America harmless against the scourge of drugs. The government stands more than willing to take them at their word. The war on drugs becomes a useful surrogate for the obsolescent Cold War, now fading into the realm of warm and nostalgic memory. Under the familiar rubrics of constant terror and ceaseless threat, the government subtracts as much as possible from the sum of the nation's civil liberties and imposes de facto martial law on a citizenry that it chooses to imagine as a dangerous rabble.

Anybody who doubts this point has only to read the speeches of William Bennett, the commander-in-chief of the Bush administration's war on drugs. Bennett's voice is the voice of an intolerant scold, narrow and shrill and mean-spirited, the voice of a man afraid of liberty and mistrustful of freedom. He believes that it is the government's duty to impose on people a puritanical code of behavior best exemplified by the discipline in place at an unheated boarding school. He never misses the chance to demand more police, more jails, more judges, more arrests, more punishments, more people serving more millennia of "serious time."

Reading Bennett's speeches, I am reminded of the Ayatollah Khalkhali, appointed by the authorities in Iran to the office of executioner without portfolio. Khalkhali was blessed with the power to order the death of anybody whom he found in the company of drugs, and within a period of seven weeks he killed 176 people. Still he failed to suppress the use of opium, and he said, "If we wanted to kill everybody who had five grams of heroin, we would have to kill 5,000 people." And then, after a wistful pause, he said, "And this would be difficult."

Zealous Coercion

In line with Bennett's zeal for coercion, politicians of both parties demand longer jail sentences and harsher laws as well as the right to invade almost everybody's privacy; to search, without a warrant, almost anybody's automobile or boat; to bend the rules of evidence, hire police spies, and attach, again without a warrant, the wires of electronic surveillance. The more obviously the enforcement of the law fails to accomplish its nominal purpose (i.e., as more drugs become more accessible at cheaper prices), the more reasons the Supreme Court finds to warrant the invasion of privacy. In recent years, the Court has granted police increasingly autocratic powers—permission (without probable cause) to stop, detain, and question travelers passing through the nation's airports in whom the police can see a resemblance to a drug dealer; permission (again without probable cause) to search barns, stop motorists, inspect bank records, and tap phones.

The polls suggest that a majority of the American people accept these measures as right and proper. Of the respondents questioned by an ABC/*Washington Post* poll in September 1989, 55 percent supported mandatory drug testing for all Americans, 82 percent favored enlisting the military in the war on drugs, 52 percent were willing to have their homes searched, and 83 percent favored reporting suspected drug users to the police, even if the suspects happened to be members of their own family. In October 1989, *Newsweek* took note of an inquisition in progress in Clinton, Iowa. The local paper had taken to printing cutout coupons that said, "I've had enough of drugs in my neighborhood! I have reason to believe that (blank) is using/dealing drugs." The paper collected the coupons for the town police, who reported the response as "excellent."

The enforcement of more and stricter laws requires additional tiers of expensive government, and of the $7.9 billion that President Bush allotted to the war on drugs in September 1989, the bulk of the money swells the budgets of the fifty-eight federal agencies and seventy-four congressional committees currently engaged, each with its own agenda and armies to feed, on various fronts of the campaign. Which doesn't mean, of course, that the money will be honestly, or even intelligently, spent. As was demonstrated all too plainly by the Reagan administration (cf. the sums misappropriated from HUD [Housing and Urban Development] and the Pentagon), the government has a talent for theft and fraud barely distinguishable from the criminal virtuosity of the drug syndicates it wishes to destroy.

Even so, and notwithstanding its habitual incompetence and greed, the government doesn't

lightly relinquish the spoils of power seized under the pretexts of apocalypse. What the government grasps, the government seeks to keep and hold. The militarization of the rhetoric supporting the war on drugs rots the public debate with a corrosive silence. The political weather turns gray and pinched. People who become accustomed to the arbitrary intrusions of the police also learn to speak more softly in the presence of political authority, to bow and smile and fill out the printed forms with the cowed obsequiousness of musicians playing waltzes at a Mafia wedding.

"The government has a talent for theft and fraud barely distinguishable from the criminal virtuosity of the drug syndicates it wishes to destroy."

And for what? To punish people desperate enough or foolish enough to poison themselves with drugs? To exact vengeance on people afflicted with the sickness of addiction and who, to their grief and shame, can find no other way out of the alleys of their despair?

Society Gains Nothing

As a consequence of President Bush's war on drugs, society gains nothing except immediate access to an unlimited fund of resentment and unspecific rage. In return for so poor a victory, and in the interests of the kind of people who would build prisons instead of schools, Bush offers the nation the chance to deny its best principles, to corrupt its magistrates and enrich its most vicious and efficient criminals, to repudiate its civil liberties and repent of the habits of freedom. The deal is as shabby as President Bush's trick with the bag of cocaine. For the sake of a vindictive policeman's dream of a quiet and orderly heaven, the country risks losing its constitutional right to its soul.

Lewis H. Lapham is the editor of Harper's Magazine, *a monthly journal of literature and opinion.*

"Those who use, sell and traffic in drugs must be confronted, and they must suffer consequences."

Drug Users Must Be Severely Punished

William J. Bennett

The drug crisis is a crisis of authority—in every sense of the term "authority."

With the weakening of political authority, the drug user, dealer and trafficker believe that the laws forbidding their activities no longer have teeth, and they consequently feel free to violate those laws with impunity.

There is a crisis of social authority: the family and our schools—those institutions responsible for keeping children occupied with redeeming pursuits and away from the easy, destructive temptations of immediate pleasure—are not performing as well as they should, as well as they once did.

Authority Crisis

There is also a crisis of moral authority: the idea that breaking the law is wrong, even when the law-breaking goes undetected, has lost its power to deter. The idea that life is not a gift but an idle plaything has become all too common.

What can be done to combat this crisis of authority? Two words sum up my entire approach: consequences and confrontation. Those who use, sell and traffic in drugs must be confronted, and they must suffer consequences.

By "consequences," I mean that those who transgress must make amends for their transgressions. This idea is central to any conception of just government. Consequences come in many forms. In terms of law enforcement, they include policies such as the seizure of assets, stiffer prison sentences, revocation of bail rights, and the death penalty for drug kingpins.

On these points I find general agreement. Yet I also find that we lack the resources to assure that consequences always follow crime. Drug dealers generally get several bites at the criminal-justice-

system apple before serving serious time. Our court dockets are too full; our jails and prisons are too full; some of our judges are less serious about drugs than are the dealers who deal them, the children who take them, and the families that are ruined by them.

Reconstituted Authority

We have to do more. We need to reconstitute authority. What those of us in Washington, in the states, and in the localities can do is exert the political authority necessary to make a sustained commitment to the drug war. We must build more prisons. There must be more jails. We must have more judges to hear drug cases and more prosecutors to bring them to trial, including military judges and prosecutors to supplement what we already have. And there must be more federal agents to investigate and solve drug crimes and break drug networks.

Still and again, though, more and tougher action will not be enough. We need to re-orient our process of justice where drugs are concerned and adopt the principle that certainty of punishment is more important than severity of punishment. Those guilty of drug offenses must believe that punishment is *inevitable*. As long as they don't, the deterrent effect of incarceration will be neutralized.

This holds true, perhaps even more true, for the non-addicted user, the so-called "casual user." Casual use is not just a matter of personal preference. It has costs—wide, horrible social costs. The suburban man who drives his BMW downtown to buy cocaine is killing himself, of course. But he is killing the city at the same time. And his "casual" use is best deterred not by empty threats of long, hard punishment, but by *certain* punishment. Compel him, as authorities are doing in Phoenix, to pay a steep fine and spend a weekend in jail. Seize his BMW right after he has bought some dope, and when he is convicted, take the car away from him for good. That is what they do in Philadelphia.

William J. Bennett, "Moralism and Realism in the Drug War," *New Perspectives Quarterly*, Summer 1989. Reprinted with the author's permission.

We are also looking at a proposal that would send the first offender, particularly the young person, to boot camp. At these camps, which are already in place in several states, including New York, Mississippi, Alabama, Oklahoma and Louisiana, the first offender gets up at 4:30 in the morning, does push-ups, runs a good bit and doesn't watch soap operas on TV, as many people do in jail. And it turns out to be a productive system. Boot camp is inexpensive, it teaches good lessons, and the recidivism rate is very, very low, because it is so grueling and so unpleasant.

Criminal Justice

Additionally, there is an area of criminal justice infrequently mobilized as a tool in the war on drugs: the juvenile-justice system. Here, too, there are innovative programs. For example, in Toledo, Ohio, parents are brought before the juvenile-justice court and made to answer for the actions of their children through civil penalties. This policy establishes the principle that parents—including live-in boyfriends and girlfriends who serve as step-parents—must bear responsibility for the behavior and activities of minors in their charge.

Here, consequences are borne not only by those minors who commit drug offenses but also by those responsible for their care and moral guidance. Minors who are non-addicted users must be taught early on that they cannot behave with impunity, and parents who have effectively turned them loose must learn why the social contract demands that they oversee and control the impulses of their children. The "certainty, not severity" doctrine is of particular merit in such situations because it sets up distinct boundaries for the behavior of our young. It sends a clear message to young people that drug use carries a swift and dear price.

"Taking an aggressive line toward drugs—forbidding their use altogether and using real authority to back up this absolute proscription—is the key to all prevention strategies."

Education programs must serve to give all Americans, but especially school children, the information they need to understand why drug use is wrong, why it is harmful to their bodies and souls, and why it is harmful to the world they live in. But education programs must also work to establish boundaries of social authority by making clear the consequences of drug use at school. Schools must have explicit policies discouraging drug use and drug dealing. Penalties must be imposed and they must be appropriate, ranging from detention to suspension to outright expulsion. No one likes to expel a child from school. But the needs of a young dealer are nothing compared to the needs of the school population on which he preys. Retaining a young dealer in school may suggest to law-abiding students that his crime is in some sense excusable, and that is a failure of basic moral education.

Drug Users' Rights

It has also been suggested that a drug user's right to a driver's license be suspended or revoked following proper due-process findings. One virtue of this approach lies in the warning it delivers to those who do not use but might be tempted to. In much of the country, drivers' licenses are an elemental freedom young people are terrified of losing.

What has been outlined is the reconstitution of legal and social authority through the imposition of appropriate consequences for drug dealing and drug use. Drug-related activities are impermissible and we are obliged to say so.

In all cases involving drug dealing and use, consequences must be established and demonstrated through confrontation. How do we reduce the demand for drugs? We must take the same aggressive posture we mean to take on the supply side, which is to confront the problem when and wherever it arises—head on.

One of the key issues in the drug war is prevention —how do we keep people from starting to use drugs? One approach to prevention is through intervention—not government intervention, but intervention family by family, neighborhood by neighborhood, church by church, school by school. Taking an aggressive line toward drugs—forbidding their use altogether and using real authority to back up this absolute proscription—is the key to all prevention strategies.

The principle of intervention through confrontation has other applications, as well—most notably as a method of treatment. We don't know as much as we would like to about how to treat drug use, and, sadly, many of our profoundly good-spirited efforts at treatment have failed to pan out. But what we do know is this: Successful programs almost always force the addict to confront and internalize the fact of his addiction.

Further, confrontation does not necessarily stop at the clinic. Take the case of a parent who has become addicted to cocaine. His family is suffering the consequences of his addiction: the rapid shifts of mood; the outbursts of violent rage; the tacit encouragement extended to husband, wife, or children to engage in similarly escapist dysfunction and despair. What is the answer to this problem? Confrontation. Ultimatum. The user must be made aware that his family no longer tolerates the addiction. He must know that, unless he enters treatment and gets himself clean, there will be dire consequences for *him*. And here the nexus between consequences and confrontation emerges—consequences can only be impressed upon the consciousness when confrontational tactics are used to impress them.

There is a great deal of talk about the rehabilitation of drug offenders, but in many cases rehabilitation is the wrong term to use. Rehabilitation implies a pre-existing state of normality, a set of learned behaviors the addict can return to once his addiction has been overcome. Yet, in too many cases, in too many places, no such normality exists. What is really needed is *habilitation*—aid, assistance, and instruction for youngsters who have been left without the most elementary lessons of morals and manners; the construction of a viable community for them to live in. Such habilitation by its very nature must proceed confrontationally. It requires demolishing bad habits and implanting good ones in their stead. In the case of 15-year-old offenders who have grown up essentially without parents, some therapists have found it necessary to serve as substitute parents, complete with a tuck-in and bedtime story at night.

"Drug use is intolerable . . .and those who use and those who sell will face certain consequences."

Community habilitation requires giving people a stake in their neighborhoods so that efforts they make to improve their wasted environs can meet with success. Indeed, confrontation by the community is key to any long-range effort at reducing drug use.

We have seen astonishing grass-roots efforts nationwide, efforts whose purpose is to salvage communities and the people who comprise them. In some cases, these efforts have been forged in blood—the blood of children whose mothers have created organizations like SO SAD (Save Our Sons and Daughters) in Detroit and MOMS (Mothers on the Move Spiritually) in Washington, DC. Their emphasis is on moral reconstruction, on arming the citizens of drug-infested neighborhoods with the strength to fight drug use and isolate their children from its temptations and ravages.

Confrontation

I believe that this same sort of confrontation is required from our spiritual leaders, the clergy, who can give their communities the most powerful reasons for saying no to drugs—reasons rooted in the deepest strains of the human soul.

There are those who say the problems of the inner city and the affluent suburb are so varied that anti-drug efforts with similar approaches cannot work. There are those who say that the cultural differences between affluent and poor, between black, white, and Hispanic are so profound that each "culture" must come up with its own approach. I say that's wrong.

It is obviously the case that someone who speaks Spanish as a first language will be more receptive to a message in Spanish. But the necessary message for rich and poor, black and white, Hispanic and Indian, is the same: Drug use is intolerable, use and the potential for use will be confronted on all fronts, and those who use and those who sell will face certain consequences.

Personal Responsibility

In the final analysis, the distinction often drawn between the "supply-reduction" and "demand-reduction" sides of the drug equation is a false one. Many things to be done on the supply side have remarkable ramifications on the demand side. As James Q. Wilson points out in his forthcoming book, *Drugs and Crime*, we do not advocate law-enforcement measures merely to apprehend and punish the guilty, though both are worthy goals.

Rather, we do so because we believe the message effective law enforcement sends will have a real impact on those who use drugs. For the so-called casual user, bringing home the potential cost of present drug use is a true deterrent to future use. And for the addicted user, who may resort to a life of crime to support his habit, the potential for certain punishment may finally lead to an acceptance of personal responsibility and a motivation to enter treatment.

Of course, to flip the argument around, successful activities on the demand side will reverberate from the inner city to the marijuana fields in California and the coca fields in South America. By reducing the profits gained from drug sales, demand-side activities will at last give supply-reduction initiatives—like crop substitution, by which coca farmers are encouraged to adopt other commodities for cultivation—a real and lasting chance to work.

From Supply to Demand

What must link all our efforts, from supply to demand, at all levels, is an ethic of personal responsibility. Those who transgress must account for their transgression. Those who spurn or resist transgression must be supported and praised. Who are our heroes in this fight? Are they those who have used and quit drugs? Quitting is great—no doubt about it. But in truth, the real heroes in our war on drugs are those who never use them, those who do all they can to keep their kids off drugs, and those who give their kids the strength to resist temptation and pressure—where it comes from, whatever guise it takes.

William J. Bennett is the commander-in-chief of the Bush Administration's war on drugs. He was Secretary of Education under Ronald Reagan from 1985 to 1988.

"Prohibition is directly responsible for the power of crack dealers to terrorize whole neighborhoods."

Punishing Drug Users Is Counterproductive

Ellen Willis

At last the government has achieved something it hasn't managed since the height of '50s anti-Communist hysteria—enlisted public sentiment in a popular war. The president's invocation of an America united in a holy war against drugs is no piece of empty rhetoric; the bounds of mainstream debate on this issue are implicit in the response of the Democratic so-called opposition, which attacked Bush's program as not tough or expensive enough. (As Senator Joseph Biden—fresh from his defense of the flag; the guy is really on a roll—put it, "What we need is another D-Day, not another Vietnam.") To be sure, there is controversy over the drug warriors' methods. Civil libertarians object to drug testing and dubious police practices; many commentators express doubts about the wisdom of going after millions of casual drug users; and some hardy souls still argue that drugs should be decriminalized and redefined as a medical and social problem. But where are the voices questioning the basic assumptions of the drug war: that drugs are our most urgent national problem; that a drug-free society is a valid social goal; that drug use is by definition abuse? If there's a war on, are drugs the real enemy? Or is mobilizing the nation's energies on behalf of a war against drugs far more dangerous than the drugs themselves?

Effective Weapons

By now some of you are wondering if I've been away— perhaps on an extended LSD trip—and missed the havoc crack has wrought in inner-city neighborhoods. One of the drug warriors' more effective weapons is the argument that any crank who won't sign on to the antidrug crusade must be indifferent to, if not actively in favor of, the decimation of black and Latino communities by rampant addiction, AIDS, crack babies, the recruitment of kids into the drug trade, and control of the streets by violent gangsters. To many people, especially people of color, making war on drugs means not taking it anymore, defending their lives and their children against social rot. It's a seductive idea: focusing one's rage on a vivid, immediate symptom of a complex social crisis makes an awful situation seem more manageable. Yet in reality the drug war has nothing to do with making communities livable or creating a decent future for black kids. On the contrary, prohibition is directly responsible for the power of crack dealers to terrorize whole neighborhoods. And every cent spent on the cops, investigators, bureaucrats, courts, jails, weapons, and tests required to feed the drug-war machine is a cent not spent on reversing the social policies that have destroyed the cities, nourished racism, and laid the groundwork for crack culture.

While they're happy to use the desperate conditions of the poor as a club to intimidate potential opposition, the drug warriors have another agenda altogether. Forget those obscene pictures of Bush kissing addicted babies (and read his budget director's lips: money for the drug war is to come not from the military budget but from other domestic programs). Take it from William Bennett, who, whatever his political faults, is honest about what he's up to: "We identify the chief and seminal wrong here as drug use. . . . There are lots of other things that are wrong, such as money laundering and crime and violence in the inner city, but drug use itself is wrong. And that means the strategy is aimed at reducing drug use." Aimed, that is, not at solving social problems but at curbing personal freedom.

Illegal Drugs

Of course, it's not all drugs Bennett has in mind, but illegal drugs. And as even some drug warriors will admit, whether a drug is legal or not has little to do with rational considerations such as how addictive it

Ellen Willis, "Hell No, I Won't Go," *The Village Voice*, September 19, 1989. Reprinted by permission of the author and *The Village Voice*.

may be, or how harmful to health, or how implicated in crime. Bill Bennett drinks without apology while denouncing marijuana and crack with equal passion; heroin is denied to terminal cancer patients while methadone, which is at least as addictive, is given away at government-sponsored clinics. What illegal drugs do have in common is that in one way or another they threaten social control. Either (like heroin and crack) they're associated with all the social disorder and scary otherness of the so-called underclass, or (like marijuana and the psychedelics) they become emblems of social dissidence, "escape from"—i.e., unorthodox views of—reality, and loss of productivity and discipline. Equally important, illicit drugs offer pleasure—and perhaps even worse, feelings of freedom and power—for the taking; the more intense the euphoria, the more iniquitous the drug. Easily available chemical highs are the moral equivalent of welfare—they undercut the official culture's control of who gets rewarded for what. And they invite subversive comparisons to the meager ration of pleasure, freedom, and power available in people's daily lives.

"The cultural changes of the '60s and '70s eroded traditional forms of authority, loosening governmental and corporate control over people's lives. And the drug war is about getting it back."

Illegal drugs, furthermore, are offenses to authority by definition. Users are likely to define themselves as rebels—or become users in the first place as a means of rebelling—and band together in an outlaw culture. The drugs are then blamed for the rebellion, the social alienation that gave rise to it, and the crime and corruption that actually stem from prohibition and its inevitable concomitant, an immensely profitable illegal industry.

From this perspective, it makes perfect sense to lump marijuana with crack—while different in every other respect, both are outlaw, countercultural drugs. From this perspective, mounting a jihad against otherwise law-abiding citizens whose recreational drug of choice happens to be illegal is not a hugely expensive, futile, punitive diversion from addressing the real problems of our urban wasteland; it goes straight to the point. After all, hard-core addicts presumably can't help themselves, while casual users are choosing to ignore two decades of pervasive antidrug moralizing. The point is that the cultural changes of the '60s and '70s eroded traditional forms of authority, loosening governmental and corporate control over people's lives. And the drug war is about getting it back.

One means of achieving this is legitimizing repressive police and military tactics. Drugs, say the warriors, are such an overriding national emergency that civil liberties must give way; of course, laws and policies aimed at curbing dealers' and users' constitutional rights will then be available for use in other "emergency" situations. Another evolving strategy is to bypass the criminal justice system altogether (thereby avoiding some of those irritating constitutional obstacles as well as the public's reluctance to put middle-class pot-smokers in jail) in favor of civil sanctions like large fines and the withholding of government benefits and such "privileges" as drivers' licenses.

Drug Testing

But so far, the centerpiece of the cultural counterrevolution is the snowballing campaign for a "drug-free workplace"—a euphemism for "drug-free workforce," since urine testing also picks up off-duty indulgence. The purpose of this '80s version of the loyalty oath is less to deter drug use than to make people undergo a humiliating ritual of subordination: "When I say pee, you pee." The idea is to reinforce the principle that one must forfeit one's dignity and privacy to earn a living, and bring back the good old days when employers had the unquestioned right to demand that their workers' appearance and behavior, on or off the job, meet management's standards. After all, before the '60s, employers were free to reject you not only because you were the wrong race, sex, or age, but because of your marital status, your sex life, your political opinions, or anything else they didn't like; there were none of those pesky discrimination or wrongful firing suits.

The argument that drug use hurts productivity only supports my point: if it's okay to forbid workers to get stoned on their days off because it might affect their health, efficiency, or "motivation," why not forbid them to stay out late, eat fatty foods, fall in love, or have children? As for jobs that affect the public safety, if tests are needed, they should be performance tests—an air controller or railroad worker whose skills are impaired by fatigue is as dangerous as one who's drugged. Better yet, anyone truly concerned about safety should support the demands of workers in these jobs for shorter hours and less stressful working conditions.

In the great tradition of demagogic saber-rattling, Bush's appeal seeks to distract from the fissures of race, class, and sex and unite us against a common enemy: the demon drug. The truth is, however, that this terrifying demon is a myth. Drug addiction and its associated miseries are not caused by evil, irresistible substances. People get hooked on drugs because they crave relief from intolerable frustration; because they're starved for pleasure and power. Addiction is a social and psychological, not a chemical, disease.

Every generation has its arch-demon drug: alcohol,

reefer madness, heroin, and now crack. Recently *The New York Times* ran a front-page story reporting that drug experts have revised their earlier belief that crack is a uniquely, irresistibly addictive drug; crack addiction, they assert, has more to do with social conditions than with the drug's chemistry. Two cheers for the experts; surely it shouldn't have taken them so long to ask why crack is irresistible to the black poor but not to the white middle class. Perhaps they will take the next step and recognize that so long as crack is the only thriving industry in the inner city—and integral to its emotional economy as well—there's only one way to win a war on drugs. That's to adopt the method the Chinese used to solve their opium problem: line every dealer and user up against the wall and shoot. And try not to notice the color of the bodies.

"If the logic of the drug war for blacks and Latinos leads to a literal police state, for the rest of us it means silence and conformity."

If the logic of the drug war for blacks and Latinos leads to a literal police state, for the rest of us it means silence and conformity. In recent years, much of the drug warriors' ideological firepower has been aimed at the '60s. Members of my generation who took any part in the passions and pleasures of those times—that is, most of us now between, say, 35 and 50—are under enormous pressure to agree that we made a terrible mistake (and even that won't help if you aspire to be a Supreme Court justice). Which makes me feel irresistibly compelled to reiterate at every opportunity that I have taken illegal drugs, am not ashamed of it, and still smoke the occasional joint (an offense for which Bush and Bennett want to fine me $10,000, lift my driver's license, and throw me in boot camp). I believe that taking drugs is not intrinsically immoral or destructive, that the state has no right to prevent me from exploring different states of consciousness, and that drug prohibition causes many of the evils it purports to cure.

Extending Freedom

According to the drug warriors, I and my ilk are personally responsible not only for the deaths of Janis Joplin and Jimi Hendrix but for the crack crisis. Taken literally, this is scurrilous nonsense: the counterculture never looked kindly on hard drugs, and the age of crack is a product not of the '60s but of Reaganism. Yet there's a sense in which I do feel responsible. Cultural radicals are committed to extending freedom, and that commitment, by its nature, is dangerous. It encourages people to take risks, some of them foolish or worse. It arouses deep

longings that, if disappointed, may plunge people into despair (surely one aspect of the current demoralization of black youth is the peculiar agony of thwarted revolution). If I support the struggle for freedom, I can't disclaim responsibility for its costs; I can only argue that the costs of suppressing freedom are, in the end, far higher. All wars are hell. The question remains which ones are worth fighting.

Ellen Willis is a contributor to The Village Voice, *a weekly New York newspaper.*

*"The way to hold individuals responsible
is to make them pay a price."*

Enforcing Drug Laws Will End the Drug Crisis

Rachel Flick

American radar in the Bahamas spotted a suspicious-looking small plane heading north. U.S. Customs and a Drug Enforcement Administration (DEA) interdiction force called Op Bat gave chase. The plane dropped a bundle that looked as if it might contain drugs into the sea, then flew on. Customs and Op Bat could not agree who should stay with the drugs and who should follow the plane. While they argued, the pilot slipped away, and a passing boat scooped up the bundle and escaped.

• New York City narcotics officers seized Santiago Martinez after he handed a buyer a heroin-filled packet from the 23 he had stashed inside his sweat shirt. The arrest was Martinez's sixth. This time, the assistant district attorney recommended a year. Martinez got 60 days. Within ten months of his release, he had been arrested on drug charges four more times.

• After he was incarcerated, Miami-based cocaine smuggler Max Mermelstein arranged delivery of a 550-kilo load of cocaine he had left in a warehouse. He simply used a prison pay phone to do it. That's how easy it is for convicted dealers to maintain their outside business.

If you get the sense from such incidents that we're accomplishing little in the so-called war on drugs, you're right. We're spending billions of dollars, yet squandering much of it in confusion, weakness, rivalry and mismanagement.

"What war on drugs?" asks Rep. Charles Rangel (D., N.Y.), chairman of the House Select Committee on Narcotics Abuse and Control. Former federal prosecutor Richard Gregorie of Florida's Southern District says he felt "a lot like the grunts in Vietnam—we are not being allowed to win."

The Bush Administration has unveiled its long-awaited strategy, calling for a get-tough attitude at every level of government—from federal agencies to the town hall. But if we are to win the drug war, we must

take a hard look at why we have been losing. It's time to fix the five failings that have bedeviled our efforts. We must:

1. Stop letting criminals' rights come first. In 1988, drug-dealing gangs controlled the Rockwell Gardens public-housing development in Chicago. They shook down terrorized tenants, held shoot-outs on the sidewalks and ran a wide-open drug market. Then, in September 1988, the Chicago Housing Authority launched "Operation Clean Sweep," which sought to stanch the drug flow by "keeping out people who don't belong." Visitors had to show identification, with only residents admitted from midnight to 9 a.m.

After the sweep of just one building, the project's crime rate dropped 32 percent. Tenants were ecstatic. Yet the American Civil Liberties Union (ACLU) sued, claiming the operation violated tenants' civil liberties. Both the curfew and the ID rule had to be abandoned.

Ultimately, the drug war is fought not in Congress or the White House, but in America's streets, schoolyards, offices, factories and housing projects. Yet, too often, when authorities on these battlegrounds try to get tough, they are accused of violating civil rights and liberties. These challenges, backed by decades of imaginative rulings from federal courts, mean that even when local authorities want to, they frequently cannot do their jobs.

Across America, police are handicapped by the "exclusionary rule," which bars critical evidence if officers even inadvertently violate search-and-seizure guidelines. When search warrants are obtained, defendants can still beat the rap.

Detroit police searched a small film-development booth and discovered three pounds of cocaine, $34,000 in currency, 11 guns and a silencer. They promptly arrested the booth operator. The police had obtained the search warrant by citing extensive evidence as to why they expected to find exactly what they did. However, a second judge declared the evidence inadequate and the search a violation of the operator's rights. He walked.

Juveniles have even more rights. In New York, the courts have ruled that juvenile offenders have the right to a trial within 90 days. If the prosecution is not ready by then, the case is dismissed—even if the delay is caused by the defendant himself.

Civil liberties should not overrule practical action against drugs, especially for minors, who need authority. Rep. Kweisi Mfume (D., Md.)—told by police, parents and teachers that beepers are the "devices of choice" for drug-dealing youths—has proposed curbing their sale to people under 21. The ACLU has threatened to sue if Mfume's bill passes. In drug-plagued Washington, D.C., where homicide has taken 27 children in 1989, the city council twice voted for a temporary curfew on youths under 17. The ACLU sued, and the curfew was struck down.

Says Detroit's U.S. Attorney Stephen Markman: "The idea that the Constitution is somehow hostile to the war on crime is a misreading of the Constitution." We have to free our elected officials to exercise their legitimate authority to protect those they represent.

2. *Build more prisons.* When the *National Law Journal* asked prosecutors nationwide to name their No. 1 problem in fighting drugs, the answer was: "Limited prison space."

One reason is that in the 1970s federal courts began applying the Constitution's ban on "cruel and unusual punishment" to prison conditions like cell size, food service, medical care, recreational facilities, staffing and supplies. These court-enforced standards have since drastically reduced the number of usable beds. Thirty-five state prison systems and uncounted local jails are under court order to reduce crowding.

To comply with such orders, massive numbers of prisoners are released. Typical, says Philadelphia District Attorney Ronald D. Castille, is the man arrested by local police in October 1987 for robbery and aggravated assault. Released on bail, he was arrested a month later for cocaine possession "with intent to deliver" and again granted bail. Ignoring trial dates, he evaded police until May 1988, when he was arrested again on cocaine-peddling charges. Because of jail overcrowding he was let go as soon as he was booked, without posting bail. Three more times in the next year, he was arrested for selling cocaine and freed because of jail overcrowding. Not until his seventh arrest, in June 1989, was he finally imprisoned.

Prisons are expensive to build and run. By 1988 the average cost nationwide to build a prison "bed" was $70,000. Maintaining a prisoner in that bed for one year runs as high as $25,000.

We will have to spend whatever it takes. The federal government, whose prison system is now 60 percent over capacity, is trying. Ten new federal prisons are under construction; several old ones are being expanded. President Bush has asked for $1.5 billion to build another 24,000 cells.

Still, new prisons take up to three years to build. In

the meantime, one inexpensive alternative supported by the Administration is "boot camps." Often set up on military bases due for closing, they emulate state programs where young offenders receive "shock incarceration." At Mississippi's Regimented Inmate Discipline Program, for instance, first-time felons awake at 5 a.m., clean their barracks, do exercises and raise the American flag. Their day is divided between classroom education and Parris Island-style drilling. The boot camp is cheap, safe and effective at reducing recidivism.

3. *Fight drugs at the source.* The coca fields of Peru's Upper Huallaga Valley are the source of half the cocaine smuggled into the United States. The crops are contained, visible and accessible. Since 1987, the United States and Peru have jointly tested herbicides for use against this crop. Yet in spring 1989, after leftist guerrillas, allied with drug interests, murdered scores of local police, Peruvian President Alan García curtailed the program.

"The boot camp is cheap, safe and effective."

Most illegal drugs consumed in the United States are produced abroad, many in identifiable areas by known people. But because the international drug fight is dangerous and diplomatically complicated, some officials here and abroad are reluctant to get involved.

Nowhere was this more striking than in the aftermath of Operation Blast Furnace in 1986, carried out in the Chapare region of Bolivia, where one-fourth of the world's coca was then grown. The Bolivian government asked U.S. troops and helicopters to help in a search-and-destroy mission against cocaine production.

While Blast Furnace lasted, "we literally shut down the coca market in Bolivia," says Thomas Kelly, deputy administrator at the DEA. Nevertheless, the operation will probably not be repeated. Why? Because the use of American troops sparked accusations that the United States had violated Bolivia's sovereignty. "I don't think another Latin American government is going to invite us to carry out law-enforcement activities that are their proper, sovereign responsibility," says a State Department official.

Problems of sovereignty are reasons to plan our attack with care, not to refuse to act. Rather than second-guess operations like Blast Furnace, we should find "ways to do this again which would not destabilize" the region, says former Assistant Secretary of State Elliott Abrams. We should not shrink from using U.S. personnel, who are sometimes the most effective drug soldiers. As soon as our soldiers departed, Bolivia's war on drugs faltered.

Most of all, we need a real plan for places like the Upper Huallaga. Any policy that does not include specific plans for attacking specific crops is a cop-out, not a strategy.

4. *Decide who's in charge.* On April 3, 1989 U.S. Customs Service agents in Mendocino County, California, were poised to nab a ship packed with ten tons of Colombian marijuana. An informant on shore was talking to the ship by radio, helping to lure the vessel to a drop-off site. But a Coast Guard unit, unaware of the operation, overheard the radio messages and cut in. The ship fled, and the bust was blown.

Federally supported drug treatment is equally confused. A Congressional investigation discovered that the states never spent $777 million in federal funds earmarked for drug education, treatment and rehabilitation. Uncle Sam's rules for using the money were too specific to be practical for the states.

With 58 federal agencies and departments involved, the drug fight has become a swamp of rivalry, misdirection, duplication and waste. In 1988, a new law finally called for one man to coordinate federal drug policy. President Bush appointed former Education Secretary William J. Bennett to be the so-called Drug Czar.

But the Bush Administration has been slow to support its new czar. For instance, in June 1989, while Bennett was still writing the Administration's policy on drug testing, Constance B. Newman, the President's choice to head the Office of Personnel Management, stated her own position. She declared at her Senate confirmation hearing that she wants to limit employee drug testing and was confirmed in part on that basis. Newman had not consulted Bennett.

If the drug czar is to exert the control his title implies, he will need more backing from Bush in situations like that one. He will also need less interference from Congress, where at least 70 committees and subcommittees oversee the drug fight. A single body in each house should be responsible. We can't win the war on drugs with every soldier acting like a general.

5. *Put the blame where it belongs.* People start taking drugs for a range of reasons. But the hard truth is that each individual is responsible for his own actions—both for starting drugs and for quitting them. Our drug policies have not acknowledged this. "We view addiction as chronic, like arthritis or diabetes, more than as a problem that can be cured," says Dr. Charles R. Schuster, director of the National Institute on Drug Abuse. One result of this outlook is that, in some cases, addiction is now considered a "handicap" under the U.S. law that protects the handicapped against job discrimination.

The way to hold individuals responsible is to make them pay a price. Currently, that price is not steep. Bob Schirn, a Los Angeles County prosecutor, says, "It's very rare that a person who has a history only of drug possession will go to prison." In New York City, most of those convicted of possessing drugs are sentenced at best to "time served"—the day or two spent awaiting arraignment. Wayne County, Michigan, Assistant Prosecutor Richard Padzieski says, "I can't say that a lot of people in Detroit fear the drug laws."

In March 1989, on the other hand, Phoenix, Arizona, launched a get-tough program—called "Do Drugs. Do Time."—with lessons for the entire nation. "We don't just take their dope and write a report," says Lt. John Buchanan of the county's drug unit. "They go to jail, and that door slams."

The cars of those who bought or consumed drugs in them are confiscated. First offenders are offered a choice between a trial or about a year of treatment, at their own expense (as much as $2000). The treatment includes compulsory drug tests.

Ben Wallace (not his real name) was a drug abuser for 12 years, shattering two marriages and ruining himself financially. But his arrest in Phoenix ended his addiction; he did not want to go to prison. "It was either 'You end it, or you go,'" he says. "I ended it."

William Bennett believes the real reason for the drug epidemic is that the 1960s and '70s are not yet behind us. In those troubled decades, Bennett says, our most influential institutions were "giving permission, even encouragement, to use drugs. Our basic institutions have still not recovered."

"We are a nation mugged."

Bennett is right. A recent drug-use survey reveals that our wavering commitment to drug enforcement has, inevitably, produced uneven and disappointing results. The strongest among us are beginning to respond to the war on drugs, but the most troubled—the young and unemployed—remain increasingly prone to the ravages of hard-core addiction.

We must never forget that the enemy we are fighting is not a chemical or a country or a social condition. Rather, it is each and every individual who sells, consumes or condones an illegal drug. The billions of tax dollars we spend to cope with the human wreckage left by drugs are being stolen from our pockets by every unpunished drug kingpin, every strutting street dealer and every "upright" citizen covertly snorting cocaine.

We are a nation mugged. We need the guts, the resolve and the righteous anger to act against the assailant. This commitment will have to come from all of us—our President, Congress, states, courts, cities and each and every American. Without it, no czar, no program and no amount of money will help.

Rachel Flick is a contributor to Reader's Digest.

"Reliance on more prisons . . . looks like dead-end spending. It's not the answer to rising crime, and it hardly solves America's drug scourge."

Enforcing Drug Laws Will Not End the Drug Crisis

Elizabeth Ehrlich, Lisa Driscoll, Wayne Greene, and Antonio Fins

Drug czar William J. Bennett calls illegal drug abuse "the enemy of the hour." His 1989 National Drug Control Strategy outlines a sweeping attack. As the war on drugs escalates, the enemy is retreating—in mainstream America at least. The task for political leaders now is to focus help where the problem is worst.

First, the good news: According to the National Institute on Drug Abuse (NIDA) survey of households, the number of Americans reporting "current" use of an illegal drug—at least once in the last 30 days— dropped 37% from 1985 to 1988. NIDA'S annual survey of high school seniors mirrors this finding. Opinion polls find rising opposition to drugs.

Away from the mainstream, however, a drug crisis rages, making the hard lives of the inner-city poor far harder. Intravenous drug use is now the largest single source of new AIDS infections. "Boarder babies" born to drug-using mothers are a sad new inner-city trial. Minorities are disproportionately hospitalized for drug-related emergencies. Dealers terrorize poor neighborhoods. Drug use is closely associated with the homeless, school dropouts, and prisoners, who aren't tracked by NIDA.

Diminishing Returns

As the two-tier pattern suggests, drug use is a symptom of complex problems—dysfunctional social institutions, lack of skills and opportunities—that call for complex solutions. But antidrug policy aimed at the inner city is in the main simplicity itself: more arrests, stiffer penalties. "I don't hear Bennett addressing the hard-core, disenfranchised addict except through law enforcement," says Karst J. Besteman, executive director of the Alcohol & Drug Problems Association of North America, a professional group. "And there's a point where law

enforcement loses its effectiveness." Certainly, highly publicized drug busts and bulging prisons seem but a frenzied display of failure.

That failure could itself prove destructive, suggests David F. Musto, a Yale Medical School physician and author of *The American Disease*, a history of narcotics control. Musto worries that mainstream America's fear and frustration could lead to harsher law enforcement and less funding for treatment. "My fear," he says, "is that we'll write off these communities rather than support institutions that would help people in them behave more like the middle class."

Yet around the country there are people with a more hopeful vision. Communities, nonprofits, and local agencies are experimenting with promising approaches in drug-abuse treatment, prevention, and local law enforcement. Most are modest in scale; few are proven "models." But with more resources, they could be nurtured, tested, and perhaps applied elsewhere. Here's a sampling:

Fahim Minkah is on patrol at the Prince Hall Apartments in drug-ravaged South Dallas. "Up there," he gestures, "that tenant sells crack." He recognizes a purple Cadillac with tinted windows: another dealer's car. As Minkah takes notes, a teenager he passes hastily gets rid of some dope.

Minkah, a community organizer and ex-Black Panther, heads AMAN-Drug Fighters, a collective of 20 black men working to chase out pushers and reduce local drug abuse. Like other grassroots groups that have sprung up in the inner cities, AMAN'S recipe is part citizen law enforcement, part neighborhood self-help, and part appeal to racial and community pride. AMAN patrols, neighbors keep watch, and posters identify dealers in the hope that publicity will drive them out. Prince Hall security guard David Ramsey says it's working. "Some drug dealers have left because of AMAN," he says.

Police street sweeps and arrests have escalated in

the inner cities, with little impact on drug abuse. Some observers blame conventional tactics, where officers swoop in and bag their prey. That leaves the drug trade to regroup—while neighbors gripe that nothing changes. But in a scattered few places, two developments may be breaking that stalemate. One is the sort of community mobilization effort AMAN represents. The other is a law enforcement innovation called "problem-oriented policing."

In problem-oriented policing, officers analyze and address community issues rather than just making arrests. That might mean getting local officials to fix street lights on a dark, drug-dealing corner. Or working with landlords on security issues. Reducing crime is viewed as a long-term proposition. The best versions get the community involved.

Foot Patrols

Tulsa police have taken the concept further than most. In 1988, officers were put on foot beats in five public housing projects with high rates of drug-related crime. They attended neighborhood watch meetings, consulted with residents, drug treatment facilities, and schools, and got city bureaucracies to act on problems from zoning violations to vermin.

Such efforts have won the police a striking degree of confidence and cooperation. In one housing project, Seminole Hills Village, tips by newly mobilized residents led to 20 search warrants in four months, 150 cocaine arrests, 130 drug evictions, and a 73% drop in violent crimes.

The approach has its skeptics. Law enforcement traditionalists pan it as more social than police work. Michael E. Clark, who heads the Citizens Committee for New York City, a nonprofit community support group, says problem-oriented policing could prove to be "a public relations shuck-and-jive act" if locals aren't brought into the process. Clark's group has, in fact, trained problem-oriented forces around the country. But it also teaches local groups to define and address drug-crime issues, to protect themselves while doing so, and to know when to turn over the job to the police.

"Police street sweeps and arrests have escalated in the inner cities, with little impact on drug abuse."

AMAN's once-cool relations with the South Dallas police are warming. Recently, AMAN helped end the police practice of releasing pushers—after confiscating their drugs—detained by the security guards landlords posted to do most after-dark policing of the area. "We're happy with any help we can get," says Levi Williams, director of the Dallas Police Dept. Office of Community Affairs.

AMAN's work goes beyond law enforcement to community rebuilding. In a new community center, AMAN members talk racial pride and self-respect as a counter to drug abuse. A job-training program is planned for 1990.

But it's not easy. Minkah, an auto mechanic, pays the bills himself. Requests to foundations to support a full-time organizer have foundered, and AMAN lost phone service because it couldn't pay the bills. Supporting such home-grown efforts may be the best investment a war on drugs could make.

In the Pottsburg Park Boys & Girls Club, Michael Waters, 24, is a wanted man. At every step, a child shouts his name and pushes schoolwork at him. Waters, the club's director, talks and praises, promising field trips and handing out quarters for video games. "Kids need to know that if they do something good, adults will notice," Waters says.

In 1987, when the Boys Clubs of America, the nation's oldest and largest philanthropy serving poor children, opened a clubhouse here, Pottsburg was the most feared housing project in Jacksonville, Fla. Many of its 250 brick units were drug dens, passing cars were attacked, shootouts were routine. Schoolbus drivers threatened a boycott, and police officers dared not enter without plenty of backup. But the new club has sparked a remarkable renaissance. And it represents Pottsburg's best shot by far to steer 300 kids from teen pregnancy, truancy, and drug abuse.

These days, "prevention and education" is on every drug warrior's lips. There was Nancy Reagan's "Just Say No" campaign. There is the Partnership for a Drug-Free America, a three-year, $1 billion public interest blitz by major advertising, media, and communications firms. Corporations are taking the message to workers. And school-based programs are proliferating.

Fail-Safe

Experts debate how well prevention programs work. Some point to declining drug abuse as proof that they do. In another view, prevention is fail-safe, with public opinion turning against drugs anyway. But most efforts have focused on kids in middle-class communities, where "experimentation is high but the frequency of serious drug problems is relatively low," says Mathea Falco, a former Assistant Secretary of State and author of *Winning the Drug War*.

In the inner cities, the prevention campaign faces tougher challenges: convincing children surrounded by instability that their choices in life matter, or preventing women giving birth from easing discomfort with crack. And although the vast majority of the disadvantaged, even in the worst settings, do resist temptation, the drug culture beckons most strongly where alternatives are few.

Can a children's crusade overcome so many demons? The Pottsburg clubhouse doesn't even bill itself as a prevention program per se. But help with homework is a big draw. "Before, you just struggled in school by yourself," says Vince Towns, 16. Recreation—sports, arts, computer instruction—also pulls kids off the streets. Staff members, rare figures of adult support, win affection, trust, and respect. Such activities themselves are preventive: They provide structure, direction, and a counterweight to the new sneakers, radios, and other blandishments of drug-dealing.

"Although the vast majority of the disadvantaged, even in the worst settings, do resist temptation, the drug culture beckons most strongly where alternatives are few."

Once youngsters are hooked on the fun, the club brings in "Smart Moves," a formal prevention program for high-risk kids ages 10 to 15. Seminars and role-playing games emphasize the dangers of drugs and teach kids to resist pressure to use or deal. And Smart Moves offers "a safe place where a child can ask how to [cope] with a relative who is involved in drugs," says Gale Barrett-Kavanagh, Boys Clubs' drug prevention director.

With a cost under $30,000 a year for staff and materials at each site, paid for by the national Boys Clubs, Smart Moves has found its way into about 200 of the organization's 1,200 sites in two years. While it's too early to gauge long-term impact, an early assessment by Columbia University social work researcher Steven Schinke glows. And "portions can be generalized and adopted by other community groups," he adds.

Schinke, who studied Pottsburg and other housing projects, also found the clubs become rallying points for adults and promote community safety. In Pottsburg, parents began helping out at the clubhouse and using the space to meet with neighbors and the police. They demanded better lighting, security, and housing improvements. And 130 cops now report to the clubhouse for weekday roll call. Drug dealing and violent crime have plummeted, and there's new optimism in the air.

A Town Pools Its Resources

Anyone giving directions to the new drug rehabilitation program in Bridgeport, Conn., warns the driver to lock the car doors. Drug dealers buzz across the street. Needles and crack vials dot the sidewalk. A six-foot cyclone fence surrounds the compound where Youth Evaluation Services (YES) has set up shop.

But there's a ray of promise behind that fence. YES, a sophisticated screening center that matches teenage drug abusers with treatment, is the linchpin of an ambitious community-wide antidrug effort.

Throughout the greater Bridgeport area, corporations, hospitals, schools, and local police are pooling resources in an experiment that aims to combine treatment, prevention, early intervention, and long-term follow-up. YES planners expect to see 300 kids in 1989, the program's first year, and ultimately, to include adults as well.

In the 1980s, treatment was the forgotten battleground of the drug war: Public funding was cut. Facilities deteriorated. Data collection suffered, and treatment research hit a nadir. The result: not only a desperate shortage of treatment, but a mismatch between new problems and available care.

Little is known about treating inner-city crack addicts, for instance, or helping the growing numbers of poor women with serious drug habits. Most treatment clinics are narrowly focused, but substances are frequently abused in combination, and psychiatric problems often complicate the picture. Many hard-core abusers need more than treatment, perhaps help dealing with family problems or job skills. But rarely do social services and drug programs intersect.

Bridgeport planners are tackling many of these issues. They are trying for more coordinated referral and more comprehensive care. Schools, peers, truant officers, social service agencies, and police departments send youngsters to YES. Families join in for counseling. Treatment is individually tailored. Where clinics usually make their own diagnoses, with results that can be self-serving, YES assigns all patients to outside programs.

"Before, referral was hit-or-miss," says Robert M. Francis, regional director of Connecticut's Children & Youth Services Dept., which has bought into the YES system. Better referral is saving money. And as the network expands, new clinics are opening.

These new sites are private, and the cost of such care—easily over $10,000 per residential stay—is out of reach for most Americans who need it. At least half of Bridgeport teenagers lack private health insurance, and medicaid covers few treatment services. YES can't do much to open new public clinics, but so far, private ones are accepting nonpaying YES clients in hopes of future referrals. No one has been turned away.

Just how much more public treatment does the U.S. need? No one seems to know. "The need is so evident, people are afraid to collect the data," says William Butynski, who heads the National Association of State Alcohol & Drug Abuse Directors. The National Institute on Drug Abuse figures about 2 million habitual users need treatment but counts only 260,000 public or private "slots" for them.

Drug czar Bennett has called for $685 million in federal treatment spending in 1990, about $240 million more than 1989 levels, plus more research funds. Such increases, says his office, could expand public capacity by 20% annually. But critics call that paltry. In 1988, the Presidential Commission on AIDS recommended that the federal government spend $15 billion over 10 years to achieve "treatment on demand" for intravenous drug users alone. And many abusers don't use needles.

"In the 1980s, treatment was the forgotten battleground of the drug war."

While policymakers debate how much is enough, there is growing agreement that the delivery system itself needs rethinking—and that communities will have to get involved. Indeed, in an effort to seed new approaches, the Robert Wood Johnson Foundation, the Nation's largest health care philanthropy, has launched a major antidrug initiative, "Fighting Back." In February 1989, citing Bridgeport's expanding effort as an early model, the Princeton (N.J.) foundation offered $26.4 million in grants to support a dozen intensive, community-wide efforts to reduce the demand for drugs and alcohol. It will look hardest at those that include dropout prevention programs, job training, and corporate involvement. Turning around the problem needs help from the feds—but it's also a job for coordination on the home front.

In the tough world of criminal corrections, one wing at New York State's Arthur Kill prison stands out. In neat dormitory rooms and in quiet halls, prisoners are doing their jobs: typing memos, organizing meetings, mopping floors. Here, one group attends an orientation lecture. There, a no-holds-barred encounter group is in full sway.

This is Stay'n Out, a model drug-treatment program for hard-core criminal drug abusers. With 140 participants at Arthur Kill in Staten Island and a smaller group in a New York women's prison, there are long waiting lists to get into the program. The cost: about $8 a day over a state prison bed. Follow-up studies boast that 77% of graduates stay clear of crime and drug-free for three years after they are released, compared with about 50% of similar state parolees.

The connection between drugs and crime is tightening. Drug trafficking and possession offenses swamp courts and prisons. In large American cities, up to 85% of arrestees test positive for drugs.

The corrections system thus offers a key site for treatment intervention—as well as an unparalleled opportunity. With nearly 1 million Americans incarcerated, a large chunk of the nation's hard-core drug users is captive for an extended time. The system is already spending heavily on them. And the link between drug rehabilitation and lower recidivism rates is of no small interest when prisons are bursting at the seams. Yet prison efforts amount to deep-sea fishing with a butterfly net. In 1987, 11.1% of prisoners were in treatment, little of it intensive or long-term.

But a handful of state prisons have had striking results with group-living programs such as Stay'n Out. Based on residential treatment communities, they isolate participants from other prisoners, reducing the influence of prison culture and enhancing a community sense.

Ronald Williams, a former heroin addict and inmate who founded Stay'n Out 11 years ago, says its focus is on improving self-esteem, attitude, and behavior. That means getting convicts, most with long histories of drug abuse, failed drug treatment, and crime to adapt to mainstream society and buy into a work ethic—in effect "habilitating" them for the first time. If these issues are addressed effectively, "you'll also stop using drugs," he maintains.

The curriculum is whatever works—service classes on AIDS, drugs, alcoholism; training in such "life skills" as how to look for a job or open a bank account. Leadership jobs go to inmates who have performed well. Counselors are former addicts and prisoners who become role models. One, Charles Cash, a Stay'n Out graduate, came back to work at Arthur Kill after his release. Now he heads the program's orientation unit.

At the heart of the program are confrontational encounter sessions to build self-awareness and weed out denial. "Sometimes it takes that to show a person the depth of his negative behavior," says Alonzo Whaley, 41. Incarcerated since 1983, he's a data clerk by morning, works with Stay'n Out in the afternoon, and takes college courses at night. "People change," he says.

Obligation

The Justice Dept. funds Stay'n Out and several other demonstration projects. Yet overall emphasis on treatment has been scant. Assistant Attorney General Richard B. Abell sees it as "a moral obligation" second to "getting the SOBs off the streets" and tackling prison overcrowding.

Bennett's national strategy lauds Stay'n Out. It would add $200 million in state and local law enforcement "drug grants" and more than double funding for federal prisons, to $1.5 billion. But observers expect most will go for more prisons, with little for more treatment.

Reliance on more prisons, though, looks like dead-end spending. It's not the answer to rising crime, and it hardly solves America's drug scourge. Indeed, it underscores a failure—of focus and imagination—that plagues federal drug policy in general and threatens to condemn the urban poor. Approaches that rebuild lives and communities, and help people take responsibility for themselves, promise to do far more.

Elizabeth Ehrlich, Lisa Driscoll, Wayne Greene, and Antonio Fins are contributors to Business Week, *a weekly business magazine.*

"Legalization would promote moderation while seeking to minimize the risk to users and the disruption of communities."

Legalization Will End the Drug Crisis

Daniel Lazare

After 20 years of troop sweeps, police actions, and military rhetoric, the evidence is all around us. The war on drugs has flopped. It's been more than ineffective—it's actually made things worse. It has caused street crime to mushroom and the murder rate to soar. It has intoxicated ghetto kids with visions of gold chains, black Mercedes, and other fruits of an underground economy. Rather than stopping drugs, it has ensured a flow of harder and harder substances onto the street.

Interdiction Policies

In the 1960s, an estimated 69,000 Americans were addicted to heroin. Today, there may be 250,000 junkies in New York City alone. Meanwhile, the cities are struggling to dig out from under a blizzard of low-priced cocaine. New and far more potent drugs are flooding the ghettos—due largely to interdiction policies that penalize traffickers in soft bulky drugs like marijuana, while actually increasing the supply of coke. In the late 1970s, federal drug prosecutors were congratulating one another over the arrest and conviction of Nicky Barnes, sentenced to life for selling 43 pounds of heroin and coke a month out of a West Harlem garage. Barnes is small potatoes compared to Rayful Edmond, recently convicted of distributing 440 pounds of coke *a week* in Washington, D.C.

This explosion did not occur despite the drug war, but because of it. Putting away druglords like Barnes backfired by disrupting a stable distribution system, replacing it with something worse, and persuading Barnes's many imitators that they would have to be more aggressive, more ruthless, more sophisticated if they were to take his place. No matter how hard the cops crack down, drug producers, importers, and street dealers manage to keep one step ahead.

"When I first started in the early '80s, a big coke seizure was 70 pounds," muses a former federal prosecutor in Miami. Nowadays, he says, busts that size are so commonplace as to be hardly worth mentioning. In 1981, federal drug agents confiscated 4,263 pounds of cocaine. By late 1989, the haul was approaching 171,000 kilos—40 times as much—not because the Drug Enforcement Administration was getting better at its job, but because smugglers have gotten better at theirs and are pushing so much more stuff through. This is the sort of private sector initiative any free market economist can appreciate. Although the feds have succeeded in pushing marijuana prices up—from $20 an ounce in the 1960s to $200 and up today—coke has plummeted from $50,000 per kilo in the late 1970s to under $10,000 in 1988. As a result of this interdiction-driven price structure, marijuana—once a "poor man's drug"— is now a gourmet item; cocaine, once reserved for the media elite, is now the lumpen proletariat's drug of choice.

Crack

The cheap, smokeable form of cocaine known as crack—said to have been invented in a Los Angeles kitchen in 1983—is simply the latest product of a process of research and development, along with ever-more sophisticated marketing, that government policies foster. Interdiction places a premium on portability and potency, encouraging dealers to switch to products that give more bang for the buck, while being easier to conceal from the police. The result: hard drugs push out soft drugs, pushers get smarter, and as cops up their firepower, dealers up theirs. Once the crack fad blows over, as undoubtedly it will, other drugs—even cheaper, more mind-blowing and more toxic—will arise to take its place. Who knows what strange fruit the drug war may bear?

This is a record of failure that's hard to beat—not that the government doesn't try. In the late '60s, New

Daniel Lazare, "The Drug War Is Killing Us," *The Village Voice,* January 23, 1990. Reprinted by permission of the author and *The Village Voice.*

York's governor, Nelson Rockefeller, unveiling what he called the toughest drug law in the world, vowed to go after not just drug lords, but users and low-level dealers as well. As a result, the courts ground to a halt as a long line of petty offenders, facing stiff prison sentences, ceased plea bargaining and demanded full-blown trials instead. In September 1988, drug czar William J. Bennett, unveiling the Bush administration's latest master plan, also vowed to go after . . . petty users and dealers. The consequence, predictably, is that plea bargaining has declined, court dockets are overcrowded, and juries are increasingly reluctant to send people to prison for possession of miniscule amounts of dope. With drug busts running at 750,000 a year nationwide—mostly for pot—prisons are bulging. In New York, where city officials are so desperate for lockup space they've begun housing prisoners on barges, drugs have displaced first-degree robbery as the number one cause of incarceration. In Washington, D.C., they account for more than half of all felony indictments.

A Form of Hysteria

So the drug war has led to more drugs, which in turn have led to more arrests and ever more feverish rhetoric out of Washington. "The more it's demonstrated that authoritarian responses don't work," observes ACLU [American Civil Liberties Union] Director Ira Glasser, "the more authoritarian they become. It feeds on itself in a way that is almost classically a form of hysteria."

The self-defeating nature of the drug war is clear from something called Operation Intercept, a massive effort launched by the Nixon administration to stop the flow of marijuana across the Mexican border. Billed as the largest peacetime search-and-seizure operation in history, Operation Intercept sent customs agents rifling through hundreds of thousands of cars and trucks for nearly three weeks in the fall of 1969. Yet while the campaign snarled traffic and tied up cross-border tourism and commerce, the drug haul turned out to be small. It did succeed, though, in triggering far-reaching changes in the marijuana business.

Stepped-up border controls forced distributors to upgrade their methods. Where previously they had relied on peasants riding public buses, in the aftermath of Operation Intercept they began switching to backcountry routes and eventually to DC-3's. As a U.S. customs agent put it in Elaine Shannon's 1988 best-seller, *Desperados,* Operation Intercept "caused the smugglers to learn to use airplanes. They started hiring pilots. And the loads got bigger." The trade also grew more professional and better capitalized. Paraquat, the herbicide that Mexican officials sprayed on marijuana fields in large quantities at American behest beginning in the late '70s, triggered another commercial revolution. The poison knocked Mexican pot off the market. But

instead of stopping the marijuana trade, it caused it to shift south to Guajira Peninsula in northern Colombia, source of the Colombia Gold that would soon become famous among American tokers. Large-scale sweeps by the Colombian military followed, whereupon marijuana cultivation, like the jet stream encountering a local storm center, shifted once again. This time it retreated deeper into the Colombian interior where it came to the attention of drug dealers in the city of Medellin.

Medellin had functioned as a heroin smuggling center in the 1950s. It was also close by the coca fields of Bolivia and Peru. As the U.S. Coast Guard and Customs Service clamped down and smuggling costs rose, it wasn't long before the major marijuana families realized there was more money in the local white powder. Cocaine began finding its way to the U.S. market in increasing quantities. The changing nature of the drug trade is illustrated by a story about Carlos Lehder. In the late '70s, this ambitious young Medellin drug entrepreneur arrived at Norman's Cay in the Bahamas to set up a trans-shipment station for drugs bound for Florida. He was irritated to find, however, a small mom-and-pop operation flying planeloads of pot. Lehder and his heavily armed associates permitted the ring to continue, but only if space was cleared on each flight for a shipment of coke. Each planeload of marijuana was worth perhaps $300,000 wholesale; the same weight in cocaine was worth $26 million. Pot was by now small-time. Coke was where the smart money was heading.

"By embarking on a crusade against pot, federal narcs triggered a series of events that eventually laid the basis for a cocaine catastrophe."

In 1982, Ronald Reagan appointed vice-president Bush director of the South Florida Task Force, a super-agency aimed at controlling the flood of hot money and drugs in and around Miami. The task force was highly effective in intercepting rusty freighters loaded with pot, but less effective against smugglers bearing valises full of cocaine. The result was to tip the market more decisively in favor of coke. In 1985, the Reaganites did coke smugglers another favor by launching a massive eradication program, Operation Delta-9, complete with troops and military helicopters, against domestic marijuana growers in all 50 states. Although pot growers tried to recoup by moving their crops indoors to greenhouses and basements, market share was lost. With a major competitor out of the way, the boys from Medellin now had the field to themselves. At some point in the mid-'80s, amid mounting horror stories of broken marriages and ruined careers, cocaine began showing signs of losing favor with the middle class. The results might have been a market glut of disastrous proportions for the cocaine cartel were it not for crack. For a few dollars a vial, it created an intense, short-lived high that proved immensely popular with the ghetto masses.

A Cocaine Catastrophe

For cocaine businessmen, the day was saved. For urban blacks and Latinos, the nightmare was just beginning. By embarking on a crusade against pot, federal narcs triggered a series of events that eventually laid the basis for a cocaine catastrophe.

Plus ça change. . . . The great historical precedent for the current impasse is, of course, Prohibition. The war on booze backfired in essentially the same way the war on drugs is boomeranging today. Besides fostering an unprecedented wave of gang violence, prohibition promoted immoderate use by tilting the market away from softer substances to harder ones. A century earlier, Thomas Jefferson had predicted as much, when he observed: "No nation is drunken where wine is cheap, and none sober where the dearness of wine substitutes ardent spirits as the common beverage."

During Prohibition, beer drinking declined in much the way pot smoking is declining today: The reason wasn't changing taste, but the effect of interdiction on supply and demand. Bootleggers refused to risk their lives for something that was 95 percent water and hops. According to data collected in the late 1920s by Irving Fisher, the famous Yale economist, a glass of beer grew to be twice as expensive as a shot of bathtub gin—meaning, in effect, that Prohibition wound up pushing drinkers toward the hard stuff. The day of having a brew or two with friends was past. The age of getting blind, blotto, buried, canned, etc. had arrived.

The upshot was a wave of drunkenness that left ordinary people aghast. As one witness observed: "Everybody drank as if there would never be another drink. If you opened a bottle, you killed it." With supplies unpredictable, bingeing became the norm. "Eat, drink and be merry," went the doggerel of the day, "for tomorrow, it may be prohibited by law." The columnist Heywood Broun called Prohibition a scheme for replacing good beer with indifferent gin. In Chicago, a Croatian immigrant complained that when working men get their hands on liquor, "they take one drink, then two, then another because they know it will be long before they can have more, and end up by spending their whole pay and then getting very sick." Added another eyewitness: "The raw liquor of those days was not the kind that induced sleep. It made people wild."

Actually, it was the *circumstances* that made people wild—the speakeasies, the illegality, the sexual frisson that comes from rubbing shoulders with gangsters and thumbing one's nose at middle class probity. With

repeal, however, the nature of alcohol consumption was transformed. People who would have killed for rotgut whiskey now breezed passed liquor stores. In a freer, more tolerant atmosphere, alcohol returned to being ordinary. Drinking increased but there's no evidence that drunkenness did. Some people had difficulty coping with the new freedom—and alcoholism remains a scourge—but taken as a whole, the social cost of drinking—as measured by corruption, enforcement expenditures, and the sheer loss of lives—went down.

Change the Demand

Hopefully, legalization would transform the demand for drugs in much the same way. Instead of the desperate desire to get as high as possible in the shortest period of time, people might grow to use drugs more carefully, discriminately, and wisely. Certainly, they couldn't use them any *less* wisely than under today's overwrought conditions.

Legalization would undercut the druglords (or at least force them to go legit). By introducing free and open competition, it would bring profits and prices down to normal business levels. Sidewalk dealers, suddenly legitimized, would have no more reason to settle their disputes with Uzis than do liquor salesmen. Whatever reasons black and Latino kids have to quit school, the desire to make big money selling crack would not be among them. And junkies would no more have to rob and steal than would a wino trying to rustle up the fistful of change needed to purchase a bottle of MD 20/20. With drugs subject to pure food and drug laws, overdoses and poisonings would decline.

"Legalization would break the cycle by stripping drugs of unnecessary moral baggage, just as decriminalization stripped fornication and booze of theirs."

Instead of expending vast sums for cops, prosecutors, judges, prison guards, etc., society would be able to finance noncoercive drug treatment by taxing hitherto forbidden substances. With the destigmatization of drugs would come a form of junkie liberation—freedom to come out of the shadows, take jobs, demand services, and organize politically against police harassment and the scourge of AIDS.

Legalization is an attempt to rise above the cycle of repression and libertinism that has characterized American culture. Historically, we have spent our off-hours reeling between the temperance hall and the tavern, between the church and the whorehouse, between abstinence and bingeing. The two poles are linked. The preacher needs the local madam to rail against on Sunday mornings, while the madam needs the preacher to insure a steady stream of neurotics in need of release on Saturday nights. Similarly, the cops need the pushers to justify their existence, while the pushers need the cops to maintain what is, in effect, an elaborate price-support system based on government intervention in the marketplace to limit competition and hold down supply.

Unnecessary Moral Baggage

Legalization would break the cycle by stripping drugs of unnecessary moral baggage, just as decriminalization stripped fornication and booze of theirs. Rather than characterizing drugs as good or evil, legalizers would have them regarded as instruments of pleasure, whose only moral content comes from how they are used. The goal is a society of norms rather than coercion. Society would attempt to set standards, just as the community does now with alcohol and tobacco. But rather than calling in the cops to break down doors, we would recognize that the choice ultimately devolves to the individual.

All of this is deeply threatening to the morality police. Which is why William Bennett, neo-conservative cultural warrior, is such a natural for the job of drug czar. As director of the National Endowment for the Humanities beginning in 1981, Bennett attempted to purge the academy of leftists, feminists, black nationalists, and anyone else exhibiting "a strong ideological bias highly critical of the government [or] the economic system." As secretary of education, he campaigned against sex education, abortion, and gay rights, and tried to impose an academic core curriculum based on the received wisdom of certain Western "classics." Now he is out to impose a similar authoritarianism with respect to drugs.

"With the explosion of crack in the inner cities, the racial nexus, always present in drug politics, underwent a twist."

As Bennett declared in a speech in Washington in May 1989: "The drug crisis is a crisis of authority—in every sense of the term 'authority.' . . . What those of us in Washington, in the states, and in the localities can do is exert the political authority necessary to make a sustained commitment to the drug war. We must build more prisons. There must be more jails. We must have more judges to hear drug cases and more prosecutors to bring them to trial, including military judges and prosecutors to supplement what we already have." Speaking on a nationwide radio call-in show in June 1989, the drug czar went himself one better by suggesting that the solution to the drug problem might actually be *beheadings*. "Legally, it's

difficult," he offered. "But . . . somebody selling drugs to a kid? Morally, I don't have any problem with that at all."

Meanwhile, Bennett & Co. have not been exactly forthcoming with the information that coke and heroin are responsible for an estimated 3-4,000 deaths a year in the U.S. Compare this toll to the 100,000 people who die yearly from alcohol, or the estimated 320,000 who die from diseases related to smoking. Not only are alcohol and tobacco legal, but the latter benefits from a wide array of government price supports and subsidies. The drug war is not directed against drug use per se; merely against the use of certain drugs the culture identifies as beyond the pale. The goal is not to get people to sober up, since certain types of intoxication are still permissible, but to get them to conform to arbitrary dictates. "Just say no," in this instance, carries a powerful subtext, especially when aimed at young people, minorities, and leftover radicals: Just do as you're told.

Chaos and Disorder

"If you want to overthrow the kind of democratic society we have, you need chaos and disorder," observes Eric E. Sterling, counsel to the House Judiciary Committee before joining the ranks of drug-war defectors in January 1989. "If you have enormous disorder and criminality and then adopt tactics to combat them that make them worse, you're playing right into the hands of those who really don't want democratic society and its inconveniences at all."

A social crisis doesn't spring up overnight; it takes years to develop. To the degree that the drug war had a beginning, it is 1875 when San Francisco adopted a ban on opium dens, aimed not so much at the drug as the Chinese immigrants who smoked it. Similar bans spread throughout the West as anti-Chinese agitation rose. In 1883, Congress raised tariffs on imported opium, then, four years later, prohibited imports altogether by Chinese (while allowing the trade to continue in the hands of "Americans"). In 1909, responding to a clamor by American missionaries and merchants opposed to the British opium monopoly in China, Congress banned smoking opium altogether. In 1914, the Harrison Narcotics Act was adopted, limiting the distribution of all opiates, including morphine and heroin, to licensed physicians. By the mid-twenties, opiates were essentially banned.

Nonetheless, as recently as World War I, opiates were favorably regarded. Many physicians viewed them as something of a wonder drug, "God's Own Medicine," as opiates were called, useful in treating everything from menstrual cramps to diarrhea. "If the entire *materia medica* at our disposal was limited to the choice and use of only one drug," observed a writer in the *Journal of the American Medical Association* in 1915, "I am sure that a great many, if not a majority, of us would choose opium." Opium derivatives such as morphine were also used to wean people off alcohol. Opium addiction was considered preferable because opiates, which produce a peaceful, calming effect, didn't interfere with physical coordination, as does alcohol, and did not lead to violent outbursts of temper. Prior to drug prohibition, they also had the advantage of being cheaper. As one medical journal pointed out, 50 cents worth of opium was enough to sustain an addict for 20 days, whereas an alcoholic needed five or 10 times as much.

Cocaine followed a similar pattern. After its introduction in this country in the 1870s and '80s, coke emerged as a popular home remedy. Rolled into small cigars, it seemed to alleviate depression. Vin Mariani, a French wine containing coca leaves, spices, and other flavorings, was world famous as a mild stimulant; the eponymous Angelo Mariani, a chemist, collected 13 volumes of testimonials from, among others, the prince of Wales, the kings of Norway and Sweden, pope Leo XIII, H.G. Wells, Jules Verne, Emile Zola, Sarah Bernhardt, Thomas Edison, and president McKinley. Coca-Cola, one of dozens of coca-based soft drinks on the market at the turn of the century, advertised itself as a temperance drink. Thus, the dominant attitude toward drugs was the opposite of the pro-alcohol, anti-opiate, anti-cocaine policies of today.

A Spreading Crisis

Since the Harrison Narcotics Act, the story has been one of spreading crisis, rising alarm, and an increasingly punitive response by the state. In 1918, a Congressional commission found that smuggling was on the upswing while addicts were burrowing deeply underground; yet, rather than reconsidering the logic of Prohibition, they recommended stepped-up enforcement. Reports of cocaine use among blacks triggered hysteria in the South in the 1930s, when many police departments switched from .32 caliber handguns to .38s in the belief that increased firepower was needed to stop coke-crazed Afro-Americans. Following repeal of Prohibition, Harry Anslinger, chief of the Federal Bureau of Narcotics (precursor to today's Drug Enforcement Administration), organized a lurid propaganda campaign to ban marijuana. Newspapers ran stories about mass murderers high on pot, while Hollywood kicked in with the 1936 camp classic, *Reefer Madness*, to the delight of contemporary campus audiences. A year later, Congress obliged by placing marijuana on the list of proscribed substances.

Thereafter, Anslinger continued operating as a one-man ministry of fear. During World War II, he accused the Japanese of spreading opium to demoralize the Chinese. During the Korean War, he accused Chinese Communists of smuggling massive amounts of heroin to "weaken American resistance." As resistance among drug users stiffened, Congress responded by steadily ratcheting up penalties—from two years to a maximum of five for drug law violations in 1914, to 10 years in 1922, to life in the 1950s. In 1966, Nelson Rockefeller, faced with pockets of persistent heroin use amid a general urban crisis, upped the ante to 15 years to life for possession of two ounces or more of "any narcotic substance," plus stiff penalties for marijuana. *Harper's* magazine predicted that 1970 would go down as "the year of the great drug panic, the year when addiction was a permanent theme in the press and on TV—when government officials and office seekers made instant headlines by pledging a 'massive attack' on the problem." But the magazine was wrong: The best was yet to come.

"Legalization would allow us to look at now-illegal substances more realistically."

In the '70s, there was tentative support within the Democratic party for drug law liberalization. A marijuana decriminalization bill sponsored by Jacob Javits and a liberal congressman named Ed Koch (shortly before he ran for mayor) got as far as legislative hearings. Eleven states decriminalized simple possession, while one—Alaska—legalized cultivation for personal use. But then, following Ronald Reagan's triumph in 1980, Democrats began backpedaling furiously. Desperate for a weapon, . . . they concentrated on outflanking the Republicans on the drug issue on the right.

In 1981, Nancy Reagan embarked on her "Just Say No" campaign, whereupon Democrats upped the ante by clamoring for a drug czar to coordinate antidrug operations. Reagan vetoed the idea in early 1983. When David Stockman tried to cut the drug war budget—arguing, as he later put it, that "no matter how many Coast Guard cutters or AWACs-type planes we deployed, the stuff still kept coming in, by boat, plane, and even parachutist"—congressional Democrats raised a howl, causing the budget director to back off. As the Reagan administration revved up its rhetoric against terrorism, Senator Joseph Biden of Delaware responded with an increasingly popular form of one-upmanship. Yes, he said, terrorism is awful. But the drug menace is even worse. " . . . [W]here are the terrorists getting their money?" he asked in 1984. "They're getting it from drugs. If you want to fight terrorism, you've got to fight drugs." Not altogether displeased at the Democratic turnabout, the Reagan administration accused Moscow not only of fostering terrorism, but, by way of Cuba and Nicaragua, fostering the drug trade as well. A new word, *narco-terrorism*, an '80s update of the old image of heroin-pushing Commies, was born.

The free-floating paranoia of the '80s thus fed on itself as Republicans and Democrats competed to see who could be most hawkish. Democrats mocked

Reagan cabinet members for their supposed inaction. Recalls Eric Sterling, whose position on the House Judiciary Committee staff placed him at the center of the storm: "If I heard them say it once, I heard it a thousand times: 'Mr. Secretary, I can't tell you the name of a single one of my constituents who has been killed by the Russians, but I can tell you thousands who have died from cocaine.' " With the death of University of Maryland basketball star Len Bias from a cocaine overdose in June 1986, the frenzy reached new heights. A survey showing that Americans cared more about drugs and health care than Star Wars or contra aid encouraged Democrats to launch new attacks. Republican pollster Richard Wirthlin drafted a lengthy memo to White House chief of staff Donald Regan advising him to consider drugs as the next major presidential initiative after tax reform. Americans were desperate for change, he advised, and would support drastic measures to achieve it. Four weeks after Bias's death, Reagan dispatched troops to Bolivia to assist local police in raids on cocaine laboratories.

"It is impossible to reach out to addicts amid a real live shooting war aimed equally at drug dealers and drug users."

With the explosion of crack in the inner cities, the racial nexus, always present in drug politics, underwent a twist. Black Democrats at all levels of government seized on the drug war and made it their own. Although a longtime opponent of the death penalty, Harlem's Charles Rangel, chairman of the powerful House Select Committee on Narcotics, ended up shepherding an omnibus antidrug bill through Congress in 1988 that contained a provision for capital punishment for drug dealers who kill. He also inserted language barring the use of federal funds to supply addicts with clean needles to prevent the spread of AIDS. In New York, black democrats who had succeeded in shouting down a Koch proposal for a clean-needles program in 1985 tried again when a scaled-down version was put forward in 1988. This time, they failed. In early 1989, Rangel raised a hue and cry against President Bush for failing to give his new drug czar William Bennett cabinet-level status—a case of a liberal, strangely enough, demanding augmented powers for one of the most rabid conservatives in national government.

At the same time, Jesse Jackson took his "Up with hope, down with dope" message to public high schools, winning praise from, among others, Senator Jesse Helms. For Jackson, who played a crucial role in drumming up liberal support for the drug war, the issue was starkly moral. As he told the Los Angeles-based *New Perspectives Quarterly* "Drugs are poison.

Taking drugs is a sin. Drug use is morally debased and sick. . . . Since the flow of drugs into the U.S. is an act of terrorism, antiterrorist policies must be applied. . . . If someone is caught transmitting the death agent to Americans, that person should face wartime consequences. The line must be drawn."

Terrorism . . . death agent . . . wartime consequences—this was the language of a political culture that had detached itself from reality and was spinning wildly out of control. Jackson and Rangel notwithstanding, minorities are the greatest victims of the drug war. Military courts such as those sought by Bennett would not be set up in the suburbs, where brokers snort an occasional line of coke and teenagers sneak off to smoke joints. Rather, they'd preside over battle zones like Washington Heights and the South Bronx. That's where the drug trade is concentrated, that's where the cops concentrate their forces, and that's where civil liberties are first to come under assault. It's also where the indirect effects of the drug war—crime, corruption, the displacement of aboveground businesses, and needle-borne diseases such as AIDS—are most intense.

Political pressures are converging on the black community, with polarizing results. While most leaders demand ever more drastic measures, some have dared to question the cultural orthodoxy. Baltimore's Kurt Schmoke, a former prosecutor, was the first big-city mayor to broach the question of legalization. State senator Joe Galiber has been the first elected official in New York. George Crockett is so far the first member of the U.S. Congress. All three are black.

Peaceful Persuasion

The alternative to the drug war is a policy based on peaceful persuasion. Instead of ostracizing junkies, throwing dealers in jail, and using the drug trade as a pretext to invade Third World nations, this approach would educate people not to do dangerous drugs, much as a broad-based anti-tobacco campaign has educated millions of Americans over the last 25 years not to smoke cigarettes. Instead of treating drugs as a criminal matter (and now a matter of national security), it would classify them as a public health problem requiring the attention of counselors and medical personnel. Just as cops now realize there is no point to throwing drunks in dry-out tanks, the abuse, harassment, and dehumanization of drug users—what maverick psychiatrist Thomas S. Szasz calls the "verminization" of those who choose to get high outside the officially approved triad of nicotine, caffeine, and alcohol—would cease. A rational policy would recognize that all drugs are not necessarily dangerous, and that drug use does not necessarily constitute abuse. On the other hand, it would recognize that, just as some people persist in smoking, some will persist in doing hard drugs. Rather than punishing those who do, legalization would promote moderation while seeking to minimize the risk to users and the disruption of communities.

Moderation has already asserted itself with regard to legal drugs. Since the health revolution of the 1970s, consumption of alcohol has declined as distilled spirits give way to wine coolers and "lite" beer. With alcohol neither vilified by bluenoses nor celebrated by the underground, it has undergone a process of demystification and deglamorization that allows most people to see booze for what it really is. Americans are drinking more decaffeinated coffee and smoking fewer cigarettes, if they smoke at all. The fact that the '80s are likely to go down in history as the decade of crack *and* the white wine spritzer says volumes about the widening gap between illegal and legal drug use in this society.

Legalization would allow us to look at now-illegal substances more realistically. Heroin, for instance, is highly addictive, although physiologically more benign when taken over a prolonged period than heavy drinking or cigarettes. It does not cause teeth to rot, appetite to decrease, stomach, intestines, and liver to cease functioning, or any of the other ghoulish effects that have been ascribed to junk by, among others, liberal Supreme Court Justice William O. Douglas. In fact, doctors have found *few* ill effects associated with heroin addiction besides those accruing from criminalization, i.e. the negative health consequence of being thrown in jail, deprived of work, poisoned by impure drugs, and hounded into poverty. For this reason, rather than forcing addicts to use methadone, which, users say, *can* have ill effects, addicts might be better off on a maintenance program of heroin. In Britain, heroin maintenance has been standard medical procedure since 1926. In this country, Dr. William Stewart Halsted (1852-1922) was a pioneer in aseptic surgery even though addicted to daily doses of morphine. Under today's more intolerant conditions he would be condemned to a life in prison or the streets. The loss to the arts—Billie Holiday and Lenny Bruce were banned from performing because of drug addiction—is as absurd as the hipster mystique that surrounds junk as a result of this policy.

Using Heroin

Meanwhile, the ban on the use of heroin as a painkiller would cease. According to John Morgan, professor of pharmacology at CUNY Medical School, heroin is medically superior to the widely used Demerol, an artificial opiate whose only advantage lies in its legality. As for marijuana: the DEA banned its use as a therapeutic substance, despite the recommendation of its own chief administrative judge, Francis L. Young, who observed . . . that pot is "one of the safest therapeutically active substances known to man." It's also useful in battling the nausea of chemotherapy, and the effects of glaucoma and epilepsy. According to John Morgan, "there has never

been a confirmed overdose due to marijuana alone," while hundreds die each year from internal bleeding brought on by aspirin. Adds Morgan: "The most effective way to kill yourself with marijuana is by having a bale drop on your head." In Holland, where marijuana has been decriminalized since the '70s, per capita consumption has declined well below U.S. levels.

"While I can treat someone for drugs, I can't treat someone with a .357 magnum bullet in his head. There's hope for a drug addict, but not for a dead man."

Finally and most horribly, there are the estimated 100,000 intravenous drug users in New York infected with human immunodeficiency virus (HIV), their 25,00 sexual partners, mainly women, who have caught it as well, and the estimated 4000 infants and children infected in utero. The HIV epidemic among IV-drug users is a direct consequence of shortsighted criminal penalties that not only outlaw drugs but needles as well. The result is to encourage addicts not to supply their own needles, but to rent used "works" where they shoot up. The state could not have designed a more effective policy for spreading the AIDS virus if it had tried.

Policies like these must end. Addicts must be given access to medical care, encouraged to use condoms, given clean needles and, ideally, high-quality heroin they can vaporize and ingest nasally so they don't have to use needles at all. All of this is as important as supplying gay men with condoms and information about safer sex. Yet virtually none of it's being done. According to public health specialists, junkies with AIDS typically receive no medical attention until they stagger into an emergency room in the final throes of the illness. While the city's needle exchange program was supplying about 300 IV-drug users with sterile hypodermics, an obvious drop in the bucket, David Dinkins has vowed that even this token effort must end.

It is impossible to reach out to addicts amid a real live shooting war aimed equally at drug dealers and drug users. Society cannot drive addicts ever deeper underground while simultaneously urging them to come out in the clean light of day to receive medical help. By verminizing junkies, the drug war encourages them to treat themselves as vermin and infect others through dirty needles or unsafe sex. The circle of destruction may widen still further as crack takes hold. The reason is a rising incidence of sexually transmitted disease, causing genital lesions that may serve as a "gateway" for the virus, as women exchange sex for crack. From junkies to their sex partners to their partners' partners, rampant drug use and a complete breakdown in medical care are spreading AIDS throughout the ranks of the city's poor.

Legalization

Legalization would be an improvement, not a panacea. It wouldn't end AIDS, simply slow its spread; it wouldn't wipe out crime, merely eliminate one major cause. People would continue to misuse drugs just as some misuse legal substances today. Addiction might rise; yet at the same time, the overall costs associated with drug use, direct and indirect, both to the user and to those around him would undoubtedly decrease. Residents of poor neighborhoods would no longer huddle in their apartments while dealers battle with guns out in the street. Ghetto kids would have less reason to look up to dealers as role models. Deprived of a perverse government support system, an overheated trade, which siphons off the ghetto's best and brightest, would disappear.

"I see these dealers standing around with their beepers and gold chains laughing," says Dr. Kildare Clarke, the Jamaican-born chief of emergency services at Kings County Hospital in Brooklyn, who is an outspoken advocate of legalization. "They look at us and say, 'These doctors don't make shit. What they make in a year, we make in a week.' For these people, the money they can make far outweighs the risk of getting shot or killed. There are some days when I have seven gunshot wounds and five stab wounds coming off the streets, and that isn't even counting the ones who go to the morgue. Yet while I can treat someone for drugs, I can't treat someone with a .357 magnum bullet in his head. There's hope for a drug addict, but not for a dead man."

Daniel Lazare is New York Editor for In These Times, *a Chicago-based socialist weekly newspaper. His articles have appeared in the periodicals* Present Tense *and* The Village Voice.

"Once a drug is legal, not only will its use increase but many of those who then use it will prefer the drug to the treatment."

Legalization Will Not End the Drug Crisis

James Q. Wilson

In 1972, the President appointed me chairman of the National Advisory Council for Drug Abuse Prevention. Created by Congress, the Council was charged with providing guidance on how best to coordinate the national war on drugs. (Yes, we called it a war then, too.) In those days, the drug we were chiefly concerned with was heroin. When I took office, heroin use had been increasing dramatically. Everybody was worried that this increase would continue. Such phrases as "heroin epidemic" were commonplace.

A Matter of Ethics

That same year, the eminent economist Milton Friedman published an essay in *Newsweek* in which he called for legalizing heroin. His argument was on two grounds: as a matter of ethics, the government has no right to tell people not to use heroin (or to drink or to commit suicide); as a matter of economics, the prohibition of drug use imposes costs on society that far exceed the benefits. Others, such as the psychoanalyst Thomas Szasz, made the same argument.

We did not take Friedman's advice. (Government commissions rarely do.) I do not recall that we even discussed legalizing heroin, though we did discuss (but did not take action on) legalizing a drug, cocaine, that many people then argued was benign. Our marching orders were to figure out how to win the war on heroin, not to run up the white flag of surrender.

That was 1972. Today, we have the same number of heroin addicts that we had then—half a million, give or take a few thousand. Having that many heroin addicts is no trivial matter; these people deserve our attention. But not having had an increase in that number for over fifteen years is also something that

deserves our attention. What happened to the "heroin epidemic" that many people once thought would overwhelm us?

The facts are clear: a more or less stable pool of heroin addicts has been getting older, with relatively few new recruits. In 1976 the average age of heroin users who appeared in hospital emergency rooms was about twenty-seven; ten years later it was thirty-two. More than two-thirds of all heroin users appearing in emergency rooms are now over the age of thirty. Back in the early 1970's, when heroin got onto the national political agenda, the typical heroin addict was much younger, often a teenager. Household surveys show the same thing—the rate of opiate use (which includes heroin) has been flat for the better part of two decades. More fine-grained studies of inner-city neighborhoods confirm this. John Boyle and Ann Brunswick found that the percentage of young blacks in Harlem who used heroin fell from 8 percent in 1970-71 to about 3 percent in 1975-76.

Heroin's Lost Appeal

Why did heroin lose its appeal for young people? When the young blacks in Harlem were asked why they stopped, more than half mentioned "trouble with the law" or "high cost" (and high cost is, of course, directly the result of law enforcement). Two-thirds said that heroin hurt their health; nearly all said they had had a bad experience with it. We need not rely, however, simply on what they said. In New York City in 1973-75, the street price of heroin rose dramatically and its purity sharply declined, probably as a result of the heroin shortage caused by the success of the Turkish government in reducing the supply of opium base and of the French government in closing down heroin-processing laboratories located in and around Marseilles. These were short-lived gains for, just as Friedman predicted, alternative sources of supply—mostly in Mexico—quickly emerged. But the three-year heroin shortage interrupted the easy recruitment of new users.

Health and related problems were no doubt part of the reason for the reduced flow of recruits. Over the preceding years, Harlem youth had watched as more and more heroin users died of overdoses, were poisoned by adulterated doses, or acquired hepatitis from dirty needles. The word got around: heroin can kill you. By 1974 new hepatitis cases and drug-overdose deaths had dropped to a fraction of what they had been in 1970.

Alas, treatment did not seem to explain much of the cessation in drug use. Treatment programs can and do help heroin addicts, but treatment did not explain the drop in the number of *new* users (who by definition had never been in treatment) nor even much of the reduction in the number of experienced users.

No one knows how much of the decline to attribute to personal observation as opposed to high prices or reduced supply. But other evidence suggests strongly that price and supply played a large role. In 1972 the National Advisory Council was especially worried by the prospect that U.S. servicemen returning to this country from Vietnam would bring their heroin habits with them. Fortunately, a brilliant study by Lee Robins of Washington University in St. Louis put that fear to rest. She measured drug use of Vietnam veterans shortly after they had returned home. Though many had used heroin regularly while in Southeast Asia, most gave up the habit when back in the United States. The reason: here, heroin was less available and sanctions on its use were more pronounced. Of course, if a veteran had been willing to pay enough—which might have meant traveling to another city and would certainly have meant making an illegal contact with a disreputable dealer in a threatening neighborhood in order to acquire a (possibly) dangerous dose—he could have sustained his drug habit. Most veterans were unwilling to pay this price, and so their drug use declined or disappeared.

Reliving the Past

Suppose we had taken Friedman's advice in 1972. What would have happened? We cannot be entirely certain, but at a minimum we would have placed the young heroin addicts (and, above all, the prospective addicts) in a very different position from the one in which they actually found themselves. Heroin would have been legal. Its price would have been reduced by 95 percent (minus whatever we chose to recover in taxes.) Now that it could be sold by the same people who make aspirin, its quality would have been assured—no poisons, no adulterants. Sterile hypodermic needles would have been readily available at the neighborhood drugstore, probably at the same counter where the heroin was sold. No need to travel to big cities or unfamiliar neighborhoods—heroin could have been purchased anywhere, perhaps by mail order.

There would no longer have been any financial or medical reason to avoid heroin use. Anybody could have afforded it. We might have tried to prevent children from buying it, but as we have learned from our efforts to prevent minors from buying alcohol and tobacco, young people have a way of penetrating markets theoretically reserved for adults. Returning Vietnam veterans would have discovered that Omaha and Raleigh had been converted into the pharmaceutical equivalent of Saigon.

"Drug use spreads in the same way any fad or fashion spreads: somebody who is already a user urges his friends to try."

Under these circumstances, can we doubt for a moment that heroin use would have grown exponentially? Or that a vastly larger supply of new users would have been recruited? Professor Friedman is a Nobel Prize-winning economist whose understanding of market forces is profound. What did he think would happen to consumption under his legalized regime? Here are his words: "Legalizing drugs might increase the number of addicts, but it is not clear that it would. Forbidden fruit is attractive, particularly to the young."

Really? I suppose that we should expect no increase in Porsche sales if we cut the price by 95 percent, no increase in whiskey sales if we cut the price by a comparable amount—because young people only want fast cars and strong liquor when they are "forbidden." Perhaps Friedman's uncharacteristic lapse from the obvious implications of price theory can be explained by a misunderstanding of how drug users are recruited. In his 1972 essay he said that "drug addicts are deliberately made by pushers, who give likely prospects their first few doses free." If drugs were legal it would not pay anybody to produce addicts, because everybody would buy from the cheapest source. But as every drug expert knows, pushers do not produce addicts. Friends or acquaintances do. In fact, pushers are usually reluctant to deal with non-users because a non-user could be an undercover cop. Drug use spreads in the same way any fad or fashion spreads: somebody who is already a user urges his friends to try, or simply shows already-eager friends how to do it.

The British Example

But we need not rely on speculation, however plausible, that lowered prices and more abundant supplies would have increased heroin usage. Great Britain once followed such a policy and with almost exactly those results. Until the mid-1960's, British physicians were allowed to prescribe heroin to certain classes of addicts. (Possessing these drugs without a doctor's prescription remained a criminal offense.) For many years this policy worked well enough because the addict patients were typically middle-class people who had become dependent on opiate painkillers while undergoing hospital treatment. There was no drug culture. The British system worked for many years, not because it prevented drug abuse, but because there was no problem of drug abuse that would test the system.

All that changed in the 1960's. A few unscrupulous doctors began passing out heroin in wholesale amounts. One doctor prescribed almost 600,000 heroin tablets—that is, over thirteen pounds—in just one year. A youthful drug culture emerged with a demand for drugs far different from that of the older addicts. As a result, the British government required doctors to refer users to government-run clinics to receive their heroin.

But the shift to clinics did not curtail the growth in heroin use. Throughout the 1960's the number of addicts increased—the late John Kaplan of Stanford estimated by fivefold—in part as a result of the diversion of heroin from clinic patients to new users on the streets. An addict would bargain with the clinic doctor over how big a dose he would receive. The patient wanted as much as he could get, the doctor wanted to give as little as was needed. The patient had an advantage in this conflict because the doctor could not be certain how much was really needed. Many patients would use some of their "maintenance" dose and sell the remaining part to friends, thereby recruiting new addicts. As the clinics learned of this, they began to shift their treatment away from heroin and toward methadone, an addictive drug that, when taken orally, does not produce a "high" but will block the withdrawal pains associated with heroin abstinence.

Whether what happened in England in the 1960's was a mini-epidemic or an epidemic depends on whether one looks at numbers or at rates of change. Compared to the United States, the numbers were small. In 1960 there were 68 heroin addicts known to the British government; by 1968 there were 2,000 in treatment and many more who refused treatment. (They would refuse in part because they did not want to get methadone at a clinic if they could get heroin on the street.) Richard Hartnoll estimates that the actual number of addicts in England is five times the number officially registered. At a minimum, the number of British addicts increased by thirtyfold in ten years; the actual increase may have been much larger.

A Real Epidemic

In the early 1980's the numbers began to rise again, and this time nobody doubted that a real epidemic was at hand. The increase was estimated to be 40 percent a year. By 1982 there were thought to be 20,000 heroin users in London alone. Geoffrey Pearson reports that many cities—Glasgow, Liverpool, Manchester, and Sheffield among them—were now experiencing a drug problem that once had been largely confined to London. The problem, again, was supply. The country was being flooded with cheap, high-quality heroin, first from Iran and then from Southeast Asia.

"Crack is worse than heroin by almost any measure."

The United States began the 1960's with a much larger number of heroin addicts and probably a bigger at-risk population than was the case in Great Britain. Even though it would be foolhardy to suppose that the British system, if installed here, would have worked the same way or with the same results, it would be equally foolhardy to suppose that a combination of heroin available from leaky clinics and from street dealers who faced only minimal law-enforcement risks would not have produced a much greater increase in heroin use than we actually experienced. My guess is that if we had allowed either doctors or clinics to prescribe heroin, we would have had far worse results than were produced in Britain, if for no other reason than the vastly larger number of addicts with which we began. We would have had to find some way to police thousands (not scores) of physicians and hundreds (not dozens) of clinics. If the British civil service found it difficult to keep heroin in the hands of addicts and out of the hands of recruits when it was dealing with a few hundred people, how well would the American civil service have accomplished the same tasks when dealing with tens of thousands of people?

Back to the Future

Now cocaine, especially in its potent form, crack, is the focus of attention. Now as in 1972 the government is trying to reduce its use. Now as then some people are advocating legalization. Is there any more reason to yield to those arguments today than there was almost two decades ago? (I do not here take up the question of marijuana. For a variety of reasons—its widespread use and its lesser tendency to addict—it presents a different problem from cocaine or heroin. For a penetrating analysis, see Mark Kleiman, *Marijuana: Costs of Abuse, Costs of Control.*)

I think not. If we had yielded in 1972 we almost certainly would have had today a permanent population of several million, not several hundred thousand, heroin addicts. If we yield now we will have a far more serious problem with cocaine.

Crack is worse than heroin by almost any measure. Heroin produces a pleasant drowsiness and if hygienically administered, has only the physical side effects of constipation and sexual impotence. Regular heroin use incapacitates many users, especially poor ones, for any productive work or social responsibility. They will sit nodding on a street corner, helpless but at least harmless. By contrast, regular cocaine use leaves the user neither helpless nor harmless. When smoked (as with crack) or injected, cocaine produces instant, intense, and short-lived euphoria. The experience generates a powerful desire to repeat it. If the drug is readily available, repeat use will occur. Those people who progress to "bingeing" on cocaine become devoted to the drug and its effects to the exclusion of almost all other considerations—job, family, children, sleep, food, even sex. Dr. Frank Gawin at Yale and Dr. Everett Ellinwood at Duke report that a substantial percentage of all high-dose, binge users become uninhibited, impulsive, hypersexual, compulsive, irritable, and hyperactive. Their moods vacillate dramatically, leading at times to violence and homicide.

Women are much more likely to use crack than heroin, and if they are pregnant, the effects on their babies are tragic. Douglas Besharov, who has been following the effects of drugs on infants for twenty years, writes that nothing he learned about heroin prepared him for the devastation of cocaine. Cocaine harms the fetus and can lead to physical deformities or neurological damage. Some crack babies have for all practical purposes suffered a disabling stroke while still in the womb. The long-term consequences of this brain damage are lowered cognitive ability and the onset of mood disorders. Besharov estimates that about 30,000 to 50,000 such babies are born every year, about 7,000 in New York City alone. There may be ways to treat such infants, but from everything we now know the treatment will be long, difficult, and expensive. Worse, the mothers who are most likely to produce crack babies are precisely the ones who, because of poverty or temperament, are least able and willing to obtain such treatment. In fact, anecdotal evidence suggests that crack mothers are likely to abuse their infants.

No Victimless Crime

The notion that abusing drugs such as cocaine is a "victimless crime" is not only absurd but dangerous. Even ignoring the fetal drug syndrome, crack-dependent people are, like heroin addicts, individuals who regularly victimize their children by neglect, their spouses by improvidence, their employers by lethargy, and their coworkers by carelessness. Society is not and could never be a collection of autonomous individuals.

We all have a stake in ensuring that each of us displays a minimal level of dignity, responsibility, and empathy. We cannot, of course, coerce people into goodness, but we can and should insist that some standards must be met if society itself—on which the very existence of the human personality depends—is

to persist. Drawing the line that defines those standards is difficult and contentious, but if crack and heroin use do not fall below it, what does?

The advocates of legalization will respond by suggesting that my picture is overdrawn. Ethan Nadelmann of Princeton argues that the risk of legalization is less than most people suppose. Over 20 million Americans between the ages of eighteen and twenty-five have tried cocaine (according to a government survey), but only a quarter million use it daily. From this Nadelmann concludes that at most 3 percent of all young people who try cocaine develop a problem with it. The implication is clear: make the drug legal and we only have to worry about 3 percent of our youth.

"The notion that abusing drugs such as cocaine is a 'victimless crime' is not only absurd but dangerous."

The implication rests on a logical fallacy and a factual error. The fallacy is this: the percentage of occasional cocaine users who become binge users *when the drug is illegal* (and thus expensive and hard to find) tells us nothing about the percentage who will become dependent when the drug is legal (and thus cheap and abundant). Drs. Gawin and Ellinwood report, in common with several other researchers, that controlled or occasional use of cocaine changes to compulsive and frequent use "when access to the drug increases" or when the user switches from snorting to smoking. More cocaine more potently administered alters, perhaps sharply, the proportion of "controlled" users who become heavy users.

The factual error is this: the federal survey Nadelmann quotes was done in 1985, *before* crack had become common. Thus the probability of becoming dependent on cocaine was derived from the responses of users who snorted the drug. The speed and potency of cocaine's action increases dramatically when it is smoked. We do not yet know how greatly the advent of crack increases the risk of dependency, but all the clinical evidence suggests that the increase is likely to be large.

No Scientific Grounds

It is possible that some people will not become heavy users even when the drug is readily available in its most potent form. So far there are no scientific grounds for predicting who will and who will not become dependent. Neither socioeconomic background nor personality traits differentiate between casual and intensive users. Thus, the only way to settle the question of who is correct about the effect of easy availability on drug use, Nadelmann or Gawin and Ellinwood, is to try it and see. But that social experiment is so risky as to be no experiment at all, for if cocaine is legalized and if the rate of its abusive use increases dramatically, there is no way to put the genie back in the bottle, and it is not a kindly genie.

Many people who agree that there are risks in legalizing cocaine or heroin still favor it because, they think, we have lost the war on drugs. "Nothing we have done has worked" and the current federal policy is just "more of the same." Whatever the costs of greater drug use, surely they would be less than the costs of our present, failed efforts.

That is exactly what I was told in 1972—and heroin is not quite as bad a drug as cocaine. We did not surrender and we did not lose. We did not win, either. What the nation accomplished then was what most efforts to save people from themselves accomplish: the problem was contained and the number of victims minimized, all at a considerable cost in law enforcement and increased crime. Was the cost worth it? I think so, but others may disagree. What are the lives of would-be addicts worth? I recall some people saying to me then, "Let them kill themselves." I was appalled. Happily, such views did not prevail.

Have we lost today? Not at all. High-rate cocaine use is not commonplace. The National Institute of Drug Abuse (NIDA) reports that less than 5 percent of high-school seniors used cocaine within the last thirty days. Of course this survey misses young people who have dropped out of school and miscounts those who lie on the questionnaire, but even if we inflate the NIDA estimate by some plausible percentage, it is still not much above 5 percent. Medical examiners reported in 1987 that about 1,500 died from cocaine use; hospital emergency rooms reported about 30,000 admissions related to cocaine abuse.

No Nationwide Plague

These are not small numbers, but neither are they evidence of a nationwide plague that threatens to engulf us all. Moreover, cities vary greatly in the proportion of people who are involved with cocaine. To get city-level data we need to turn to drug tests carried out on arrested persons, who obviously are more likely to be drug users than the average citizen. The National Institute of Justice, through its Drug Use Forecasting (DUF) project, collects urinalysis data on arrestees in 22 cities. As we have already seen, opiate (chiefly heroin) use has been flat or declining in most of these cities over the last decade. Cocaine use has gone up sharply, but with great variation among cities. New York, Philadelphia, and Washington, D.C., all report that two-thirds or more of their arrestees tested positive for cocaine, but in Portland, San Antonio, and Indianapolis the percentage was one-third or less.

In some neighborhoods, of course, matters have reached crisis proportions. Gangs control the streets, shootings terrorize residents, and drug-dealing occurs in plain view. The police seem barely able to contain matters. But in these neighborhoods—unlike at Palo Alto cocktail parties—the people are not calling for legalization, they are calling for help. And often not much help has come. Many cities are willing to do almost anything about the drug problem except spend more money on it. The federal government cannot change that; only local voters and politicians can. It is not clear that they will.

"In some neighborhoods, of course, matters have reached crisis proportions. Gangs control the streets, shootings terrorize residents, and drug-dealing occurs in plain view."

It took about ten years to contain heroin. We have had experience with crack for only about three or four years. Each year we spend perhaps $11 billion on law enforcement (and some of that goes to deal with marijuana) and perhaps $2 billion on treatment. Large sums, but not sums that should lead anyone to say, "We just can't afford this any more."

The illegality of drugs increases crime, partly because some users turn to crime to pay for their habits, partly because some users are stimulated by certain drugs (such as crack or PCP) to act more violently or ruthlessly than they otherwise would, and partly because criminal organizations seeking to control drug supplies use force to manage their markets. These also are serious costs, but no one knows how much they would be reduced if drugs were legalized. Addicts would no longer steal to pay black-market prices for drugs, a real gain. But some, perhaps a great deal, of that gain would be offset by the great increase in the number of addicts. These people, nodding on heroin or living in the delusion-ridden high of cocaine, would hardly be ideal employees. Many would steal simply to support themselves, since snatch-and-grab, opportunistic crime can be managed even by people unable to hold a regular job or plan an elaborate crime. Those British addicts who get their supplies from government clinics are not models of law-abiding decency. Most are in crime, and though their per-capita rate of criminality may be lower thanks to the cheapness of their drugs, the total volume of crime they produce may be quite large. Of course, society could decide to support all unemployable addicts on welfare, but that would mean that gains from lowered rates of crime would have to be offset by large increases in welfare budgets.

Proponents of legalization claim that the costs of having more addicts around would be largely if not entirely offset by having more money available with which to treat and care for them. The money would come from taxes levied on the sale of heroin and cocaine.

To obtain this fiscal dividend, however, legalization's supporters must first solve an economic dilemma. If they want to raise a lot of money to pay for welfare and treatment, the tax rate on the drugs will have to be quite high. Even if they themselves do not want a high rate, the politicians' love of "sin taxes" would probably guarantee that it would be high anyway. But the higher the tax, the higher the price of the drug, and the higher the price the greater the likelihood that addicts will turn to crime to find the money for it and that criminal organizations will be formed to sell tax-free drugs at below-market rates. If we managed to keep taxes (and thus prices) low, we would get that much less money to pay for welfare and treatment and more people could afford to become addicts. There may be an optimal tax rate for drugs that maximizes revenue while minimizing crime, bootlegging, and the recruitment of new addicts, but our experience with alcohol does not suggest that we know how to find it.

The Benefits of Illegality

The advocates of legalization find nothing to be said in favor of the current system except, possibly, that it keeps the number of addicts smaller than it would otherwise be. In fact, the benefits are more substantial than that.

First, treatment. All the talk about providing "treatment on demand" implies that there is a demand for treatment. That is not quite right. There are some drug-dependent people who genuinely want treatment and will remain in it if offered; they should receive it. But there are far more who want only short-term help after a bad crash; once stabilized and bathed, they are back on the street again, hustling. And even many of the addicts who enroll in a program honestly wanting help drop out after a short while when they discover that help takes time and commitment. Drug-dependent people have very short time horizons and a weak capacity for commitment. These two groups—those looking for a quick fix and those unable to stick with a long-term fix—are not easily helped. Even if we increase the number of treatment slots—as we should—we would have to do something to make treatment more effective.

One thing that can often make it more effective is compulsion. Douglas Anglin of the University of California at Los Angeles, in common with many other researchers, has found that the longer one stays in a treatment program, the better the chances of a reduction in drug dependency. But he, again like most other researchers, has found that drop-out rates are high. He has also found, however, that patients who enter treatment under legal compulsion stay in the program longer than those not subject to such pressure. His research on the California civil-commitment program, for example, found that heroin users involved with its required drug-testing program had over the long term a lower rate of heroin use than similar addicts who were free of such constraints. If for many addicts compulsion is a useful component of treatment, it is not clear how compulsion could be achieved in a society in which purchasing, possessing, and using the drug were legal. It could be managed, I suppose, but I would not want to have to answer the challenge from the American Civil Liberties Union that it is wrong to compel a person to undergo treatment for consuming a legal commodity.

Drug-Education Programs

Next, education. We are now investing substantially in drug-education programs in the schools. Though we do not yet know for certain what will work, there are some promising leads. But I wonder how credible such programs would be if they were aimed at dissuading children from doing something perfectly legal. We could, of course, treat drug education like smoking education: inhaling crack and inhaling tobacco are both legal, but you should not do it because it is bad for you. That tobacco is bad for you is easily shown; the Surgeon General has seen to that. But what do we say about crack? It is pleasurable, but devoting yourself to so much pleasure is not a good idea (though perfectly legal)? Unlike tobacco, cocaine will not give you cancer or emphysema, but it will lead you to neglect your duties to family, job, and neighborhood? Everybody is doing cocaine, but you should not?

Again, it might be possible under a legalized regime to have effective drug-prevention programs, but their effectiveness would depend heavily, I think, on first having decided that cocaine use, like tobacco use, is purely a matter of practical consequences; no fundamental moral significance attaches to either. But if we believe—as I do—that dependency on certain mind-altering drugs *is* a moral issue and that their illegality rests in part on their immorality, then legalizing them undercuts, if it does not eliminate altogether, the moral message.

"I wonder how credible [drug-education] programs would be if they were aimed at dissuading children from doing something perfectly legal."

That message is at the root of the distinction we now make between nicotine and cocaine. Both are highly addictive; both have harmful physical effects. But we treat the two drugs differently, not simply because nicotine is so widely used as to be beyond the reach of effective prohibition, but because its use does not destroy the user's essential humanity. Tobacco shortens one's life, cocaine debases it. Nicotine alters one's habits, cocaine alters one's soul. The heavy use of crack, unlike the heavy use of tobacco, corrodes those natural sentiments of sympathy and duty that constitute our human nature and make possible our social life. To say, as does Nadelmann, that distinguishing morally between tobacco and cocaine is "little more than a transient prejudice" is close to saying that morality itself is but a prejudice.

Now we have arrived where many arguments about legalizing drugs begin: is there any reason to treat heroin and cocaine differently from the way we treat alcohol?

There is no easy answer to that question because, as with so many human problems, one cannot decide simply on the basis either of moral principles or of individual consequences; one has to temper any policy by a common-sense judgment of what is possible. Alcohol, like heroin, cocaine, PCP, and marijuana, is a drug—that is, a mood-altering substance—and consumed to excess it certainly has harmful consequences: auto accidents, barroom fights, bedroom shootings. It is also, for some people, addictive. We cannot confidently compare the addictive powers of these drugs, but the best evidence suggests that crack and heroin are much more addictive than alcohol.

"The government cannot legislate away the addictive tendencies in all of us. . . . But it can cope with harms when the harms are still manageable."

Many people, Nadelmann included, argue that since the health and financial costs of alcohol abuse are so much higher than those of cocaine or heroin abuse, it is hypocritical folly to devote our efforts to preventing cocaine or drug use. But as Mark Kleiman of Harvard has pointed out, this comparison is quite misleading. What Nadelmann is doing is showing that a *legalized* drug (alcohol) produces greater social harm than *illegal* ones (cocaine and heroin). But of course. Suppose that in the 1920's we had made heroin and cocaine legal and alcohol illegal. Can anyone doubt that Nadelmann would now be writing that it is folly to continue our ban on alcohol because cocaine and heroin are so much more harmful?

And let there be no doubt about it—widespread heroin and cocaine use are associated with all manner of ills. Thomas Bewley found that the mortality rate of British heroin addicts in 1968 was 28 times as high as the death rate of the same age group of non-addicts, even though in England at the time an addict could obtain free or low-cost heroin and clean needles from British clinics. Perform the following mental experiment: suppose we legalized heroin and cocaine in this country. In what proportion of auto fatalities would the state police report that the driver was nodding off on heroin or recklessly driving on a coke high? In what proportion of spouse-assault and child-abuse cases would the local police report that crack was involved? In what proportion of industrial accidents would safety investigators report that the forklift or drill-press operator was in a drug-induced stupor or frenzy? We do not know exactly what the proportion would be, but anyone who asserts that it would not be much higher than it is now would have to believe that these drugs have little appeal except when they are illegal. And that is nonsense.

Social Harm

An advocate of legalization might concede that social harm—perhaps harm equivalent to that already produced by alcohol—would follow from making cocaine and heroin generally available. But at least, he might add, we would have the problem "out in the open" where it could be treated as a matter of "public health." That is well and good, *if* we knew how to treat—that is, cure—heroin and cocaine abuse. But we do not know how to do it for all the people who would need such help. We are having only limited success in coping with chronic alcoholics. Addictive behavior is immensely difficult to change, and the best methods for changing it—living in drug-free therapeutic communities, becoming faithful members of Alcoholics Anonymous or Narcotics Anonymous— require great personal commitment, a quality that is, alas, in short supply among the very persons—young people, disadvantaged people—who are often most at risk for addiction.

Suppose that today we had, not 15 million alcohol abusers, but half a million. Suppose that we already knew what we have learned from our long experience with the widespread use of alcohol. Would we make whiskey legal? I do not know, but I suspect there would be a lively debate. The Surgeon General would remind us of the risks alcohol poses to pregnant women. The National Highway Traffic Safety Administration would point to the likelihood of more highway fatalities caused by drunk drivers. The Food and Drug Administration might find that there is a nontrivial increase in cancer associated with alcohol consumption. At the same time the police would report great difficulty in keeping illegal whiskey out of our cities, officers being corrupted by bootleggers, and alcohol addicts often resorting to crime to feed their habit. Libertarians, for their part, would argue that every citizen has a right to drink anything he wishes and that drinking is, in any event, a "victimless crime."

However the debate might turn out, the central fact would be that the problem was still, at that point, a small one. The government cannot legislate away the addictive tendencies in all of us, nor can it remove completely even the most dangerous addictive substances. But it can cope with harms when the harms are still manageable.

One advantage of containing a problem while it is still containable is that it buys time for science to learn more about it and perhaps to discover a cure. Almost unnoticed in the current debate over legalizing drugs is that basic science has made rapid strides in identifying the underlying neurological processes involved in some forms of addiction. Stimulants such as cocaine and amphetamines alter the way certain brain cells communicate with one another. That alteration is complex and not entirely understood, but in simplified form it involves modifying the way in which a neurotransmitter called dopamine sends signals from one cell to another.

When dopamine crosses the synapse between two cells, it is in effect carrying a message from the first cell to activate the second one. In certain parts of the brain that message is experienced as pleasure. After the message is delivered, the dopamine returns to the first cell. Cocaine apparently blocks this return, or "reuptake," so that the excited cell and others nearby continue to send pleasure messages. When the exaggerated high produced by cocaine-influenced dopamine finally ends, the brain cells may (in ways that are still a matter of dispute) suffer from an extreme lack of dopamine, thereby making the individual unable to experience any pleasure at all. This would explain why cocaine users often feel so depressed after enjoying the drug. Stimulants may also affect the way in which other neurotransmitters, such as serotonin and noradrenaline, operate.

"If . . . the legalizers prevail anyway, then we will have consigned millions of people, hundreds of thousands of infants, and hundreds of neighborhoods to a life of oblivion and disease."

Whatever the exact mechanism may be, once it is identified it becomes possible to use drugs to block either the effect of cocaine or its tendency to produce dependency. There have already been experiments using desipramine, imipramine, bromocriptine, carbamazepine, and other chemicals. There are some promising results.

Tragically, we spend very little on such research, and the agencies funding it have not in the past occupied very influential or visible posts in the federal bureaucracy. If there is one aspect of the "war on drugs" metaphor that I dislike, it is its tendency to focus attention almost exclusively on the troops in the trenches, whether engaged in enforcement or treatment, and away from the research-and-development efforts back on the home front where the war may ultimately be decided.

I believe that the prospects of scientists in controlling addiction will be strongly influenced by the size and character of the problem they face. If the problem is a few hundred thousand chronic, high-dose users of an illegal product, the chances of making a difference at a reasonable cost will be much greater than if the problem is a few million chronic users of legal substances. Once a drug is legal, not only will its use increase but many of those who then use it will prefer the drug to the treatment: they will want the pleasure, whatever the cost to themselves or their families, and they will resist—probably successfully—any effort to wean them away from experiencing the high that comes from inhaling a legal substance.

Society After Legalization

No one can know what our society would be like if we changed the law to make access to cocaine, heroin, and PCP easier. I believe, for reasons given, that the result would be a sharp increase in use, a more widespread degradation of the human personality, and a greater rate of accidents and violence.

I may be wrong. If I am, then we will needlessly have incurred heavy costs in law enforcement and some forms of criminality. But if I am right, and the legalizers prevail anyway, then we will have consigned millions of people, hundreds of thousands of infants, and hundreds of neighborhoods to a life of oblivion and disease. To the lives and families destroyed by alcohol we will have added countless more destroyed by cocaine, heroin, PCP, and whatever else a basement scientist can invent.

Human character is formed by society; indeed, human character is inconceivable without society, and good character is less likely in a bad society. Will we, in the name of an abstract doctrine of radical individualism, and with the false comfort of suspect predictions, decide to take the chance that somehow individual decency can survive amid a more general level of degradation?

I think not. The American people are too wise for that, whatever the academic essayists and cocktail-party pundits may say. But if Americans today are less wise than I suppose, then Americans at some future time will look back on us now and wonder, what kind of people were they that they could have done such a thing?

James Q. Wilson is Collins professor of management and public policy at the University of California at Los Angeles. He is the author of Thinking About Crime *and* Bureaucracy.

The U.S. Military Should Be Used to Fight Drug Trafficking

Dick Cheney

Editor's note: This viewpoint is adapted from a news briefing at the Pentagon on September 18, 1989. At the news briefing Cheney presented a prepared statement and then answered questions from a group of assembled reporters.

The Department of Defense is an enthusiastic participant in the nation's drug control effort and can make a substantial contribution if its assets are used intelligently and efficiently. For the past several years, the Department of Defense has been embarked on a program to counter the problem of illegal drugs. Since taking on that mission, we've committed over 72,000 flying hours and nearly 7,000 ship days in support of the anti-drug effort. We established Joint Task Force Four in the Caribbean and Joint Task Force Five in the Pacific to help stem the flow of drugs from the south and the west. We are also expanding the coverage of radar at our borders.

One main foreign policy goal of this administration and this president is to reduce the flow of illegal drugs into the United States and if possible, to eliminate it. The president recently issued his national drug control strategy. I want to explain in greater detail the role of the Department of Defense in that strategy.

Our specific mission is to protect national security. There can be no doubt that international trafficking in drugs is a national security problem for the United States. Therefore, detecting and countering the production and trafficking of illegal drugs is a high-priority, national security mission of the Department of Defense.

Under the leadership of President George Bush, there is now recognition that the drug problem is not just for the department alone to fight. He knows that the only way to deal with it is to combine interdiction with treatment, education, prevention and enhanced

law enforcement. We also need to make clear that the Defense Department is not a law enforcement agency. We do not enforce domestic criminal laws, nor can we solve society's demand problems. But there is much that we can do without usurping the police role.

We will work on the drug program at every phase—at the source, in the delivery pipeline and in support of federal, state and local law enforcement agencies. In countries where the plants are grown and the raw materials are converted into drugs, we can provide economic and security assistance, training and operational support for host country forces and assistance to law enforcement agencies in stopping the export of drugs.

We will work hard to stop the delivery of drugs on their way to the United States and at our borders and ports of entry. Deploying appropriate elements of the armed forces with the primary mission of cutting off the flow of drugs should help reduce the flow of drugs into the country over time. At the very least, it will immediately complicate the challenge of getting illegal drugs into America and increase the cost and risk of drug smuggling.

Law Enforcement

At home, we will help law enforcement agencies and the National Guard with training, reconnaissance, planning and logistics. We will step up efforts to stop drug use by DoD personnel, a program that has reduced drug abuse by more than 80 percent in the last eight years.

The president has directed the department to act as the lead agency in providing better communications and intelligence cooperation among agencies of the federal government in fighting the drug problem.

Therefore, I have sent a message to all the commanders in chief of the unified and specified commands informing them that reducing the flow of drugs into the United States is a high-priority, national security mission. My message directs these

Dick Cheney, "DoD and Its Role in the War Against Drugs," *Defense 89,* November/December 1989.

commanders to plan how they intend to carry out that mission in their particular areas of responsibility.

I believe that our military forces have the capability to make a substantial contribution in the area of successful drug interdiction, and I am asking them to make the necessary preparations to carry out that responsibility. . . .

"Reducing the flow of drugs into the United States is a high-priority, national security mission."

I'm asking the Atlantic Command to prepare a plan for a substantial Caribbean counternarcotics task force, with appropriate planes and ships to help reduce the flow of drugs from Latin America.

I am asking Forces Command for a plan to deploy appropriate forces to complement and support the counternarcotics work of U.S. law enforcement agencies and cooperating foreign governments. That effort will focus especially on the southern border with Mexico.

I am asking the North American Aerospace Defense Command to plan to increase detecting and monitoring of illegal drug traffic to the United States.

I've also asked Southern and Pacific commands to plan to combat the production and trafficking of illegal drugs in conjunction with cooperating host countries in their areas of responsibility.

I've also asked DoD civilian and military leaders to immediately find ways to better support the president's national drug strategy, including ways to increase the effectiveness of host country forces. I've proposed several steps consistent with national policy, available resources and our national values and law. These actions include studying the possibility of installing mobile radars in countries where drugs are grown and processed; exploring the opportunities to train counternarcotics forces of cooperating foreign countries, including greater use of mobile training teams; arranging to detail military personnel to federal law enforcement agencies to provide liaison, help train and do planning as appropriate; continuing and expanding where appropriate our support of the counternarcotics effort of the National Guard as it provides support for the states; and reviewing the potential for the department to provide temporary overflow facilities when federal, state or local authorities need more jail and prison space.

Questions and Answers

The Department of Defense is an enthusiastic participant in the nation's drug control effort. We have significant resources at our disposal. We can make a substantial contribution to our national effort if we use our assets intelligently and efficiently. This

guidance is intended to make that happen.

Q. Many of the complaints in the building center on the fact that the military is being asked to do more with less. How can you respond to that?

A. The fact of the matter is the president has made it clear this is an important priority for him; I've made it clear that it's an important priority for me; Congress has made it clear that it feels very strongly that we need to be more actively involved in the counternarcotics effort. There is money being added to our budget for that purpose.

There is no question this involves some tradeoffs and choices. We'll have a much better feel for exactly what kind of tradeoffs we're talking about once we see the detailed plans coming in from the commanders in chief. But, as in all of our other missions, the department has to make choices. We cannot do everything we would like to do all of the time. We have limited resources. The point of the directive that I've issued is to make it clear to everyone in DoD—civilian and military alike—that this is a high-priority, national security mission for us. It, therefore, deserves a greater allocation of resources in terms of time and energy and effort and perhaps equipment and troops and personnel than has been true in the past.

Military Costs

Q. Have you put a cost on this, a price for what it's going to cost? And how will this affect the military's ability to do its other job, providing for the national defense of the country?

A. First of all, we don't have a specific cost figure at this point.

With respect to our ability to perform our other missions, I don't see this as in any way in conflict with our basic mission of defending the country. When you have reached a point where you have the kinds of problems that we see today in our society as a result of illegal narcotics trafficking; . . . when you have the government of a friendly country, Colombia, seriously threatened by the cartel, financed in this case by billions of dollars provided by Americans who use drugs illegally, I think you've got a serious national security problem.

Again, you have to make some tradeoffs. It may be, for example, that we'll find deploying resources and assets in this area, whether it's in the Caribbean or perhaps in assisting law enforcement agencies along the southern border, means those units will not be available for other purposes, probably training and exercises.

But there are some benefits. For example, if you go to the North American Aerospace Defense Command, they like the idea of having the role of being actively involved in the interdiction effort as it relates to illegal air traffic coming into the United States. It gives them a real target to work, and the same skills they require in their normal, basic, national security assignment are very appropriate in this regard. You can't make a clear-cut choice. I cannot say, though, that this will not mean that it's more difficult for us to do some of our other things. Our basic mission is still to defend the country. That will continue, and this is an added responsibility.

Q. Will it change the operations tempo in the Med, for instance, in the Mid-East or in other parts of the world?

A. I doubt it. We're talking about basically using resources and assets that are available here in the United States.

Q. It's been DoD policy to cooperate in interdiction missions and so forth if it coincided with training. Is that still going to be the policy, or are you going to go beyond training?

A. I think we'll go beyond training.

Q. How quickly do you expect to see results from this program, and how will you measure success?

A. I guess I would like to come back to the proposition that there is no quick, easy answer to the drug problem. It has been with us for a long time, and it's gotten much worse lately. If we're going to be successful, it will be because we have a broad-gauged strategy that addresses the production in the host countries, the problem of transiting the drugs into the United States and then the problem of consumption within the United States itself. We are not responsible for all of those phases, but we have contributions we can make in each one of them.

The Department of Defense ought to be judged in terms of its ability to cooperate in the broad-gauged strategy the president has laid out for us. It's going to take years and the cooperation of millions of Americans. It's going to take the best efforts of law enforcement agencies and the military and educational facilities and rehabilitation centers and all the other elements in our society that can contribute to this effort. And it's going to take a fundamental change in public attitude.

"There have been requests that we are meeting in Colombia and elsewhere for training and operational assistance in terms of communication and intelligence."

Q. Are you for or against shooting down aircraft that fail to heed warnings to land and are suspected of carrying drugs? And what more would you have our active duty military doing on the ground in countries that ask for our help? In other words, where would you draw the fire break between advising and participating?

A. We have no authority to shoot down aircraft coming into the United States. We haven't sought such authority, and I think you have to be very careful about proceeding on that basis. Obviously, the first time you made a mistake you would have severe problems. There are various and sundry regulatory schemes that can make it easier for us to do our mission, but the idea we would go out and willy-nilly shoot down unidentified aircraft strikes me as not a very good one.

No Troops Involved

With respect to drawing the line in terms of U.S. military personnel on the ground in foreign countries, I think there's a very clear line out there right now. There has been no request from any host country, any Latin American country, for example, for the active use of American combat personnel. There have been requests that we are meeting in Colombia and elsewhere for training and operational assistance in terms of communication and intelligence.

We're doing that. The president's policy is very clear on this point, though. U.S. military personnel are not to accompany host country troops on operations. We aren't flying their helicopters for them. We are not traveling with their units as advisers into the field when they're out on operational assignments. It's an appropriate division of responsibility. This effort is going to be successful only if the host countries, the producing countries, aggressively address the problems in their own societies that lead them to produce illicit drugs for the U.S. market.

Q. The president wants to increase funds for the interdiction effort $313 million for fiscal 1990. I realize that you shied away from giving even a ballpark figure, but is that the quantity generally of funds available? Or are you talking about wholesale diversion of funds from what was thought to be other military purposes into this effort to complement them?

A. It's very difficult for me to put a specific dollar figure on it. The relative level of effort compared to what has been done in the past will be significantly greater.

Q. Your plan calls for fairly heavy interdiction. The president's drug plan really does not. There's not much extra spending for interdiction on the grounds, apparently, that it hasn't been that effective in the past. In view of that, why this emphasis?

A. This is not exclusively an interdiction package.

I think the impression is that in years past we've had policies that dealt only with interdiction. We didn't deal with the demand side in the United States, and we didn't have any really successful cooperative programs overseas. Now, thanks in part to the courage of President Virgilio Barco in Colombia, for example, you've got a very aggressive program under way. The United States and this department are moving very, very aggressively to support that effort. . . .

I think with respect to interdiction that we can help. It's not the sole solution to the problem. I hope that our interdiction efforts will be more successful in the future because we've got more aggressive efforts under way in host countries and a greater willingness for them to cooperate with our efforts. I think they're, frankly, probably more interested in cooperating now because it appears finally that the United States is beginning to address the demand side at home.

None of those areas, none of the policies that deal with only one of those areas, is going to solve the problem. By the same token, you're not going to solve the problem if you ignore any one of them.

The Interdiction Role

The interdiction role is most appropriate for the department and has been assigned by the president, and by the Congress. Specific statutory language says the Department of Defense will be the lead agency in performing the interdiction mission. That's the mandate of the Congress of the United States. I've got an obligation to carry it out.

Q. Have the Andean countries been more lenient as far as the role U.S. special forces can play in their territories?

A. What's required any time you have one of these relationships develop is a willingness on the part of the host country to have a U.S. military presence in the form of training teams, for example. Those individuals and units then perform missions under guidance established by me at the direction of the president. That guidance is clear and specifically provides that they will not accompany the host country units on operational missions. That is in the national security defense directive that the president signed out with respect to our aid to the Andean nations, and that is the policy.

Q. Mr. Secretary, you said earlier that the Department of Defense is an enthusiastic participant in the drug enforcement program. Is that your evaluation or is that the expression from your commanders who have been reluctant in the past to get the armed forces into this?

A. In any department this large, you're going to find a wide variety of opinions on any given issue. There has been, though, this constantly repeated refrain I've seen in the press that the military is reluctant to get involved in the war against drugs.

I haven't found that to be the case. In fact, my experience has been that when you provide firm guidance as to what our policy and objectives are, then the response of our military leadership is very affirmative in figuring out how to get on with the job in the best way possible.

Senior military personnel, members of the Joint Chiefs and Joint Staff have been consulted extensively as we've pulled together specific guidance and direction. They will continue to be heavily involved in the process. I am sure that just as you can find differences among the civilians in the department, you can find differences among the military in the department about how we should proceed and how actively we ought to be involved.

Q. Approximately how many armed forces personnel will be sent to the Andean countries to implement the strategy? And have you suggested any kind of a cap on that?

A. We haven't suggested any kind of a cap. You deal with individual responses that come in terms of the kind of assistance that needs to be provided. There is no hard and fast number on it. The Southern Command basically coordinates these kinds of requests. If you add up all of Latin America together—not just the three Andean countries that are the most directly involved—we're talking about a few hundred people that at any given time are involved in these kinds of activities. There is a desire to be as helpful as possible. We're not trying to keep a secret from anybody. We have an active program of support for the host countries in terms of their efforts to stamp out the illegal drug trade. I hope we'll be successful in that effort.

"We just have to do everything we can to make certain that our people have the kind of protection they deserve if we're going to ask them to undertake these kinds of missions."

With respect to the security of our personnel involved in this mission, obviously there is some risk. Sending military personnel into Latin America to support the efforts of the host countries to stamp out the drug trade and in effect thwart the efforts of the cartel is a dangerous business. I hope none of our people is hurt in the process, but I can't guarantee it.

Our personnel go into the area with rules of engagement that allow them to defend themselves. The basic responsibility for providing security for them in those host countries, like Colombia, rests with the local military. We work as aggressively as we can with them to see that adequate precautions are taken.

I come back to the proposition that this can be a risk mission given the nature of our adversaries, and we just have to do everything we can to make certain that our people have the kind of protection they deserve if we're going to ask them to undertake these kinds of missions.

Dick Cheney became the Secretary of Defense in May 1989. From 1978 to 1989, he was a member of Congress representing Wyoming. Cheney was previously an official in the administrations of Richard Nixon and Gerald Ford.

The U.S. Military Should Not Be Used to Fight Drug Trafficking

Ted Galen Carpenter and R. Channing Rouse

Two events in December 1989 indicate that the Bush administration is dramatically escalating the war on drugs in Latin America and intends to have the U.S. military play an extensive role in that effort. The first was the invasion of Panama, which was at least partially motivated by anger at the Noriega regime's alleged drug-trafficking activities. The second was a White House decision to station an aircraft carrier battle group in the waters off Colombia to intercept drug shipments. Both episodes suggest that a hemispheric drug war may become the successor to the cold war—with potentially calamitous consequences for both the United States and its Latin American neighbors.

Enlisting the military in the crusade against drugs is the logical outcome of the hysteria that has been generated in the United States, and it is a confession that all previous methods of fighting drugs have failed. Since the beginning of the 1970s when President Richard M. Nixon first proclaimed America's war on drugs, Washington has employed a variety of strategies in that struggle. At various times it has emphasized vigorous interdiction efforts, directing the Customs Service and the Coast Guard to prevent the flow of illicit drugs into the country. On other occasions, it has waged well-publicized campaigns against domestic drug producers, especially marijuana growers. It has encouraged and helped fund enhanced state and local law enforcement efforts to arrest and imprison street pushers. In recent years it has revived the strategy (largely abandoned in the mid- and late 1970s) of attempting to intimidate casual users. The advocacy of widespread drug testing and mandatory fines and jail terms for casual users, under the theory of "zero tolerance," is the latest manifestation of that approach.

Ted Galen Carpenter and R. Channing Rouse, "Perilous Panacea: The Military in the Drug War," The Cato Institute *Policy Analysis*, February 15, 1990. Reprinted with permission.

In addition to its domestic campaigns, Washington has sought to curtail the supply of drugs at the source. Most of that effort throughout the 1980s was directed at the Andean countries of South America, where the bulk of the cocaine and marijuana that comes into the United States originates. Washington has pursued its supply-side strategy in diverse ways. It has trained and equipped indigenous anti-drug police and paramilitary forces, assigned agents of the Drug Enforcement Administration to assist the governments of drug-producing countries, and funded crop substitution programs in an attempt to persuade Andean peasants to switch from drug crops to legal alternatives.

Those multifaceted initiatives have had one thing in common: they have had no discernible beneficial effect on the "drug problem" in the United States. Despite an increase of nearly 400 percent in federal spending on anti-drug efforts during the 1980s—from $1.2 billion in 1981 to more than $5.7 billion in 1989—usage is actually higher now than it was at the beginning of the decade (although it has declined slightly since 1985). Moreover, the bulk of what little decline has taken place in the last half of the 1980s has occurred among casual marijuana users—certainly the least serious component of the drug problem. Most troubling of all, the violence associated with the black market in drugs has continued to escalate.

As proponents of the war on drugs have seen all of their strategies fail, they have begun to exhibit intense frustration. That frustration is translated into a desperate search for "tougher" measures that will, somehow, achieve the victory that has thus far proven so elusive.

The Military as a Panacea

It is indicative of the desperation of drug war partisans that their hopes now revolve around an expanded role for the military. The belief that the military can succeed where civilian agencies have failed has gradually but inexorably gained popularity. As early as 1981 Congress passed legislation authorizing the president to employ the military in the drug war, albeit in a limited fashion, by amending the Posse Comitatus Act of 1878, which prohibited the use of military personnel to enforce civilian laws. In 1981 it appeared that most members of Congress were interested primarily in using troops to bolster the interdiction effort along the coasts and the U.S.-Mexican border.

Some drug war enthusiasts soon began to advocate an even wider role for the military. In May 1984, for example, Sen. Paula Hawkins (R-Fla.) proposed sending American troops to South America; she urged President Ronald Reagan to "offer whatever resources are necessary including U.S. military personnel to the government of Colombia in their war on illegal drugs." A few years later, a *Washington Post* staff writer suggested deploying the National Guard on the streets of the nation's capital to stem the drug trade and the growing violence associated with it—an idea that was endorsed by some members of the city council.

Until recently, however, most Americans seemed wary about involving the military in the domestic phase of the war on drugs. Critics pointed out that military forces are trained to seek out and destroy an enemy in wartime; they are not trained in the nuances of civilian law enforcement, much less the subtleties of constitutional law. Equally important, uniformed leaders and most civilian officials in the Department of Defense resisted attempts to conscript their institution because they believed that it would divert attention and resources from the military's primary mission—protecting the United States from the Soviet Union and other foreign enemies. As cold war tensions have eased as a result of Mikhail Gorbachev's more conciliatory foreign policy and internal reforms, however, the credibility of that justification for declining to enlist in the war on drugs has diminished.

"One of the weapons that appeals to U.S. officials is the threat of 'decertification.'"

A crucial step in involving the military in the anti-drug effort came in April 1986 when President Reagan signed a National Security Decision Directive (NSDD) declaring drug trafficking a threat to the security of the United States. From that point on, supporters of the drug war redoubled their calls for the military to play an expanded role. . . .

In the summer of 1986 the United States dispatched six high-performance Black Hawk helicopters and 160 troops to Bolivia to assist the government of that country in its attempt to eradicate a network of cocaine-processing laboratories. American forces

participated in the eradication effort—Operation Blast Furnace—for more than four months before they were withdrawn. It should be noted that their departure was largely the result of intense opposition from important segments of the Bolivian populace, not of opposition at home.

Although administration spokesmen denied that Operation Blast Furnace was meant to be the prototype for similar measures elsewhere in Latin America, reports circulated that the administration had approached the governments of Colombia, Ecuador, and Peru about using U.S. troops. It is striking that the Bush administration's Andean Initiative of the summer of 1989 explicitly included a role for the U.S. military in two of those countries. It was clear that some drug war enthusiasts saw Operation Blast Furnace as the long-awaited first step toward greater use of the military in the campaign against narcotics. . . .

Coercing the Latin Americans

The Bush administration's plans to have the U.S. military participate in drug eradication efforts in Latin America are unfortunate. To be sure, the administration insists that there are no current plans to use American forces in a combat capacity. But both Bush and Secretary of Defense Richard Cheney have pointedly refused to rule out an eventual combat role. Their refusal understandably disturbs Americans who recall that the massive Vietnam intervention also began with the shipment of hardware and the dispatch of small numbers of military advisers. Nor can they take much comfort from the ambiguous phrasing of Bush's pledge of military aid to the Andean countries:

> Our message to the drug cartels is this: The rules have changed. We will help any government that wants our help. When requested, we will for the first time make available the appropriate resources of America's military forces.

In particular, one might ask what is meant by "appropriate resources?"

Administration leaders insist that the United States will provide assistance only on the request of the host governments, implying that this is another limitation on America's military involvement. But those who are familiar with Washington's ability throughout the cold war to pressure small client nations into "requesting" assistance will be skeptical about the effectiveness of that caveat. The president and Congress have already displayed a willingness to use coercive measures to "encourage" nations that produce or export drugs to accede to U.S. demands. One of the weapons that appeals to U.S. officials is the threat of "decertification." The 1986 Anti-Drug Abuse Act made U.S. economic and military assistance, the granting or continuation of most-favored-nation trade status, and U.S. support for World Bank loans contingent on a government's "certified cooperation" with the United States in drug eradication efforts. The president's

1989 national drug control strategy report affirmed that "in bilateral relationships with illegal drug producing and transit countries," the United States "must emphasize the requirement for cooperation with our anti-drug efforts . . . we must be prepared to decertify countries that willfully permit drug traffickers to continue operations within their national territory." With the United States possessing such vital leverage, many Latin American nations would be hard pressed to decline U.S. "offers" of military assistance in the war on drugs.

Indeed, one must question whether, in any case, requests for military aid from drug-producing countries would be genuine or merely made in acquiescence to a policy demanded by Washington. For example, more than two months before the Colombian government requested emergency military aid, the Bush administration had signaled its intent to provide increased levels of military as well as economic aid to the Andean countries to combat drug trafficking. In the immediate aftermath of the Luis Carlos Galán assassination, Attorney General Richard Thornburgh emphasized that the United States would seriously consider sending troops if the Colombian government requested it to do so. Two weeks later White House Chief of Staff John Sununu stated that the administration would probably approve direct U.S. military involvement if Bogota reversed its position and requested such assistance.

Even the most obtuse officials in Bogota could scarcely have failed to pick up such repeated hints. The Bush administration's none-too-subtle pressure placed the government of Virgilio Barco in a difficult position. Barco responded by asking the United States for military equipment and, as an apparent concession to Washington, a limited number of "advisers" while placating nationalist feelings in his own country by reiterating that there was no need for U.S. combat forces. By pressuring the Andean governments to permit even a limited U.S. military role in the campaign against drug trafficking, the Bush administration is ignoring the long-standing antipathy of Latin American *populations* to a U.S. troop presence in their countries. Such a visible display of power is likely to reawaken memories of "Yankee imperialism"—memories that are not slumbering too soundly to begin with. . . .

Incentives for the Military

The incentives for the military to join the war on drugs have shifted markedly. As the cold war winds down, members of the national security bureaucracy, those who profit from a large military establishment, and cheerleaders for "inspiring" national crusades all appear to see the drug war as a useful substitute. Using the military to combat drug trafficking both in the United States and in other countries creates a justification (or more accurately a pretext) for maintaining bloated military spending and personnel levels.

A striking correlation appears to exist between the ebbing of the cold war and the military's willingness to participate in the drug war. The Pentagon now faces the prospect of sizable losses in personnel and cherished weapons systems, as well as prestige and power, unless it has an alternative mission. Retired Army chief of staff General Edward Meyer, for example, concedes that "the end of the cold war makes it inevitable that the Army will shrink far below the 772,000 on duty today." The drug war is a plausible alternative mission. To at least a limited extent, a heightened role in attacking Latin American drug trafficking can fill a void—the drug lords can replace the Soviet evil empire as the "necessary enemy."

"A striking correlation appears to exist between the ebbing of the cold war and the military's willingness to participate in the drug war."

One sign of a change of attitude among members of the national security bureaucracy is that outright opposition to military involvement in the drug war has been largely replaced by emphasis on increased funding as a condition for involvement. Pentagon spokesman Dan Howard exemplified that position when he stated, "We're prepared to do more. But that requires resources." An analysis by the Joint Chiefs of Staff indicated that $14 billion is needed to purchase 66 additional surveillance aircraft (AWACS) and that $6.2 billion is needed for effective operation of border patrol planes and ships.

Another sign of changing sentiment is the attitude of Secretary of Defense Cheney. In marked contrast to his predecessors, he is receptive to the idea of greater military participation in the drug war. He quickly implemented Bush's NSDD in September 1989 by establishing new guidelines for an expanded role. The purpose of his directive, Cheney stressed, was "to make clear to everyone in the Department that this is a high national security mission for us, and therefore it deserves greater allocation of resources in terms of time and energy and perhaps equipment and troops and personnel than has been true in the past."

Shortly thereafter, Admiral William Crowe, the departing chairman of the Joint Chiefs of Staff, delivered forceful farewell comments in which he emphasized the military's willingness to do battle against the new threat to national security and asserted that the American people would have to give up some of their liberties if the nation was to win the war on drugs. The willingness of Crowe, generally regarded as the most politically astute JCS member in many years, to explicitly embrace the drug war signaled that the officer corps' resistance to a high-profile role for the military in that struggle was rapidly dissipating.

The accelerating pace of involvement in the Andean region, as well as a probable role in trying to seal the southern U.S. border, gives the Pentagon an ideal justification for retaining at least some of the troops that are likely to be withdrawn from Central Europe and other cold war frontiers. Already, the Bush administration's drug strategy calls for an "unspecified number of military advisers" and troops to train Latin American authorities and law enforcement personnel, and a senior administration official stated that "several hundred" U.S. personnel may be deployed to Peru, Bolivia, and Colombia. Moreover, there is no assurance that U.S. involvement will be confined to those levels.

> *"The war on drugs in Latin America provides an alternate justification for maintaining an extensive U.S. capability for low-intensity warfare."*

Participation in the Andean Initiative also has opened a way for the military and its defense industry allies to justify the procurement of questionable weapons systems. Defense consultant Dov Zakheim, a former deputy undersecretary of defense, touts the V-22 Osprey—a hybrid fixed-wing aircraft and helicopter used to transport troops—as an "innovative response" to demands for military operations "in scenarios where precise measurement of benefits is impossible." Zakheim leaves little doubt about the scenario he has in mind. He notes that the danger of a NATO [North Atlantic Treaty Organization]-Warsaw Pact war is increasingly remote and that the Osprey would make little sense in that setting in any case. Zakheim observes, however, that "the United States finds itself involved in an unanticipated conflict, a drug war that threatens to consume ever greater defense resources for programs whose effectiveness cannot be measured in the old, conventional ways." Coincidentally, the Osprey had been earmarked for extinction by economy-minded officials in the Bush administration, in spite of feverish lobbying on the part of the Marine Corps, and it is ominous that Congress refused to delete it from the military budget. As the military role in fighting drug trafficking expands, requests for superfluous personnel and weapons systems may prevail, despite the easing of cold war tensions.

The drug war offers another, more subtle, potential benefit to the national security bureaucracy. During the latter stages of the cold war, U.S. military doctrine emphasized the need to engage and prevail in low-intensity conflicts. As the Soviet Union withdraws its ground troops from many Third World countries—such as Afghanistan—the U.S. military is hard pressed to make a compelling argument that intervention is needed to counter a Soviet threat. Yet Washington considers Fidel Castro, Daniel Ortega, and other "independent" communist leaders—as well as Libya and other noncommunist terrorist states—a continuing menace to U.S. security, however difficult it might be to convince the American people of that proposition.

The war on drugs in Latin America provides an alternate justification for maintaining an extensive U.S. capability for low-intensity warfare. Operation Blast Furnace proved to be an ideal exercise for honing such skills. The troop deployments connected with the Andean Initiative give the United States an ongoing military presence in a region where low-intensity conflicts are occurring and are likely to continue to occur. By providing technical expertise and equipment to Latin American militaries U.S. officials are able to further yet another objective—strengthening allied forces that might be needed in low-intensity conflicts. That motive may have been the reason so much of the Andean Initiative assistance was directed to the military establishments in the recipient countries even though the police forces have had the primary responsibility for antidrug efforts.

William von Raab, customs commissioner under the Reagan administration, has been a prolific source of proposals for escalating the war on drugs. For example, he ordered his agency to confiscate the passports of U.S. citizens accused of attempting to bring drugs into the country—a move that was countermanded by the State Department. On another occasion, he even suggested giving authority to military and law enforcement agencies to shoot down aircraft *suspected* of carrying drugs. The Reagan Justice Department—not generally considered an ardent defender of civil liberties—considered that proposal an "absolutely crazy" idea.

It is a measure of how far the drug war hysteria has escalated that Sen. Mitch McConnell (R-Ky.) introduced von Raab's "crazy" idea as an amendment to the FY [Fiscal Year] 1990 military spending bill. Moreover, over the vehement objections of Sam Nunn and most other members of the Armed Services Committee, the Senate passed the McConnell amendment. That action was taken despite a GAO [General Accounting Office] study that underscored the danger of victimizing innocent parties. The GAO study found that of the 337 suspected drug-smuggling planes that the Customs Service forced to land over two years, only 134 had drugs on board.

Eroding Civil Liberties

Such erosions of constitutional liberties are a direct product of viewing the drug problem as a "war." Those who use that analogy have created a war hysteria that has potentially calamitous consequences.

The extent of that hysteria can be gauged by the results of a *Washington Post/ABC News* poll taken immediately after Bush's address to the nation in early September 1989. The survey discovered that

• 62 percent of respondents were willing to give up "a few" freedoms in order to curb drug use;

• 67 percent would allow police to stop cars at random to search for drugs;

• 52 percent would allow the police to search without court order the homes of people suspected of selling drugs, even if some homes were searched by mistake;

• 71 percent would make it against the law to show the use of illegal drugs in the movies; and

• 74 percent endorsed Bush's plan to send military advisers to Colombia.

"Contrary to the belief of the drug war enthusiasts, victory will not be achieved by adopting the panacea of military intervention."

Americans should resist the war hysteria and the dangerous measures being suggested to win the war on drugs. It is possible that if we were willing to convert the United States into a police state, the flow of drugs *might* be substantially reduced—although when authorities cannot prevent prison inmates from obtaining drugs, even that proposition is questionable. In any case, there is no possibility of achieving something that has never existed in the nation's history: a "drug-free America." A particularly sobering realization is that despite having been one of the most repressed and regimented societies on earth during the pre-Gorbachev period, the Soviet Union now concedes that it has a serious drug problem. That situation suggests that a willingness of Americans to sacrifice their hard-won liberties on the altar of the drug war would be not only shortsighted but ultimately futile. It is time for even hard-core supporters of the war on drugs to ask themselves if they really want a society in which warrantless searches become routine, individuals can be stripped of their property before trial, innocent air travelers can be blown out of the skies by overzealous officials, privacy scarcely exists, and detention centers and boot camps dot the landscape. That is precisely the direction the drug war is taking America.

The United States can weaken the international drug cartels and terrorist organizations (as well as domestic criminal enterprises) without destroying constitutional liberties, making enemies throughout Latin America, or entangling the U.S. military in a dangerous, unwinnable conflict. Legalization of drugs would wreck the now lucrative black market and dramatically reduce the flow of revenue to trafficking organizations. It would undermine the cartels by eroding their enormous profit margins and permitting the entry of honest businesses into the field. The result would be fewer drug-related violent street crimes. Legalizing drugs would have the same impact on criminal drug-trafficking organizations that the repeal of Prohibition had on powerful U.S. bootlegging organizations.

Avoiding Another Unwinnable War

Even those Americans who are not yet prepared to endorse legalization should recoil from the drug war hysteria that is being generated in the United States. Columnist Tom Wicker observes perceptively:

> Like any other war, it's sure to produce a dangerous wartime mentality that "anything goes" in pursuit of victory. . . . What will happen to public and Congressional attitudes if a supposed war—like the war in Vietnam—drags on endlessly with marginal achievements and no apparent hope of victory? Some will give up, no doubt; but many, perhaps more, will call for escalation, new weapons, more troops, tougher tactics—victory at any price.

Americans should view with great skepticism the proliferating schemes to use the military to wage that "war." The military is ill-equipped by training and temperament to handle domestic law enforcement functions, especially if a semblance of constitutional freedoms is to be preserved. Nor will it succeed in stopping the importation of drugs. No military establishment, not even one as large and sophisticated as that of the United States, can effectively seal borders across which 355 million people, 635,000 air flights, and 8 million freight containers pass each year.

A military solution in the international phase of the drug war is equally improbable. Coercing the Andean countries to wage a war against the cartels is dangerous and shortsighted, since they must defy powerful domestic political and economic constituencies—as well as well-armed opponents. Even more foolhardy is the idea of having the U.S. military play a direct role in that conflict. Such a course will undermine the legitimacy of fragile democratic governments and damage the reputation of the United States throughout the hemisphere in addition to enhancing the power of the already bloated and expensive U.S. national security bureaucracy.

Protecting Liberty

Contrary to the belief of the drug war enthusiasts, victory will not be achieved by adopting the panacea of military intervention. The proper function of the military in a democratic republic is to protect the liberty and security of the people from the armed forces of threatening states—a daunting enough task in a complex and often volatile international environment. It should not wage moral crusades or become a super law enforcement agency. A society that values individual liberty must oppose any effort to expand the military's power beyond its rightful, constitutionally established sphere.

Despite the hype and alarmist rhetoric, drug trafficking does not constitute a serious threat to national security, nor is the drug problem in the United States the moral equivalent of war. Given the probable consequences of enlisting the military in the war on drugs, and especially of deploying U.S. troops in the source nations of Latin America, it is more likely to be the moral—and operational—equivalent of America's disastrous Vietnam intervention. The outcome will be a dangerous erosion of liberty at home and the return of American soldiers in flag-draped coffins from an unwinnable crusade abroad.

Ted Galen Carpenter is the director of foreign policy studies at the Cato Institute, a research organization in Washington, D.C. R.Channing Rouse is an associate defense policy analyst at the Cato Institute.

"A powerful drug syndicate had been using Cuba as a transshipment point for illegal narcotics shipments to the United States since 1978."

Cuba Is Involved in Drug Trafficking

Joseph D. Douglass Jr.

At dawn on July 14, 1989, one month after he was arrested, Gen. Arnaldo Ochoa Sanchez was executed by firing squad along with three other Cuban officers. Ochoa was one of Cuba's most popular army officers. A recipient of the Hero of the Republic medal, his career dates back thirty-one years to the revolution, when he was a member of the famed Camilo Cienfuegos brigade. In 1979 he commanded the Cuban forces in Ethiopia, and subsequently, the Cuban advisers in Nicaragua and the fifty thousand Cuban troops in Angola.

Ochoa was found guilty of helping Colombia's Medellin drug cartel smuggle cocaine into the United States. His trial, which was conducted in secret, began on June 26. The star witness was Gen. Raul Castro, the minister of defense and Fidel Castro's deputy and likely successor. Raul Castro denounced Ochoa and called for exemplary punishment. All members of the military tribunal who sat in judgment also denounced Ochoa. The military prosecutor, Gen. Juan Escalona, in his conclusion said Ochoa had "betrayed his people, his fatherland and Fidel . . . and cast a slur on the prestige and credibility of the revolution."

Trial and Sentencing

The trial and sentencing was conducted with dispatch. Along with Ochoa, thirteen other officers were charged. Four, including Ochoa, would be sentenced to death; the rest would receive long prison terms. There was no defense. All of the accused pleaded guilty. Nor was any news media coverage allowed. The only information that has been available, including televised segments of the trial, is that which was released by the official Cuban news ministry.

The arrest, trial, and execution of Ochoa followed seven years of highly publicized and embarrassing reports in the United States on the involvement of Cuban officials in drug trafficking. The publicity began in November 1982 when the U.S. attorney in Miami indicted the noted Colombian drug trafficker, Jaime Guillot-Lara, and eight accomplices, including four ranking Cuban officials: Rene Rodriguez-Cruz, a senior official in Cuban intelligence and member of the Cuban Communist Party Central Committee; Aldo Santamaria-Cuadrado, a vice-admiral in the Cuban navy and also a member of the Central Committee; Fernando Ravelo-Renedo, former Cuban ambassador to Colombia, current Cuban ambassador to Nicaragua; and Gonzalo Bassols-Suarez, former minister-counsel of the Cuban Embassy in Colombia.

Over the six years that followed the first indictment, an impressive array of testimony on Cuban involvement in drug trafficking has been placed in the public record. The testimony comes from captured drug traffickers, covertly recorded drug trafficker conversations, former Cuban intelligence officers, and former high-ranking officials from Cuba and other countries where Cuba was also involved in drug trafficking.

Their testimony reveals a wide range of official Cuban involvement in drug trafficking. Marijuana is grown in Cuba. The production is described as an official state operation protected by special military forces. Cuba is known to maintain several training camps for would-be-terrorists. The camps are run by Cuba's military intelligence service. Cocaine is reported to be readily accepted as tuition payment. Safe haven and transshipment facilities are provided for drug traffickers by Cuban authorities. Smugglers are not only given free passage through Cuban airspace and territorial waters, they are escorted and protected by Cuban military forces. The smugglers are also permitted to land and shift cargo to smaller boats and planes in preparation for their final dash into the United States or to the Bahamas prior to their final run into the United States. Cuban intelligence has

Joseph D. Douglass Jr., "Drug Trafficking and the Castros," *Global Affairs,* Winter 1990. Reprinted with permission.

inserted agents into the United States, agents who were then directed by Cuban intelligence to organize drug distribution networks and return the profits to Cuba. Cuban leaders, specifically Raul and Fidel Castro, were said to have arranged to have Nicaragua join the ranks of trafficking nations. Cuban military and intelligence advisers assisted the Nicaraguans in setting up drug operations. Cuba has also provided assistance and military security forces to help protect drug operations in other countries, such as Surinam, and various islands throughout the Caribbean. . . .

Extensive Cuban Involvement

It was not until the Miami indictment of November 1984 that drug trafficking began to receive some attention. Since that indictment, there has been a steady stream of information, reports, and first-hand eyewitness accounts of extensive Cuban involvement in drug trafficking.

One of the individuals who testified at the 1983 trial following the indictment of Guillot was Mario Estevez Gonzalez. Estevez was a Cuban intelligence (*Direccion General de Inteligencia* or DGI) agent who was infiltrated into the United States during the Mariel boatlift. He testified that he was directed by his DGI superior to make contact with drug traffickers in Bimini and the United States and to "load up the United States with drugs."

"Cuban leaders, specifically Raul and Fidel Castro, were said to have arranged to have Nicaragua join the ranks of trafficking nations."

During his drug trafficking career Estevez imported over 270 kilograms of cocaine from Cuba; sold this cocaine to individuals in Miami, Chicago, Ohio, New Jersey, New York, and other cities; and took the money he was paid to Cuba where he delivered it to the Cuban government. It was during one such trip that Rene Rodriguez-Cruz, a senior DGI official and a ranking member of the Cuban Communist Party Central Committee—one of the Cubans in the 1982 indictment—put his arm on Estevez's shoulder and told him how nice it was now that Cuba had "a drugstore in the United States."

The Cubans' drug operation also became tied to their revolutionary terrorist activities in Latin America, especially those in Colombia. The manner in which narcotics trafficking and revolutionary or terrorist organizations operate together is easily appreciated. Terrorist or revolutionary groups provide protection for the drug traffickers. The drug traffickers help finance the terrorists and revolutionaries and furnish them with information (intelligence) and transportation assistance.

Colombia's Marxist M-19 revolutionaries have close ties to Cuba and various drug traffickers, the more highly publicized of which is the collection known as the Medellin Cartel, which also has close ties to Cuba, Nicaragua, and other countries. The principal linkage between the Medellin Cartel and the M-19, as explained by Jose I. Blandon Castillo, former consul general of Panama, is Cuban Ambassador Fernando Ravelo-Renedo—another of the Cubans in the 1982 indictment. Ravelo works for Manuel Pineiro Losada, head of the Americas Department of the Central Committee of the Communist Party of Cuba and former head of the DGI. The Americas Department has special responsibility for subversive and sabotage operations in the Western Hemisphere, including disinformation, terrorism, and drugs. . . .

Maj. Florentino Aspillaga Lombard was a career officer in the Cuban DGI until his defection to Vienna on June 6, 1987, from Czechoslovakia, where he was stationed. He confirmed that a powerful drug syndicate had been using Cuba as a transshipment point for illegal narcotics shipments to the United States since 1978. He further stated that operational security and protection was provided by Jose Abrahantes Fernandez, a Castro deputy and minister of Interior. None of the drug-related activities could have been carried out without the personal approval of Fidel Castro, he explained. Two days after the military tribunal had called for Ochoa's death, Abrahantes was fired and Gen. Abelardo Colome Ibarra was appointed the new minister of Interior. Abrahantes was fired because of his agency's involvement in the scandal, which more likely means he was fired for not maintaining sufficient operational security.

In 1988, the role of Cuba in drug trafficking was again confirmed, this time by Maj. Juan Antonio Rodriguez Menier, an officer in Cuban intelligence who defected from Budapest, Hungary, in January, 1987, where he had been chief of security at the Cuban Embassy. He explained that the Cuban government participated both directly and indirectly in narco-trafficking and that the Special Troops were used to coordinate operations. Rodriguez quoted the chief of the DGI, Gen. German Barreiro, as saying that "drugs are the best way to destroy the United States." Their primary target was American youth. By undermining the will of American youth to resist, the United States could be destroyed "without firing one bullet. The foundation of any army is the youth and he who is able to morally destroy the youth, destroys the army."

Castro's Drug Trafficking

During an interview on Cuba's involvement on August 25, 1989, Rodriguez stated that Fidel Castro was personally aware of the drug trafficking and that in the case of one Cuban company that was in the drug business, Cimex, Castro received 80 percent of the hard currency profits. Because of their control over foreign operations, these activities could not have been carried out without the approval of both Fidel and Raul Castro, Rodriguez added. His knowledge of Castro's involvement went back to 1982, when he first learned of Castro's personal involvement from a high-ranking official of Cuba's Ministry of Interior. "Fidel is not doing that only for money," he explained. "His philosophy is to use anything to destroy the United States. For example, drugs are regarded as the best way to destroy the American society without troops or guns because the younger people who are the future leaders, if they are drug addicts, they are very weak."

"Ochoa's trial and execution was a show staged for the benefit of U.S. officials, and quite possibly, Cuban citizens."

In March 1989, two Colombian drug dealers pleaded guilty to moving cocaine into Florida through Cuba. Videotaped evidence contained conversations of how the Cuban military and civilian officials aided the traffickers. Reinaldo Ruiz and his son Ruben are shown telling a U.S. Drug Enforcement Administration (DEA) informant how Cuba guarantees the success of cocaine loads run through the island and how the money paid for the service goes to Fidel Castro. . . .

Later Developments

The latest data on Cuban drug trafficking to emerge . . . were provided by Jose Luis Llovio-Menendez, the highest-ranking civilian defector from Cuba. Llovio-Menendez provided to the press his notes on a series of telephone conversations he had with Colonel de la Guardia. De la Guardia headed a secret office in the Ministry of Interior. His last call came in May 1989, shortly before the arrest of Ochoa, *et al*. He told Llovio-Menendez that he had been ordered to head Cuba's drug trafficking operations, but that he knew he would be abandoned by Castro if the smuggling operation was uncovered. The order came from Abrahantes, the minister of Interior, who "doesn't do anything that isn't ordered by the Chief [Castro] . . ." De la Guardia was executed along with Ochoa two months later.

Ochoa's trial and execution was a show staged for the benefit of U.S. officials, and quite possibly, Cuban citizens. Blame for Cuba's past activities was placed on a few individuals, who were portrayed as corrupt, and on the United States for recruiting those citizens and for not bringing appropriate information to the attention of Cuban officials.

What is perhaps least surprising is that even before the beginning of the last act, and with evidently no consideration for the events of the past, specifically the collection of evidence on the role of Fidel and Raul Castro and the Cuban Communist Party, security ministries, intelligence and military services in drug trafficking, members of the U.S. Congress who are certainly well aware of the facts began calling for the U.S. government to ignore what has transpired and use the occasion to work jointly with Cuba to curb drug trafficking.

The U.S. and Cuba

This same thought was also contained in a long speech delivered by Fidel Castro several days prior to the executions, in which he asked for talks with the United States to help combat drug smuggling. Given the history of Cuba's involvement in drug trafficking, how can anyone who is serious about the problem view Castro's remarks as anything other than a staged dramatic reading.

As for the U.S. response, both the State Department and DEA expressed immediate interest in testing Castro's call for a "common battle" in the war on drugs and providing current intelligence on suspected drug flights to Cuba. This should come as no surprise. For over fifteen years, the U.S. government has been providing information on U.S. techniques for catching drug traffickers and intelligence on suspect traffickers to officials of nations such as Bulgaria, which has been widely reported to be officially running drugs against the West.

Is it any wonder that the drug problem in the United States has grown so bad and that U.S. efforts to combat the trafficking have been so notably unsuccessful?

Joseph D. Douglass Jr. is a defense analyst and author of numerous books on national security affairs, including Red Cocaine: The Drugging of America.

"Recent White House attempts to frame Fidel Castro and the Cuban government as kingpin cocaine traffickers should be viewed with deep suspicion."

Cuba Is Not Involved in Drug Trafficking

Jon Reed

Recent White House attempts to frame Fidel Castro and the Cuban government as kingpin cocaine traffickers should be viewed with deep suspicion in the light of an ongoing 30 year program of disinformation and covert warfare designed to destroy the Cuban Revolution. In the wake of the spectacular July 1989 trial and execution of General Arnaldo Ochoa and three other high-ranking Cuban military officers for cocaine smuggling and black market profiteering, the U.S. has tried to revive previously discredited charges of Castro's involvement in the international drug trade. Such charges have run all the way from a preposterous claim of a meeting between Che Guevara and Salvador Allende in 1961 to plan the undermining of the U.S. system by importing drugs to recent allegations of a conspiracy between Castro, Nicaragua and the Medellin Cartel.

The White House has ignored Castro's repeated offers to cooperate with the U.S. in drug interdiction, and seems to have conveniently forgotten Cuba's close cooperation with the Carter administration in the late 1970's, when the Cubans seized numerous ships and aircraft carrying contraband drugs. The Bush administration has planted stories in the mass media claiming that Castro scapegoated Ochoa and the others in order to head off a mythical Soviet-backed coup d'etat (to force glasnost on the Cubans) and to hide his own role as Latin American drug kingpin. According to *The New York Times,* General Ochoa "may have been leading a group of dissidents and planning some type of action against the Cuban government."

There is little evidence to support the existence of a "Cuban Connection." As an August 1989 article in *The New York Times* by Juan Mendez of Americas Watch points out, the Medellin Cartel works hand-in-hand, not with left-wingers, but rather with the chief U.S. allies in Colombia—the military and police authorities. Left-wing guerrilla cooperation with these drug cartels, so-called "narco-terrorism," is either minimal or nonexistent.

No Cocaine in Cuba

Visiting Cuba, it is obvious that there's no significant cocaine or crack problem on the island. The main problems are economic stagnation and political over-centralization, direct results of the White House's 30 year war against the Cuban revolution. The economic consequences of a normalization of relations with the U.S. would go a long way toward solving the country's major problems. If the travel blockade were lifted, the Cuban tourist industry would boom. If the Cubans could freely trade with the U.S., there would be no "hard currency" crisis. If U.S. peace activists and ordinary citizens could freely travel to the island, there would be a significant upsurge in solidarity and crosscultural communication. With close cooperation between the U.S. and Cuba, the fundamental right-wing roots of the Medellin Cartel and international cocaine trafficking would become evident. These are the real reasons why the Bush team wants us to believe that Castro and the Latin American left are at the root of our problems.

The achievements of the Cuban revolution are impressive and undeniable: in education, in health care, in combating racism, in providing employment and eliminating poverty, and most of all in creating an anti-imperialist consciousness and commitment in the majority of the island's 10 million people. It's hard to imagine a more exciting or uplifting place to visit. As part of a rousing send-off for an international delegation, several thousand young Cubans have massed on Calle 23 (23rd Street) dancing to a live Afro-reggae band and turning the Vedado neighborhood into an impromptu carnival. Fascinated by the multiethnic composition of the crowd and the

Jon Reed, "U.S. Drug Information Campaign Targets Cuba," *Northern Sun News,* December 1989. Reprinted with permission of *Northern Sun News,* 1519 E. Franklin Ave., Minneapolis, MN 55404.

exuberant energy of the dancers near me, I am forcefully reminded of all the good things about the Cuban revolution: its internationalism, its emphasis on youth, and its vibrant Afro-Cuban culture.

As my Cuban compañera reminds me, many of the young men and women in the crowd have recently returned from volunteer duly in Angola, fighting against the South African army and the Unita mercenaries of Jonas Savimbi. After 13 years of bloody war, many Cubans believe that Angola's enemies have finally been defeated. Without the Cuban volunteers, the Angolans probably would have been defeated by the U.S.-backed counterrevolution— a fact widely acknowledged in the Third World.

After months of traveling through the war-battered cities and villages of Central America, it's a relief to see so many beautiful, smiling faces. It's reassuring to look at a well-dressed and healthy crowd. Standing in the shade of tropical foliage that borders the Cuban Pavilion, I try to make myself heard above the amplified sound system, asking several women dancing beside me what they think about the trial and execution of General Ochoa. . . .

"It's terrible. I can hardly believe it," a woman in jeans tells me, shaking her head. "Ochoa was a war hero in Angola and a long-time associate of Fidel."

"As I watched the testimony of the accused officers on television," the other young woman added, "I didn't know what to think. . . . How could this have happened?"

Protecting the Revolution

Everyone I talk to on the streets is careful not to blame Fidel, who after 30 years in power remains very popular. But my questions stimulate an uneasy guardedness, a defensiveness arising out of the average Cuban's desire to protect the image of the revolution. People are willing to criticize lower level Communist Party bureaucrats for corruption and inefficiency, but not the top leadership.

One very articulate Cuban I spoke with off the record felt sorry for Ochoa and the others—defending their actions by pointing out that perhaps they were only trying to earn badly-needed hard currency in order to be able to continue financing Cuba's anti-imperialist activities in Africa and Central America. He reminded me that the Soviet Union can no longer afford to provide large sums of money for its allies in the Third World. Since drug trafficking is obviously used as an important fundraising tool by the CIA [Central Intelligence Agency] and its allies, perhaps Ochoa and the others believed that they were justified in using "any means necessary" to raise needed funds. Most people, however, blamed Ochoa and the others for trying to enrich themselves personally and for staining the reputation of the Revolution.

The majority of Cubans I spoke with seemed genuinely shocked when I told them about the terrible social and political effects of the crack epidemic in the United States. No one was able to answer me when I asked why the Cuban press still supported General Noriega uncritically, when it is clear that he was involved in money-laundering and cocaine smuggling, worked hand-in-hand with the Medellin Cartel, and had a long record of cooperation with the Reagan administration and the DEA [Drug Enforcement Administration]. One person speculated that perhaps Noriega had played the role of a "double agent," working with the DEA and the Bush/North network in order to be able to expose them later. Why else would the U.S. be trying so hard to get rid of him now?

"The White House is happy to promote the myth of left-wing narco-terrorism and the 'Cuban-Nicaraguan Connection.' "

The "Colombianization" of inner cities in the U.S. is not a myth. It is a troubling reality which must be addressed by the left. President Bush's "War on Drugs" speech, nationally-televised on September 5, 1989, makes it clear that the administration plans to make this issue a centerpiece of reactionary, bipartisan politics. The coke epidemic of the late 1980's has done more to fuel racism and to destroy Black, Latino, and youth community consciousness than perhaps any other domestic counterinsurgency tool that could have been devised by the CIA. Not only does this multi-billion dollar industry provide strategic funds for a worldwide network of contras, death squads, and right-wing dictatorships, its social and political effects are poisoning everyday efforts to build a broad-based radical movement in the United States.

The CIA and Drug Dealing

As Jesse Jackson and others have pointed out, every misguided, desperate crack addict is a loss to the Movement—a potential political activist who may never have the opportunity to become involved. This is the real reason that the White House is happy to promote the myth of left-wing narco-terrorism and the "Cuban-Nicaraguan Connection" while hiding the fact that the CIA and its "secret teams" have been directly involved with major right-wing heroin and cocaine syndicates for the last 40 years—from the Corsican Mafia and right-wing Laotian tribes to the Afghan contras and the Guatemalan military high command. From the standpoint of the National Security State, the North American-European crack epidemic is a phenomenon to be prolonged for as long as possible. It divides and weakens opposition forces while providing a demonic replacement for the traditional "Evil Empire"—the Soviet Union.

While police and military-affiliated drug lords in Colombia and Central America bolster counterinsurgency campaigns through assassinations and kidnapings of left-wing grassroots leaders, violence, robbery and gang warfare have reached epidemic proportions in many North American urban areas, stimulating racist attacks and reactionary calls for police-state repression. While a crack dealer shoots down and kills former Black Panther leader Huey Newton, "gangbanging" and Miami Vice stereotypes have replaced Malcolm X and Che Guevara as role models for youth.

National polls indicate that the cocaine epidemic has begun to destabilize the United States. Fearful citizens rank drugs as the country's number one problem. If the public won't support sending U.S. combat troops into Latin America to fight the FMLN, the Sandinistas, or the Colombian guerrillas, then perhaps they will support armed counterinsurgency disguised as a War on Drugs. If, as a 1986 Gallup poll suggests, most North Americans would support a normalization of relations with socialist Cuba, perhaps this dangerous tendency can be reversed by painting the Castroites as crack wholesalers. If sending the Green Beret into Honduras, Costa Rica, Guatemala, and Mexico is too unpopular, then the White House will be glad to send in an army of militarized DEA thugs instead.

More Military Intervention

In the absence of a propaganda and action offensive by the left, government calls for increased funds for police and military intervention have an undeniable attraction. Instead of demanding the controlled legalization of drugs and recognizing the crack epidemic as a deep-rooted socioeconomic and medical problem, we are asked to support sending combat troops to Colombia and Peru and to sanction widespread spraying of deadly herbicides in the war zones of Guatemala. Instead of qualitatively improving economic opportunities for disadvantaged youth or pumping the huge funds needed into drug rehabilitation programs, what the bipartisan hard-liners suggest is the imposition of police state measures in the ghetto and the society at large. If present trends continue, we can expect White House denunciations of ghetto violence and left-wing "narco-terrorism" to increase—especially as the myth of the "communist menace" loses its rationale in the Gorbachev era.

Even though evidence uncovered by the Christic Institute and investigative reporters demonstrates that the drug godfather is really former CIA director Bush and his death squad allies across the globe, we on the left have been losing the propaganda battle of the War on Drugs. Public receptivity to Bush's recent disinformation campaign surrounding the drug scandal in Cuba is a depressing indication of just how far we on the left have to go if we are to point our finger at the socioeconomic causes of the crack epidemic and clean up the biggest crack house in the hemisphere, the White House.

Jon Reed is the Northern Sun News *correspondent in Havana, Cuba.* Northern Sun News *is the newspaper of Northern Sun Alliance, a Minneapolis organization that opposes nuclear weapons, U.S. intervention in other countries, and supports recycling and environmental conservation.*

bibliography

The following bibliography of books, periodicals,
and pamphlets is divided into chapter topics
for the reader's convenience.

Addiction

Robert Ackerman — *Perfect Daughter: Adult Daughters of Alcoholics*, Deerfield Beach, FL: Health Communications, 1989.

Melody Beattie — *Beyond Codependency*. Center City, MN: Hazelden, 1989.

Maureen Dowd — "Addiction Chic," *Mademoiselle*, October 1989.

Susan Forward with Craig Buck — *Toxic Parents*. New York: Bantam Books, 1989.

E. Nelson Hayes, ed. — *Adult Children of Alcoholics Remember*. New York: Harmony Books, 1989.

Rosalie Cruise Jesse — *Children in Recovery*. New York: W.W. Norton & Company, 1989.

Morris Kokin and Ian Walker — *Women Married to Alcoholics*. New York: William Morrow and Company, 1989.

Art Levine — "America's Addiction to Addictions," *U.S. News & World Report*, February 5, 1990.

Theodore McCarrick — "The Church's Concern About Substance Abuse," *Origins,* November 2, 1989.

Linda Marsa — "Addiction and IQ," *Omni*, October 1989.

Larry Martz — "A Dirty Drug Secret," *Newsweek*, February 19, 1990.

Gerald S. May — *Addiction and Grace*. New York: Harper & Row, 1989.

Lisa J. Moore — "Codependency," *U.S. News & World Report*, September 11, 1989.

Mark A. Schuckit — "Alcohol, Drugs and the Elderly," *Drug Abuse & Alcoholism Newsletter*, April 1989. Available from the Vista Hill Foundation, 3420 Camino del Rio North, Suite 100, San Diego, CA 92108.

Mark A. Schuckit — *Drug and Alcohol Abuse*. 3rd ed. New York: Plenum Medical, 1989.

Charles M. Sell — *Unfinished Business: Helping Adult Children Resolve Their Past*. Portland, OR: Multnomah Press, 1989.

Peter Steinglass with Linda Bennett, Steven Wolin, and David Reiss — *The Alcoholic Family*. New York: Basic Books, 1989.

Carol Tavris — "Just Another 'Disease' to Soothe Powerlessness," *Los Angeles Times,* March 15, 1990.

Carol Tavris — "The Politics of Codependency," *The Family Therapy Networker*, January/February 1990. Available from The Family Therapy Network, 8528 Bradford Rd., Silver Spring, MD 20901.

David Treadway — "Codependency: Disease, Metaphor, or Fad?" *The Family Therapy Networker*, January/February 1990. Available from The Family Therapy Network, 8528 Bradford Rd., Silver Spring, MD 20901.

Joe Vaughn — *Family Intervention: Hope for Families Struggling with Alcohol and Drugs*. Louisville, KY: Westminster/John Knox Press, 1989.

Carol J. Verburg — *Substance Abuse in America*. Washington, DC: National Academy Press, 1989.

Arthur Wassmer — *Recovering Together*. New York: St. Martin's Press, 1989.

Alcoholism

James Alsdurf — "Alcoholism: Is It a Sin After All?" *Christianity Today*, February 3, 1989.

Louie Anderson — *Dear Dad*. New York: Viking Penguin, 1989.

LeClair Bissel — "When the Alcoholic Is a Woman," *The Catholic World*, July/August 1989.

Garth Bray — "Alcohol Labeling: Shortchanging the Public," *Multinational Monitor*, June 1989.

Arthur L. Caplan — "Is Alcoholism a Disease?" *Medical Humanities Review*, July 1989.

The Catholic World — "The Many Faces of Alcoholism," July/August 1989.

Lily Collet — "After the Anger, What Then?" *The Family Therapy Networker*, January/February 1990. Available from The Family Therapy Network, 8528 Bradford Rd., Silver Spring, MD 20901.

Paul Farhi — "A Drug by Any Other Name," *The Washington Post National Weekly Edition*, January 8-14, 1990.

Herbert Fingarette — "Willful Misconduct?" *American Legion Magazine*, January 1989.

Norman Fleishman and Diana Fleishman — "Beer Ads: Fuel for the Drug Bonfire," *The Humanist*, November/December 1989.

Richard J. Frances — *Concise Guide to Treatment of Alcoholism and Addictions*. Washington, DC: American Psychiatric Press, 1989.

David L. Gonzalez — "Very Personal Computing," *Newsweek*, August 28, 1989.

Enoch Gordis et al. — "Alcoholism Treatment Research: New Directions for an Old Problem," *Journal of the American Medical Association*, September 22-29, 1989.

Trish Hall "A New Temperance Is Taking Root in America," *The New York Times*, March 15, 1989.

Eleanor Harris "Not Just My Brother's Problem," *Glamour*, February 1989.

Jean Kinney "America's Silent Epidemic," *American Legion Magazine*, January 1989.

Gerald L. Klerman "Treatment of Alcoholism," *The New England Journal of Medicine*, February 9, 1989.

Melvin Konner "Study on Alcoholism Shows the Roots of Sexism Are Seriously Flawed," *Los Angeles Times*, February 19, 1990.

Joanne Lipman "Foes Claim Ad Bans Are Bad Business," *The Wall Street Journal*, February 27, 1990.

Earl M. *Physician Heal Thyself!* Minneapolis: CompCare Publishers, 1989.

William Madsen "Thin Thinking About Heavy Drinking," *The Public Interest*, Spring 1989.

Joseph P. Newhouse and Emmett B. Keeler "Make Drinkers Pay the Social Costs of Imbibing," *Los Angeles Times*, April 30, 1989.

Edward E. Rosenbaum "Alcohol: Everyone's Problem," *New Choices*, February 1989.

Scott Russell Sanders "Under the Influence," *Harper's Magazine*, November 1989.

Jeffrey A. Schaler "Alcoholism, Disease, and Myth," *Skeptical Inquirer*, Winter 1990.

Steven Schenker and K. Vincent Speeg "The Risk of Alcohol Intake in Men and Women," *The New England Journal of Medicine*, January 11, 1990.

Ronald K. Siegel *Intoxication*. New York: E.P. Dutton, 1989.

Lloyd H. Steffen "Rethinking Drinking: The Moral Context," *The Christian Century*, July 19-26, 1989.

Pat Taylor and Karen Lieberman "Alcohol and Health," *Multinational Monitor*, June 1989.

Gail Unterberger "Twelve Steps for Women Alcoholics," *The Christian Century*, December 6, 1989.

Jacqueline Wasser "The Thinking Girl's Guide to Drinking," *Mademoiselle*, September 1989.

Case Study: Drug Addiction and Pregnancy

Garry Abrams "Drug Orphans," *Los Angeles Times*, September 21, 1989.

Michael D. Bayles "Prenatal Harm and Privacy Rights," *National Forum*, Fall 1989.

Beryl Lieff Benderly "Saving the Children," *Health*, December 1989.

Barry Bearak "Hooked and Pregnant: A Time Bomb," *Los Angeles Times*, August 22, 1989.

Douglas J. Besharov "Crack Children in Foster Care," *The American Enterprise*, January/February 1990.

Douglas J. Besharov "Cracked-Up Kids—Right from the Start," *The Washington Post National Weekly Edition*, September 11-17, 1989.

Sandra Blakeslee "Crack's Toll Among Babies: A Joyless View, Even of Toys," *The New York Times*, September 17, 1989.

Charles Robert Burton "Fetal Drug or Alcohol Addiction Syndrome: A Case of Prenatal Child Abuse?" *Willamette Law Review*, vol. 25:223, Winter 1989.

Morris E. Chafetz "Alcohol and Innocent Victims," *The Wall Street Journal*, March 5, 1990.

Wendy Chavkin "Help, Don't Jail Addicted Mothers," *The New York Times*, July 18, 1989.

Mark Curriden "Holding Mom Accountable," *ABA Journal*, March 1990.

Jean Davidson "Drug Babies Push Issue of Fetal Rights," *Los Angeles Times*, April 25, 1989.

Susan Diesenhouse "Punishing Pregnant Addicts: Debate, Dismay, No Solution," *The New York Times*, September 10, 1989.

Michael Dorris *The Broken Cord*. New York: Harper & Row, 1989.

Howard W. French "For Pregnant Addicts, a Clinic of Hope," *The New York Times*, September 29, 1989.

Ted Gest "The Pregnancy Police, on Patrol," *U.S. News & World Report*, February 6, 1989.

Barbara Kantrowitz "The Crack Children," *Newsweek*, February 12, 1990.

Charles Leershen "Pregnancy + Alcohol = Problems," *Newsweek*, July 31, 1989.

Paul Marcotte "Crime & Pregnancy," *ABA Journal*, August 1989.

Michele L. Norris "Growing Up in a World of Crack," *The Washington Post National Weekly Edition*, September 11-17, 1989.

Diana Roberts and Robert M. Pinkerton *Women, Drugs, and Babies: Guidelines for Medical and Protective Services' Response to Infants Endangered by Drug Abuse During Pregnancy*. Salem, OR: Oregon Department of Human Resources, Children's Services Division, 1989.

Elisabeth Rosenthal "When a Pregnant Woman Drinks," *The New York Times Magazine*, February 4, 1990.

Andrea Sachs "Here Come the Pregnancy Police," *Time*, May 22, 1989.

Elizabeth L. Thompson "The Criminalization of Maternal Conduct During Pregnancy: A Decisionmaking Model for Lawmakers," *Indiana Law Journal*, vol. 64:357, 1989.

U.S. Senate U.S. Congress. Senate. Committee on Labor and Human Resources and Committee on the Judiciary. *Impact of Drugs on Children and Families*. One Hundred and First Congress. First session. 1990. Senate hearing 101-397.

U.S. Senate U.S. Congress. Senate. Committee on Labor and Human Resources. Subcommittee on Children, Family, Drugs and Alcoholism. *Drug Addicted Babies: What Can Be Done?* One Hundred and First Congress. First session. 1990. Senate hearing 101-396.

Ellen Willis "The Wrongs of Fetal Rights," *The Village Voice*, April 11, 1989.

International Drug Trafficking

Peter Andreas "U.S. Drug Policy and the Andean Cocaine Industry," *World Policy Journal*, Summer 1989.

David Asman "Man in the Middle of Drug Trafficking," *The Wall Street Journal*, September 25, 1989.

Bruce Michael Bagley "Dateline Drug Wars: Columbia—The Wrong Strategy," *Foreign Policy*, Winter 1989/1990.

James A. Baker III — "Narcotics: Threat to Global Security," *Current Policy*, No. 1251, February 20, 1990. Available from the United States Department of State, Bureau of Public Affairs, PA/DAP, Room 5815A, Washington, DC 20520-6810.

Diane K. Bartz — "U.S. Drug Policy in Region Eradicates Itself," *In These Times*, September 6-12, 1989.

Joseph Contreras — "Anarchy in Colombia," *Newsweek*, September 11, 1989.

Richard B. Craig — "Are Drug Kingdoms South America's New Wave?" *The World & I*, November 1989.

Brian Crozier — "The Castro Connection," *National Review*, March 5, 1990.

Ken Dermota — "Can Colombia Bargain with Cocaine Kingpins?" *In These Times*, December 6-12, 1989.

Hernando de Soto — "Property Rights: The Way Out for Coca Growers," *The Wall Street Journal*, February 13, 1990.

Joseph D. Douglass Jr. — "Drug Trafficking and the Castros," *Global Affairs*, Winter 1990.

Mathea Falco — "Beating the Next Drug Crisis," *World Monitor*, February 1990.

John J. Fialka — "Cleaning Up," *The Wall Street Journal*, March 1, 1990.

Richard L. Fricker — "A Judiciary Under Fire," *ABA Journal*, February 1990.

Jeff Gerth — "C.I.A. Shedding Its Reluctance to Aid in Fight Against Drugs," *The New York Times*, March 25, 1990.

Gustavo Gorriti — "Coca Won't Die Easily in Peru," *Los Angeles Times*, September 19, 1989.

Guy Gugliotta — "Beating Back the Cocaine Kings," *U.S. News & World Report*, February 19, 1990.

Guy Gugliotta and Jeff Leen — *Kings of Cocaine: Inside the Medellin Cartel*. New York: Simon & Schuster, 1989.

Douglas Jehl — "U.S. Plans More Pressure on Mexico to Block Cocaine," *Los Angeles Times*, December 2, 1989.

Jo Ann Kawell — "Sending in Army Could Drag U.S. into Morass," *In These Times*, October 25-31, 1989.

Rensselaer W. Lee — "Cocaine Mafia," *Society*, January/February 1990.

Rensselaer W. Lee — *The White Labyrinth: Cocaine and Political Power*. New Brunswick, NJ: Transaction Publishers, 1989.

William R. Long — "Colombia's Drug Lords Concede They Lost the War," *Los Angeles Times*, January 8, 1990.

Ed Magnuson — "More and More, a Real War," *Time*, January 22, 1990.

Richard Morin — "Americans and Colombians Stand a Gulf Apart on Fighting Cocaine," *The Washington Post National Weekly Edition*, February 12-18, 1990.

Robert F. Nagel — "The Myth of the General Right to Bail," *The Public Interest*, Winter 1990.

Gabriel G. Nahas — *Cocaine: The Great White Plague*. Middlebury, VT: Paul S. Eriksson, 1989.

Serge Sabourin — "From the Cold War to the Drug War," *New Perspectives Quarterly*, Fall 1989.

The Washington Spectator — "The Drug Cartel: Beating the Rap," August 15, 1989.

War on Drugs

Fred Barnes — "Bennett the Drug Czar: An Agenda," *The American Spectator*, April 1989.

Sara Sun Beale — "Get Drug Cases Out of Federal Court," *The Wall Street Journal*, February 8, 1990.

Georgette Bennett — *Crime Warps: The Future of Crime in America*. New York: Doubleday, 1989.

Business Week — "Some Winning Maneuvers in the War on Drugs," November 27, 1989.

James Cook — "The Paradox of Antidrug Enforcement," *Forbes*, November 13, 1989.

Ken Dermota — "Drug Warriors March to Different Drums," *In These Times*, January 17-23, 1990.

Kenneth R. Feinberg — "Drug Enforcement: Criminal Division," in *America's Transition: Blueprint for the 1990s*, edited by Mark Green and Mark Pinsky. New York: Democracy Project, 1989.

Gerry Fitzgerald — "Dispatches from the Drug War," *Common Cause Magazine*, January/February 1990.

Barbara Flicker — "To Jail or Not to Jail," *ABA Journal*, February 1990.

Michael S. Gazzaniga — "The Federal Drugstore," *National Review*, February 5, 1990.

Reuben Greenberg and Arthur Gordon — *Let's Take Back Our Streets!* Chicago, IL: Contemporary Books, 1989.

Edward S. Herman — "The 'War' on Drugs?" *Zeta*, November 1989.

John W. Johnstone Jr. — "The War on Drugs: Saying 'Yes' to Getting Involved," *Vital Speeches of the Day*, March 15, 1989.

David A. Kaplan and Karen Springen — "Kansas City Doesn't Just Talk," *Newsweek*, February 5, 1990.

Louis Kraar — "How to Win the War on Drugs," *Fortune*, March 12, 1990.

Los Angeles Times — "Drugs—the Real Needs," September 7, 1989.

Michael Massing — "The Two William Bennetts," *The New York Review of Books*, March 1, 1990.

Waltraud Queiser Morales — "The War on Drugs: A New U.S. National Security Doctrine?" *Third World Quarterly*, July 1989.

Tom Morganthau and Mark Miller — "The Drug Warrior," *Newsweek*, April 10, 1989.

Jefferson Morley — "Contradictions of Cocaine Capitalism," *The Nation*, October 2, 1989.

The New Republic — "Crackmire," September 11, 1989.

Daniel Porter — "Just Say No to Giving Inner Cities a Bad Rap," *In These Times*, January 24-30, 1990.

William Safire — "War on the 'War'," *The New York Times*, September 11, 1989.

Robert Schwebel — *Saying No Is Not Enough*. New York: Newmarket Press, 1989.

David Shribman — "Turning Off," *The Wall Street Journal*, January 25, 1990.

Vern E. Smith — "A Frontal Assault on Drugs," *Newsweek*, April 30, 1990.

Thomas Szasz — "Lay Down Your Arms," *Free Inquiry*, Spring 1990. Available from the Council for Democratic and Secular Humanism, 3159 Bailey Ave., Buffalo, NY 14215.

Arnold S. Trebach	"Can Prohibition Be Enforced in Washington?" *The Truth Seeker*, September/October 1989. Available from *The Truth Seeker*, PO Box 2832, San Diego, CA 92112-2832.
George F. Will	"Drugs Are a Crisis of American Behavior," *Conservative Chronicle*, September 20, 1989. Available from *Conservative Chronicle*, PO Box 11297, Des Moines, IA 50340-1297.
Terry Williams	*The Cocaine Kids: The Inside Story of a Teenage Drug King*. Reading, MA: Addison-Wesley, 1989.
Steven Wisotsky	"Rethinking the War on Drugs," *Free Inquiry*, Spring 1990. Available from the Council for Democratic and Secular Humanism, 3159 Bailey Ave., Buffalo, NY 14215.
The World & I	"Drug Legalization: Now or Never?" May 1990.
Emily Yoffe	"How to Legalize," *Mother Jones,* March 1990.
Marty Zupan	"A Hard Sell," *Reason*, April 1989.

index